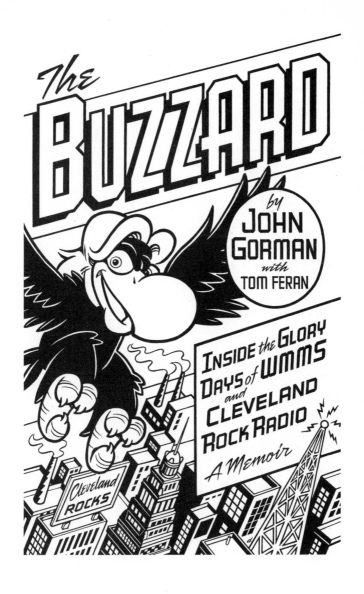

The BUZZARD

by
JOHN GORMAN
with
TOM FERAN

INSIDE the GLORY DAYS of WMMS and CLEVELAND ROCK RADIO
A Memoir

Cleveland ROCKS

GRAY & COMPANY, PUBLISHERS
CLEVELAND

Gray & Company, Publishers
www.grayco.com

Library of Congress Cataloging-in-Publication Data
Gorman, John
The Buzzard : Inside WMMS and the glory days of FM rock radio /
John Gorman with Tom Feran.
p. cm.
ISBN-13: 978-1-886228-47-4 (hardcover)
1. Gorman, John   2. Disc jockeys—Ohio—Cleveland—Biogra-
phy.   3. WMMS (Radio station : Cleveland, Ohio) I. Feran, Tom.
II. Title. III. Title: Inside WMMS and the glory days of FM rock
radio.
ML429.G675A3 2007
791.44'3—dc22
[B]   2007039778

Printed in the U.S.A.
10 9 8 7 6 5 4 3 2 1

For Nafcica

CONTENTS

Foreword ix

Find Me 1
Welcome to Cleveland 3
Radio Architect 16
A New Identity 24
"That's MY Station!" 32
Number One 40
It's Still a Business 52
Hatching the Buzzard 61
The World Series of Rock 72
Got-ta Got-ta Get Down! 80
"We Don't Go to Work; We Go to War" 89
Continuous Party 98
The Switch 109
The Voice of Rock and Roll 113
Moving On Up 124
The Buzzard and The Boss 131
Coffee Break Concerts 139
Beatles Blitz 148
Chimps, Rats, and Buzzard Killers 154
Into the '80s 165
Pride of Cleveland 176
Video Stars, Radio Stars 182
"Bring the Next One On" 192
Your Modern Music Station 202
Buzzardland 209

Taking the Fight To the Airwaves 216

Choosing Sides. 225

"WMMS Can Call Itself Anything It Wants" 236

Departures and Divisions 246

The Rock Stops Here 255

Know Your Close 264

End of an Era 275

Acknowledgments 280

Cast of Characters 283

Index 285

FOREWORD

Back in 1969, when I was living in Boston, I was dialing around on my AM car radio one afternoon, when I came across one of the area's many suburban stations, WNTN. Instead of hearing their usual mix of swap and shop listener call-ins and the warbling of Jack Jones, I was astonished to hear an album track by Traffic. Then something by Cream that was not the overplayed "Sunshine of Your Love." An album cut by the Byrds. Somebody over there knew their music.

By that time, I was already conducting "free form album rock" shows on WTBS-FM, the non-commercial station of the Massachusetts Institute of Technology in Cambridge, just over the river from Boston. It was artistically satisfying, and we were gaining a reputation as the hippest station in town, but there was no compensation except for some free records and an occasional club pass.

But now, here's a commercial station, WNTN, and on AM yet, playing a distinctively free-form album rock mix. Commercial stations actually pay you a salary to appear on the air and play music. And I knew this music.

The station was a daytime-only facility, and—this being early spring—their hours of operation would expand through the up-coming weeks and they certainly would need another show host. Off I went to find the station.

WNTN was housed in a tiny, rundown house, incongruous in the middle of an industrial area across the street from the city incinerator and next door to the Coca-Cola plant. I soon found out that the sole on-air host, a market veteran named Phil Christie, actually had much of the music suggested to him by the station's music director. Where was he? "Oh, he's around back in the parking lot," Phil remarked. "His name is John Gorman."

Out back, there was this sorry looking Opel automobile, and an individual in complete frustration. I introduced myself and complimented him on his music selection, then asked what the trouble was with the car. He had never changed a tire before, at least not on this metric nightmare. I changed his tire, and our lives changed. I became the afternoon guy on WNTN and we got to be pretty tight.

Later, when I accepted a job in Cleveland in the original rebuilding phase of WMMS in 1971, I knew who we needed to eventually hire as music director. Later, when I became program director, I brought John to town. To be honest, I knew that I would soon have to make a choice between being a program director and doing a big daily show, and John was my ace in the hole if I chose the latter. I chose the latter.

John became program director and it fit him like a glove. Or should I say a pair of brass knuckles. He was the most driven, determined and obsessed individual that I have ever worked with in radio.

He has been called many things by many people, some of which are probably true. But there is one thing that no one can deny: WMMS was one of the most accomplished, unique and distinguished radio stations of its day, a completely hand-made operation, and the guiding hand was John. He knew how to motivate and galvanize a staff (get a load of those memos), had a terrific marketing sense, knew how to work the system, and understood that a radio station had to be rich with distinctive features, great personalities, and one show-stopping special event after another, both on air and in the streets.

A typical week at WMMS might find Rodney Dangerfield on Kid Leo's show live in the studio taking phone calls, Matt the Cat hosting Lou Reed playing a set on the Coffee Break Concert broadcast live from the Agora, Betty Korvan playing exclusive tracks from the new Rolling Stones album, and Jeff and Flash, with Ruby Cheeks cutting up with Phil Proctor and Pete Bergman of the Firesign Theatre. Shelley Stile would be off interviewing Paul McCartney. Dia might have Robert Plant as a surprise phone-in. The inimitable all-night institution BLF Bash playing Funkadelic's "Maggot Brain" every Saturday at 1 a.m., Len Goldberg's mind-blowing station IDs, David Helton's original art ads and TV commercials, Steve Church's eclectic Sunday night talk show *Livewire* and Murray Saul's explosive and clever weekend "get downs" all told you that this was no typical cookie-cutter radio station. And behind the whole thing was John. More more more. We can do more. Let's show those phonies on the coasts how its really done. Let's make some history.

We sure did.

Sometimes we wanted to kill him, but, in the end, nobody can deny that John kept us—the airstaff, an amazing promotion, production and sales team, as well as an outstanding engineering department—at the top of our game.

And for those of you who only care about such things, go look up the ratings.

—Denny Sanders

AUTHOR'S NOTE

The events described in this book occured between July 3, 1973 and August 15, 1986. All details are based on my personal experience and are drawn from my memory and my collection of memos, correspondence, and press clippings. This is my life as I remember it.

Memories are subject to distortion. To ensure the accuracy of mine, I called on many people who provided invaluable assistance. They are listed in the acknowledgments at the end of the book.

PROLOGUE

FIND ME

My first week at radio station WMMS I met Tom Bracanovich, the chief engineer of both WHK and its sister station, or, as he would tell you, "the FM, too." He reminded me of George Gobel, the crew-cut comedian of the 1950s.

WHK's studios were bright, spacious, and—unlike the WMMS studio, which was a quarter of their size—freshened by working air-conditioning. The WMMS studio was small and dirty. Every square inch was cluttered with albums, tapes, carts, reference books, speakers, wires, wires, and more wires. Layers of dust and grime coated record cabinets, speakers, the clock, and the wires that snaked everywhere.

"You know what FM stands for?" Bracanovich asked me. "Find Me! FM means Find Me. How many radios have FM on them?"

"Some . . ."

"FM's an option no one gives a shit about."

I'd heard this before. As a proponent of FM radio, and of what was being called the "Progressive Rock" and "Album Rock" formats, I was ready to shoot back some statistics. "Tom, over half of home radios have an FM band."

"That doesn't mean they listen to FM," he retorted. "And how many cars have FM?"

"Maybe twenty-five percent." I was guessing.

"Bullshit!" Tom said. "Try maybe ten percent."

I said that Congress would eventually pass a bill for FM, similar to legislation of a decade earlier that required new television sets to carry the UHF channels above 13.

He scoffed. "It will never happen. It will never, never, ever, ever happen. When you kids grow up, you'll grow out of your rock and roll and you'll be listening to AM radio."

I bit my tongue. Why confuse him with the facts? I had thirteen years ahead of me to prove him wrong.

This book is about a chain of events that gave birth to a radio format—one that would send a supercharged life-force into the "Find Me" frequency; serve as a generation's political statement and banner of identity; and, for an elite few, make millions and even billions of dollars. And it's the story of how one manic, drug-induced, sex-crazed, take-no-prisoners, renegade-warrior radio station helped revive an American city that had been written off as dead.

Thirty years later, wherever I go, I find people who know of the station I helped create. I get e-mail and letters from people I've never met, in places I never visited, who were in one way or another turned on or influenced by the Buzzard. We created something that still survives—and an era of radio that took on a life of its own.

CHAPTER 1

WELCOME TO CLEVELAND

Fourth of July 1973. Welcome to Cleveland. There was a dead pigeon on the windowsill of my room overlooking Public Square in the Sheraton-Cleveland Hotel. Despite several calls to the front desk, the pigeon remained part of the decor for three long, hot, muggy days. It matched the desolate street scene below. Sure, this was a holiday, but still—at 10 a.m. there was not a single car or person on the street.

I'd come from Boston, the city I loved, to take the new job of music director at WMMS—a promising, "free-form" radio station whose program director and morning host, Denny Sanders, was an old friend in need of help.

Metromedia, WMMS's former owner, had recently sold its Cleveland properties to Malrite Broadcasting, a small company relocating from suburban Detroit. Most of the staff, fearing an inevitable format change, had resigned. Denny was now program director, trying to keep the station on the air with a limited staff hired largely from the Cleveland State University station.

The clock was ticking. Malrite's purchase of WMMS had been held up when a community group, led by activist Henry Speeth and a young councilman named Dennis Kucinich, convinced the Federal Communications Commission that the station's progressive format provided a unique public service. Malrite, which planned to change it to country, agreed to retain progressive rock for one year, starting in January 1973. If the station failed to generate revenue and ratings, Malrite would be free to change.

Denny asked if I was interested in coming to Cleveland. I was. It sounded like a challenge and, maybe, fun.

Malrite was putting me up at the Sheraton-Cleveland for my first two weeks of employment. I was expected to find a place to live in that time. What furniture I had wasn't worth the trouble of moving, and I hadn't owned a car for months because Boston's extensive transit system made one unnecessary. I had rented a small truck to move my records, books, files, and clothes, and I'd be searching for a furnished apartment on a bus or train route.

The Sheraton-Cleveland was frayed and musty. The hallway connecting to the Terminal Tower reeked of urine. The gutters on Public Square were littered with trash. Twelve blocks up Euclid Avenue, I was amazed to see a department store, Halle's. It was the only sign of life in an area whose name, Playhouse Square, appeared suited only to history. Its theaters were boarded up, seemingly abandoned.

I drove my rented truck to the WHK-WMMS studios on Euclid Avenue near East 55th Street to meet Denny, who was waiting in the parking lot off Prospect Avenue. The building's once-imposing facade at 5000 Euclid Avenue recalled the time, a generation earlier, when it was a glittering broadcast center, complete with auditorium and theater marquee.

Now it could have been a struggling old factory. The WHK call letters, on a vertical marquee, were grimy, and there wasn't even a sign for WMMS. The back of the building was tarpaper. To its left on Euclid stood a bank; on the right was a Blepp-Coombs Sporting Goods store with Indians and Browns jackets in the window. The view didn't improve inside the stations' dingy lobby. It was a place where the woman who ran a small snack stand died behind the counter as she was closing up one evening, and no one noticed or cared until the stench became unbearable.

There were two other cars in the lot. One belonged to Hal Fisher, the general manager. Lugging a briefcase overflowing with papers, he was wrapping up a half day of work on this holiday morning. "You must be John Gorman," he said as he shook my hand. "Welcome aboard. I'm looking forward to working with you."

I hauled boxes upstairs, to the stuffy loft that was the music library and my office, while Denny got some paperwork out of the way, and decided to pass on a station tour in favor of lunch. My primary concern was finding a furnished apartment, and I pulled out the *Plain Dealer* classifieds as we waited for corned beef sandwiches at Hatton's Deli, a few blocks down Euclid.

The next day, my first on the job, I took the bus down Euclid and got an early start. Waiting for Denny to finish his morning show, I headed upstairs to the music library, switched on the intercom for WMMS. The library hadn't been a priority. Few albums were filed alphabetically or in the correct cabinet, and I found box upon box of unopened albums. I spent an hour trying to make sense of it. In a desk drawer, I found a faded copy of a months-old clipping from *Scene* magazine, a local entertainment tabloid, criticizing the station for losing its past glory. On the intercom in the background, a song ended and a deep voice—like the voice of God—boomed from the speakers. "This is . . . Len Goldberg . . . on W-M-M-S. Good mornin' to you. Here's Van Morrison." This guy did middays? He made Isaac Hayes sound like Alvin and the Chipmunks.

Denny walked in, his show over, and brought me down to the studio to meet Len. If Central Casting was looking for a mad cave dweller, Len would have been the essential choice. His thick head of hair was a veritable jungle, and his full beard matched. Small, square reading glasses perched on his nose, and he had on well-worn bib overalls over a blue T-shirt. His voice could rattle windows like a passing freight train.

"The music department is completely fucked up," he said. "Half this fucking library is scratched to shit, and there's a lot of things I want to play that we don't have. You want a list? I'll give you a list." He paused and took a hit of pot from a tiny pipe, probably to see my reaction. Although surprised, I pretended that I saw that sort of thing every day. "Meet JC yet?" he asked. "My advice to you is not to let JC run this fucking radio station. If you are the music director, you should run the fucking department the way you see fit. Understand? You do that and we'll get along just great."

We walked down the hall toward the archaic production studio, and I met the new production director, Jeff Kinzbach—six feet tall, rail thin, with shoulder-length hair. Then I followed Denny to a claustrophobic office in the back of the FM sales office and met the sales manager, Walt Tiburski. He proposed a Cleveland tour to visit a few clients and record labels, immediately suggesting a date and time.

My next order of business was to meet John Chaffee, Malrite's national program director, who had approved my hiring. From phone conversations, I pictured a conservatively dressed executive in his early 30s. Short, dark hair, light to medium build.

"We call him JC," Denny said. "JC is brilliant, brilliant in his own way. He's very product oriented."

I asked what he looked like. "Like a hippie on *Dragnet*," Denny said. "You know how *Dragnet* stereotyped everyone. Just think of how *Dragnet* would portray a hippie. He wouldn't look like a real hippie. He would look like a Jack Webb version of a hippie. A stereotyped character."

At that instant, someone who looked exactly like a hippie from *Dragnet* entered the hallway. Graying, shoulder-length hair. A slightly wild, medium-length beard. Dark, piercing eyes. A two-piece outfit, not exactly a suit, of a peculiar fabric in a medium blue hue. Cuban-heeled boots. A furry shoulder bag. JC, extremely courteous, welcomed me "on board" and marched toward the back of the building.

Denny suggested lunch at Hatton's. As we pulled out of the parking lot, he cranked up the radio—"Evil Woman" by Spooky Tooth. Then it happened. "Eeeeee-vil (click) Eeee-vil (click) . . . Eeeevil (click)." Len Goldberg, in his best burning bush voice, boomed through the speakers, "If anyone from the music department is listening, we need a new copy of that Spooky Tooth album"—followed by a loud crack.

"Denny, did he just break the album on the air?"

"Hmmm. Sounds like it, doesn't it?"

On my second morning, I walked up the stairs to the music office loft, opened the door, and turned on the light. Someone was sleeping on the couch in the corner. He was tall, thin, had shoulder-length hair and a beard. "Whuttufuck, whuttufuck," he mumbled.

That was my introduction to Kid Leo. Denny had left him a note to meet me. For Leo, the best way to do that was to stick around after his 2 a.m.–6 a.m. show. He was groggy and tired, but we exchanged pleasantries. He asked me about Boston—"Are they all eggheads and weirdos up there?"—and I asked him about Cleveland. We talked music. Being roughly the same age, we shared similar reference points, and he was extremely knowledgable—from New Music through Top 40, garage bands, and rhythm and blues. He grew up listening to WJMO—"they had this jock, Michael 'Da Lover' Payne—an' sometimes WIXY, KYW-KYC, 'NCR, 'MMS. 'MMS is what got me interested in radio."

I soon met the rest of the staff and started to settle in. With the exception of a quick hello, however, I had no interaction with Milton Maltz, the president and essentially the owner of Malrite Communications. The office help called him "Grouchy," after one of the Seven Dwarfs. Others called him "Little Napoleon," "The Tiny Tyrant," and "The Mean Midget." Terms of endearment. Everyone feared his explosive temper. It was considered normal to hear his snarling shouts emanating from the stairway to Malrite's corporate suite. If Maltz was meeting in Hal Fisher's office, one could easily hear his bellows in the second-floor music loft directly above it.

Only JC appeared to have a true rapport with Maltz. He called him Milt. Fisher called him Mr. Maltz. I doubted he even knew who I was until the afternoon I collided with him as I came down the stairs from the music loft, and he stormed out of Fisher's office with Fisher and JC behind him.

"WE-E-E were just talking about you," Maltz said. Snarled, actually. It was his way of speaking. Teeth bared, lips drawn back in a scowl, he punched up certain words and drew them out dramatically, a character out of Dickens. "How LONG before YOU feel we will have the NUMBER ONE FM? You need to create GOALS. GOALS.

"You have a number of BASS-tards in this town," he said. "Sons of BITCH-ezz who will FIGHT to preserve the status quo. You have to PUSH THEM OUT OF THE WAY. SEIZE THEIR AUDIENCE! Give them no oppor-TOON-ity to counterattack. That's how you will win."

He turned and walked away. In unison, Fisher and JC said, "Thank you, John."

There was plenty of work to be done. What came first, for me, was instituting new policies for the music department.

The "free form" format had no guidelines at all. I could add anything I wanted, which was a recipe for disaster. Because WMMS was adding about fifteen albums a week, the chances for all of them to get airplay were low, and individual tracks could not get enough airplay to become familiar to listeners. To be successful, we needed to pick from the best of the bunch, and not become top-heavy in any one genre of rock.

I broke the music into separate categories—New, Up and Coming, Hot, and Recurrent—and added a separate entry for singles in advance of their album release. Under that system, we could control how much music got added and played. It would give us a more consistent sound, and allow a full variety of new songs from current and new artists to get decent exposure and rotation. I also gave the airstaff input into music selection by asking them to vote on new releases, after providing every full-time announcer a copy of every new album we received.

We called for reports from area record stores, though they were often tainted. Columbia was the biggest offender. Virtually every album it released hit the top five in sales immediately, and when you'd see an album in the top five by an unknown artist who was getting little or no airplay—Dr. Feelgood, for example—you knew something was amiss. Eventually, we learned how it worked: Columbia would provide these stores with twenty-five free copies, known as "cleans," for a top-five store report. That meant a 100 percent profit for the record store, and artists whose albums were provided in the trade for a false report did not receive royalties from their sale. The "free" albums and goods the label provided the record store were charged against the artists' royalties. With new contesting and giveaway practices in place, we began giving away concert tickets with Belkin Productions. I would contact the labels and match up tickets with the performers' latest album releases, adding a "WMMS—with new rock first" tag to our on-air giveaway sheets.

Noticing that the Friday entertainment supplements of the *Plain Dealer* and *Cleveland Press* carried news, gossip, and charts from area stations, I typed a weekly press release listing our album and ticket giveaways, scheduled interviews, and details of special programming—anything to get the WMMS call letters and rounded-off "101 FM" frequency into print. If a jock had a particular favorite track or album, I listed that, too. And while the station had shunned as "too commercial" a listing in the week's top twenty for WIXY, WGCL, WNCR, WJMO, WABQ and CKLW, I thought we should join the party. We provided a top twenty album list compiled from a combination of airplay, requests, and pure guesswork on my part, and sent a copy to Jane Scott at the *Plain Dealer*. WMMS was the only station listing albums.

There always seemed to be problems between WMMS and *Scene* magazine, which at that time was a locally owned magazine that covered music clubs and concerts. I made a courtesy call to editor Jim Girard, who connected me with someone identified only as the "decision maker." After I inquired about a possible trade with *Scene*, in which we would run a number of spots for them each in exchange for a quarter-page print ad for WMMS, Decision Maker said, "We only do those deals with stations that have ratings." When

I asked about the weekly ad for WPIC-FM from Sharon, Pennsylvania, he claimed it was Youngstown's top-rated rock station. I knew better. Decision Maker hung up without saying good-bye. Don't get mad—get even. I took note of an ad in *Scene* displaying a Nazi swastika for the N.S. Bookstore, which sold Nazi books, patches, posters, and rings—and sent letters to other advertisers I felt would be most affronted by it. N.S. Bookstore was conspicuous by its absence in future editions. Touché.

We were aiming at Cleveland's mass audience—the baby boom bulge of young teens to twenty-five-year-olds—and I believed we needed to serve as an adult Top 40, a true rock station station playing all genres of rock music. I'd done my homework on Cleveland and its rich rock radio history, from Alan Freed at WJW through WHK, KYW, and WIXY, plus CKLW, WAKR, and any of the other stations that influenced the area. As with my native Boston, its history was a cut above average, on par with some of the greatest radio markets in the country. WMMS was billed as the place "Where Music Means Something," and the slogan applied to Cleveland in general. (Our listeners also knew it as an acronym for Weed Makes Me Smile, but that was not used on the air.)

To be successful, WMMS had to be more than just another radio station. In an early memo to the staff, I wrote that we should grow into Cleveland's full-service pop-culture station. We needed other stations to play our game, and deceive them into assuming we were underpaid, undertalented, naive kids with an FM our owners didn't know what to do with. We'd play that same hand with corporate.

Otherwise, who was to say, once we turned the station into a ratings-proven moneymaker, that Malrite wouldn't discard the staff for the next round of younger, cheaper talent. We had to set up our own protection, personally and collectively, to protect our own asses and assets.

When Mick Jagger, Keith Richards, and Marianne Faithfull were busted for pot in early 1967, and Jagger and Richards were given to-be-determined jail sentences, the Who vowed to record only Jagger-

Richards compositions until the two were freed. The band hurried into the studio and recorded versions of "Under My Thumb" and "The Last Time," which were rushed to Radio Caroline, the pirate radio station broadcasting from a ship off the English coast. Mel Phillips, who was programming Boston's WRKO, landed a copy and put it into rotation. I wanted to program a progressive rock station with the same passion and street smarts.

This new WMMS would embrace the moment. I felt we had to ride trends, knowing when to jump on and off. Let college radio initiate new trends, as they should; we should be attuned to the latest novelties and fads. Knowing our timing—when to embrace and, equally important, when to close—would save us during the Disco Invasion, which we would not ignore either. Novelty records were mostly ignored by album radio. Cheech and Chong, the Firesign Theatre, the Bonzo Dog Band, Monty Python, George Carlin, and Murray Roman were as close as the format got to comedy and novelty. I felt we should break that trend. The format was in desperate need of a sense of humor and a heavy injection of novelty. I recalled Peter Sellers's narration of the Beatles' "Help" from the Top 40 of the 1960s—never a hit, but a track with its moment of curiosity and novelty. I also ended self-indulgent music segues like looping together tunes with the same theme or word in the title—like "White Bird" to "White Rabbit" to "White Room."

When people recalled their favorite stations, they referenced the disc jockeys: Joey Reynolds, with his theme song sung by the Four Seasons to the tune of "Sherry." Murray the K's Swingin' Soiree and "submarine races." Jerry G's "alligator counting." Cousin Brucie's "cousins," and Arnie "Woo Woo" Ginsberg, "Woo Woo for you-you." I coveted that for WMMS. We had to be personality radio. Everyone needed a style, a hook, and signature lines.

I loved disc jockey nicknames. It was Murray The K, not Murray Kaufman; Cousin Brucie, not Bruce Morrow. It was "Emperor" Joe Mayer. I rejected pre-fab "Ron Radio" nom de plumes. I vowed that if I had to change a name, it would either be close to the original or way, way out there. I had a head start with Kid Leo, who named himself after Kid Jensen, a popular British radio DJ, and his friend Matt the Cat, whose name took a little more work.

Matthew Lapczynski was working weekends as a part-timer. Born in Belgium, he'd immigrated with his family to the United States in the 1950s, stopping first in Massachusetts and then settling in Cleveland's Slavic Village. He was soft-spoken—just this side of too soft—but his music selection was the most mainstream on the station. He joined WMMS on April 21, 1973, the day after his twentieth birthday, and within three and a half months he had worked every shift on the station except morning drive.

His family had moved to Cleveland and settled in Maple Heights when his father accepted a position at the Immaculate Heart of St. Mary Church in Cleveland as church organist. Matt was also fluent in Polish.

Matt's initiation to radio came by way of a friend who ran a pirate radio station out of his home. The station, which ran a Top 40 format and became the unofficial voice of Chanel High School, had a fairly powerful signal. It often changed frequencies to confuse the FCC. Listeners were notified when the frequency changed. A radio engineer heard the station and notified the FCC, which shut the station down but did not prosecute.

I liked him, but not the one-name air name Matthew, which sounded too progressive rock sixties. I wouldn't have minded Lapczynski, except I knew it would get butchered in ratings diaries. This is the reason why "on-air" names tend to be simple and easy to recall. Denny, Matt, and I had lunch to discuss a name, but every suggestion sounded "too radio." Matthew Williams, Matthew Thomas, Matthew Martin. Lapczynski, tall and rail thin, ordered a chocolate fudge sundae for dessert. He scooped up a chunk of vanilla ice cream, ran the spoon around the inside the glass dish to pick up some extra fudge, put the spoon to his lips, stopped, and examined it. There on the spoon was a sharp, nearly invisible sliver of glass.

"Look," he said. "I almost swallowed that."

"Lucky you," I said. "You're like a cat—using up one of your nine lives." Silence. "Matt the Cat! Matt the Cat. What about that name?"

Denny liked it. Lapczynski thought it sounded stupid, and not believable. And Kid Leo was? It's show biz, I told him. It fit, it wasn't derogatory or offensive, it was catchy, it rhymed, and it didn't sound like "Ron Radio." Besides, listeners might feel they knew him a bit better because of a perception that Matt the Cat was his nickname.

On the first day he used it, he got hang-up calls saying, "Matt the Cat—pussy!" from the usual suspects who complained about everything. Ride it out, I suggested. It would work. Look at Leo, with his share of late-night callers saying, "Kid Leo, huh? Prizefighter? I'll come down there and kick your ass." I made sure the Saturday schedule changed "Matthew" to "Matt the Cat," which was how he signed on that afternoon. Within a couple of weeks, the name was established, and the peanut gallery harrassers moved on to another element of WMMS to complain about. A few years later, a research study showed "Kid Leo" and "Matt the Cat" among the most recognized staff names on Cleveland radio.

Being known and recognized was important. I wanted our staff to be out in public, to be on TV, to get their pictures in the paper. I wanted listeners to place voices with names instantly. No surprises, and none of that "you don't look anything like you sound" on my air talent. I wanted them to be rock stars in their own right, respected, even loved.

I spent hours discussing radio with Leo, Matt, Kinzbach, announcers David Spero and Steve Lushbaugh, John Chaffee, and Walt Tiburski and Joel Frensdorf in sales—their likes, dislikes, and perceptions of regional radio. What had attracted them to it? Its music was a soundtrack to life. Our generation used radio differently than our parents. We'd been both weaned on and contaminated by television. We were the instant gratification generation. For us, the line between entertainment and reality was blurred.

My single greatest influence was satirist Stan Freberg, who mastered the art of using the imaginative aura of radio. He described a flotilla of helicopters carrying a giant maraschino cherry to drop on a mountain of whipped cream. With the right script, direction, and production, you could create any vision you wished. I wanted WMMS to sound like it was coming from a state-of-the-art studio, not the pit we worked in.

I devoured every trade paper and kept tabs on every format. I analyzed the Top 40 page, the Country page, the Middle-of-the-Road page. I perused playlists regardless of format, and studied victorious radio stations. The word "soundtrack" kept coming back to me. We had to be that 24/7 soundtrack, and "full service" for our listeners. When I wasn't scanning trades, I was reading any book I could find on administration and leadership. They weren't so common in 1973. Dale Carnegie was—and to most, should be—the bible of direction. I didn't always follow his suggestions, and more often than not, that would be a mistake. I read and listened to lectures by Zig Zigler and Gunther Klauss.

And I studied Cleveland. I spent hours reading old issues of the *Plain Dealer* and *Cleveland Press* on microfilm at the public library. The city's political and social mood in the 1970s would become a primary explanation for the success of WMMS. To my surprise, I learned Cleveland was not really midwestern like Kansas City or Chicago. If anything, Cleveland and Cuyahoga County had more in common with the Northeast than Columbus, which has far more in common with Indianapolis and Cincinnati. Like most major industrial cities of the Northeast and Midwest, its post–World War II boom had gone bust. It had to find new reasons to be meaningful to the rest of the world. For forty long years, the region failed, coming perilously close to morphing into Southeast Detroit. Cleveland lacked any postwar shaping of its urban neighborhoods, roads, and public transportation. Its crippled school system was among the first to rupture. The region suffered from poor city and county services, and widespread political corruption shaped an environment that invited little investment in the city from the private sector. Cleveland's racial polarization was among the nation's worst.

Nationally, Cleveland was a joke. The locals knew it, and the young despised it. To the rest of the country, it was a burning river,

Mayor Ralph Perk accidentally setting his hair on fire, his wife skipping an invitation to the White House to go bowling. Downtown was dying. Even the sports teams added to the national joke. Art Modell, King Midas in reverse, was dismantling the once great Cleveland Browns. The Indians' pennant and contention years were a distant memory. There was little to root for. I reminisced about growing up in the 1950s in Boston, a city with comparable problems—appalling services, inadequate and poorly supplied schools, little if any downtown renewal or construction. There was no life north of New York City in those days, but Boston had turned around. If Boston could, why not Cleveland?

One of my first objectives became making WMMS the Cleveland cheerleader for the next generation. While other media played up doom and gloom, we would champion Cleveland as a city rebuilt on rock and roll—a memorable place to have fun and party, a city with immense potential and the best rock audience on the planet. We would turn every Cleveland liability into an asset.

CHAPTER 2

RADIO ARCHITECT

I was twelve when I put my first radio station on the air. I built it from one of those Lafayette AM radio hobby kits that were supposed to broadcast only a few hundred feet. I rigged it to reach a few blocks and set up in my attic, which had a view of the surrounding neighborhood. One summer day, I noticed my neighbor Zeke Kissell sitting on his stoop listening to a Red Sox game on his transistor radio. I tuned my transmitter to the same frequency as the station carrying the game and said, "Zeke, you're a bum." Zeke, a Polish immigrant who was a little unsure of the language and the technology behind radio, couldn't figure out why his radio was talking to him. After making a few more comments, I heard a voice shout my own name. It was my father, standing in the doorway. I didn't know that he was also listening to the Sox game on *his* radio. Radio Free Southie, as I called it, was off the air.

I grew up in South Boston, a poor, rough Irish neighborhood on a peninsula separated by water from the rest of Boston. In its poverty and insularity, it sometimes seemed separated by decades as well. We lived in a home my father inherited when my grandmother died. My father, who was born in the house in 1909, spent endless hours trying to rehabilitate it. We didn't have a telephone. We didn't have an automobile. Everyone used public transportation.

South Boston was a birthplace of saints and sinners, from John F. Kennedy's spiritual and political advisors, Cardinal Richard Cushing and Speaker of the House of Representatives John W. McCormack, to organized crime leader James "Whitey" Bulger, long one of the FBI's ten most wanted criminals. Street gangs governed everyday life and commerce in Southie, which was divided into territories run by gangs from the immediate neighborhood—the Saints, the Blackhawks, the Cavaliers, the Mullens, the Pedros, the Stompers, the Bottlers. Gang fights and rumbles were the norm, everyone carried a knife, and guns were not uncommon. Crimes ranged from petty theft to murder.

I had three close friends I met in junior high school: Tom Gosse, John Grant, and Tony Liebl. Our fathers worked blue-collar jobs and our mothers cleaned downtown office buildings in the evening. We all lived in neighborhoods surrounded by housing projects and gang turfs. We weren't bad kids. At least a quarter of the kids I went to grade school with did reformatory school time, but we avoided trouble.

Living between gang territories gave us advantages and disadvantages. On one hand, we did not have to run with a pack. On the other, we had no real protection. If we found ourselves in a gang situation, we had to fight our way out ourselves and could not rely on backup.

We decided to create the illusion of being part of a large gang.

Our first attempt was to call the gang the Truckers, complete with an elaborate story that involved us smuggling stolen copper wire to be fenced on the black market. Seizing an opportunity to solidify our reputation and avoid direct challenge from other gangs, Tom Gosse spilled the beans about us to a school counselor—knowing from experience that counselors could not keep secrets, and that any confidence shared with one would be on the street within the week. Tom wove an amazing tale about the Truckers, and the story spread fast.

After a few months, we tired of the name. It didn't have the cool ring of other gang names. We had to reinvent ourselves. Inspiration came on Sunday, September 15, 1963. I remember, because it was the day Tony Liebl's older brother, who had recently bought a car, took us to see the Blue Angels at the South Weymouth Naval Air Base. It was a rare treat to be in a car, and it was the farthest any of us had been from South Boston without our parents.

The TV networks opened their fall season that night, and I watched *Arrest and Trial*, a new cops-and-court show starring Ben Gazzara and Chuck Connors. If you grew up in Boston in the 1960s, you knew as much about Connors's brief moment as a Boston Celtic as you did about his role in *The Rifleman*. The show dealt with a teenage gang that had gone too far. Their name was the Barracudas. Cool name. I looked up Barracuda in the dictionary. That was it.

On Monday morning, it was unanimous. We would be the South Boston Barracudas—a gang supposedly built from remnants of the Truckers, including some guys from "downtown," after the Feds started closing in and some of the guys had to leave town for a while.

The following Saturday, the four of us stocked up on spray paint. On Sunday night, we met at John Grant's house, sneaked into the schoolyard of Patrick F. Gavin Junior High, and sprayed the entire wall with "South Boston Barracudas." We added our names, and copied more names from album covers, newspapers, and magazines. When a gang "advertised," the standard practice was for its graffiti to list the names of all members. By the time we were finished, we had about sixty names attached to the Barracudas.

The next morning, when we returned to the school yard to line up and enter the building, we were cool. It kept us out of trouble for the rest of the school year. We didn't need protection. We were protection, as far as the others were concerned.

That was my first brush with being part of what I would call a "great illusion," and—although I didn't know it at the time—with audience research, marketing and promotion, organization, and competition.

We played Southie for what it was worth, but our lives and goals extended far past its boundaries. We took the "T" downtown, and if we didn't have the money, we walked. We spent hours at the Boston Public Library, reading and studying on our own. We prowled the bookstores and coffeehouses of Harvard Square. Our interests went beyond picking up girls and having winos cop booze for us— although we did that, too. We knew of a life beyond Southie.

Of all my interests, radio was number one. I was attracted to a radio career by the time I was nine. It was my constant companion and soundtrack. I collected the Top 40 charts from local radio stations and studied them weekly, wondering why a certain tune would be number three on one chart and number seven on another. One winter Sunday, I asked my father how disc jockeys could change records so quickly on a turntable. He explained how studios had two to three turntables, in addition to tape machines and other equipment, and by the end of the afternoon I had jerry-rigged two turntables to one amplifier, allowing me to segue singles at home.

My father insisted that if I wanted to make something of my life, I should get a good education and go beyond the limits of South Boston. "Don't be like me," he would often say. He took home $50 a week from his job supervising the receiving docks for Jordan Marsh, one of Boston's four downtown Boston department stores. He must have mentioned to the truck driver making record deliveries that his young son was interested in music. As a result, once or twice a week, my father would bring home a few 45 RPM singles. It was my reward, back then, for being "good." In a few short years, I had a fairly large collection. Many of the singles were DJ copies, with colorless, generic-looking white labels. My father told me the vinyl was more durable than on commercially sold singles.

When I hit my teens, my interest in both music and radio went into overdrive. Living less than a mile from the Atlantic Ocean, I could pick up stations from New York City, upstate New York, even Canada. Transistor radios and earphones made radio portable, and I listened every waking hour. I learned which smaller-market stations were used as barometers and proving grounds for new records, and which big stations, like WINS in New York, were first with "exclusives"—especially after Beatlemania and the British Invasion separated the cool from the uncool and opened a new level of competition.

My father gave me an inside track on that, too. His dock received all the magazine shipments for the Jordan Marsh bookstore, and I casually asked one day if he could get any music magazines. It turned out that the magazine distributor had begun importing British magazines to meet the demands of Beatlemania. My father would bring them home. In school the following day, I would report on the next big band breaking out of England—the one we'd hear next on the radio.

I had to see how a radio station worked. The first opportunity came courtesy of WBZ, which had what it called a "Sundeck Studio"—a long trailer converted into a fully functioning portable studio. Unlike the radio remotes of today, the disc jockeys were on site, playing records on turntables and commercials on cartridge machines. I was mesmerized by being able to view an actual show taking place—and also learned that few disc jockeys resembled my audio impressions of their appearance. Sometimes, it was an unusual dichotomy, because they usually sported blazers with the station's logo on the breast pocket. Here they were playing the hippest, coolest new music, yet their clothes were so . . . so . . . cheesy. More illusion.

What inspired and impressed me most about radio was when a disc jockey would go against the grain, by breaking format or seeming to break the rules. It would get everyone talking about that disc jockey and that radio station. It was something I wouldn't forget.

WBZ's remotes also allowed me an occasional opportunity to meet one of the disc jockeys. I always had questions ready. I'd ask about the playlist, the selection, the rotation, and the way Boston stations seemed to monitor what was being played in Worcester or Providence. I always got a raised eyebrow and the same response: "You ask some pretty serious questions."

I was fifteen when I landed my first legitimate job in radio, as a paid intern. I was not an on-air person, nor did I want to be. My first love was behind the scenes, handling the programming, the music, and the scheduling. I wanted to be a radio architect.

·   ·   ·

Denny Sanders and I met in early 1970. I was working part-time at WNTN, an AM station in suburban Boston that was licensed only for daytime broadcasting, sunrise to sunset.

I was only nineteen, but it was my third station. The first was WORL, a small daytimer in downtown Boston, where I got a part-time job with the music department while still in high school. That's where I learned to program a radio station, though it was no match for Boston's powerhouse Top 40s. After it changed to a soft music format, I tried for a similar position at WBCN, the city's first album-rock station, where I made some good contacts but, at eighteen, was considered too young for a job.

I caught a break from Phil Christie, a journeyman disc jockey who worked for some of Boston's biggest stations until a serious automobile accident set his career back. He was working in smaller markets when Boston's WHDH-FM changed to album rock and hired him as program director. They delayed hiring a full staff during an unrelated license challenge, and he hired me to program music on the station's automated system. After the station was put up for sale and changed format, I was out of work and started writing for *Fusion*, a Boston-based magazine that tried to go up against *Rolling Stone*.

Christie called from WNTN a year later, in the summer of 1969, asking me to write a proposal to change its format to rock. I did, and the general manager agreed to rock from 2 p.m. to sundown on weekdays and all day Saturday. (WNTN ran ethnic progamming on Sunday.)

Denny visited early the next spring, knowing the station would need an additional person to cover the longer on-air hours as broadcast days lengthened. (I couldn't do it. If you heard my voice you'd know why. I love radio, but some people are best kept behind the scenes.) Denny had hosted shows on MIT's college station, WTBS, and his aircheck (an on-air "audition") won the job. We hit it off immediately.

WNTN was situated in a tiny house in an industrial section of Newton across from the town dump. When it rained, the basement flooded and we'd get knocked off the air. Its antenna was a lightning rod, and Denny and I once saw our hair stand on end, seconds before a lightning bolt hit within a few feet of us. But the station's signal blanketed Greater Boston, and we were able to build some audience. Most cars had only AM radios, and our progressive rock format was a rarity on AM.

Denny and I, with newscaster Ken Currier, wrote a proposal and business plan to pitch our format to almost every FM station in town. None bit. Worse for us, in 1971 Vice President Spiro Agnew threatened sanctions up to license loss for stations playing songs with anti-war lyrics or drug references. That was enough for WNTN's owner, a staunch Republican, to pull the plug on rock. Phil Christie landed an overnight shift on Boston's powerful WBZ, with Denny, Ken Currier, and me as coproducers. Then he moved on to other projects, and Ken moved away.

I went back to writing for music magazines and got a job with the Commonwealth of Massachusetts. Denny did fill-in shifts on WBCN. We launched our own music magazine, *Cabinessence*, named after a Brian Wilson song. It folded after two issues.

Then Denny heard about an opening in Cleveland at WMMS—a quasi-Top 40 station evolving to progressive rock. We drove to Cleveland for his interview, and he moved there a few weeks later. I continued to pitch Boston stations, and we made a pact that whoever found an ideal station would contact the other.

By 1972, I was running out of fortitude. I won a lucrative promotion with the Massachusetts Department of Public Works, which paid the bills and would give me a free education, but I didn't like working for the state. If you were politically connected, you did nothing; if you weren't connected, you learned how to be, and did nothing. And with Denny and Phil Christie gone, I soured on radio.

Driving from Cambridge to Boston one night, I turned on the radio, which I'd rigged with a hand-dialed FM converter, and happened on a new station, WVBF. An energetic jock with a grizzled voice who called himself "Benevolent Bill" and "BLF" was playing current or recent album tracks in a format similar to the up-tempo, high-gloss version of album radio that Denny and I had pitched to every station in town but this one. I couldn't believe what I was hearing. It was inspiring. I decided that somehow, some way, somewhere, I'd be back in radio.

In early 1973 I called Denny—who was just about to call me. I agreed to join him at WMMS. We'd do there what we weren't able to do in Boston. We believed we could do a mass-appeal album-rock station, where we could play the best progressive and mainstream cuts and even some Top 40 hits and oldies. We'd play progressive rhythm and blues. We'd sound like we were having fun. We'd jump on every fad, regardless of how weird or off-the-wall it might be. Our goal was to be a pop culture station, and the best rock and roll station in America.

CHAPTER 3

A NEW IDENTITY

Administrative work wasn't the reason Denny loved radio, and it was taking a visible toll on his health. He was working from five in the morning until nine or ten every night. In September he asked JC if I could become the new program director; Denny would take the 6 p.m.–10 p.m. air shift and get the new title of creative services director. JC offered me the PD position and a whopping $25 raise, from $150 to $175, with another $25 in the spring. Not much, and not enough to buy a dependable car. As program director, I wouldn't be able to leave between 6 p.m. and 7 p.m. to catch the bus home. I'd have to be at the station nights and weekends and cover concerts and clubs. JC agreed to provide a company car, at least through spring. Deal.

Label reps called with congratulations, some sending fruit baskets and bottles of wine. What they really wanted to know was who the new music director would be, and if I, unlike Sanders, would join the decision-making process for adds and rotations. Whose asses would they have to kiss, in other words. Even Milton Maltz made a rare journey up the hall, to what was about to be my new office, and told me his legendary, "I applied for a job here a few years ago, they TURNED ME DOWN, now I OWN IT" story. He closed with the line, "Your DES-tin-ee and this RAY-DEE-O station are LINKED!"

Denny took the next two weeks off. When he came back, he looked years younger. He began evolving into his role as the "professor of rock," and as one of radio's most artistic and inventive announcers anywhere.

I suggested that Kid Leo replace me as music director. JC vetoed it because of what he perceived to be Leo's limited musical tastes, and asked if I knew anyone from Boston. I called Kenny Greenblatt at WBCN, a sales manager and a good friend. Greenblatt was plugged in to the progressive rock industry and would have a lead on a possible candidate. He suggested Debbie Ullman, WBCN's first female announcer, who once did mornings at the station. "You don't want her doing music," he said, laughing. "She's the epitome of a hippie chick. She'd bury you in granola music. But I always thought she sounded pretty good on the air—and unless you're ready to shell out big bucks, Debbie may be the best you can get."

I took note of that, needing a new morning show, but more important was finding a music director. "Got one for you," he said. "Donna Halper." She was doing a Sunday afternoon folk show on WCAS, a daytime station in Cambridge that was barely making ends meet with folk music, light rock, and brokered shows (whose distributors buy an hour or more of air time to run their own programming). Its call letters represented the suburbs it served: Watertown, Cambridge, Arlington, and Somerville. Most locals aware of its existence called it "Wickass," the joke being that the Somerville border was the ass end of Cambridge. "She's been over here a million times lookin' for work," Kenny said. "She's, how can I put it, not really our style. She can be a real yenta. Check her out first. She could drive you crazy."

Debbie Ullman and Donna Halper both agreed to terms, sight unseen, after three or four phone interviews—Ullman was hired to take over mornings from Denny, and Halper as music director with a weekend shift or two. I scheduled Kid Leo for Saturday nights, from 6 p.m. to midnight. His music selection was part of what I wanted for the WMMS sound, and Kid Leo was real. It may have been the character Larry Travagliante portrayed while on the air, but it came from the heart.

Lawrence James Travagliante was born in 1950 and raised in

Cleveland's industrial southeast side, around Buckeye Road and Woodland Avenue. Half Italian, half Polish, he was educated in Catholic schools—Immaculate Heart on Lansing, then Our Lady of Lourdes High School ("It was either gonna be Lourdes or Holy Name, because I wasn't going to go to an all-boys school"), where he acquired the nickname "Leo" from a hard-of-hearing nun. He borrowed "Kid" from a well-known British DJ named Kid Jensen.

He'd grown up listening to legendary disc jockeys like Pete "Mad Daddy" Myers, Johnny Holliday, Jim Stagg, Jerry G, Joey Reynolds, and Michael "The Lover" Payne. He was a business major at Cleveland State University, learned he didn't need to be a communications major to work at its radio station, WCSB, and signed up for work. He became part of a group that was ready when Denny had to fill airshifts on WMMS.

We had only one inadequately rigged production studio. Because commercial clients often waited until the Friday deadline to turn in ad copy, there were times when production deadlines couldn't be met—even with Jeff Kinzbach laboring all day, and Steve Lushbaugh taking over at 5 p.m. until his on-air shift at 10 p.m.. In those rare cases, I would reluctantly let commercial copy be delivered live. On Leo's first Saturday shift, Audio Warehouse turned in copy too late to get produced. But because the sales staff was selling WMMS on "lifestyle," without benefit of ratings, and because our rates were not easy for many clients to swallow, I agreed to run it live.

For Leo, the live spot was a disaster. It was not well written, and he tripped over a dozen words while stumbling in and out of his developing Kid character. (Leo did not talk off the air in the same style he did on WMMS.) JC heard it and was incensed that I would allow Leo to deliver live copy. When I arrived at the office Monday morning, an envelope was taped to my door, with a typewritten note from JC on a torn piece of yellow legal paper: "Where is this man's head? I did not recognize his music. He could not read live copy. This man will never amount to anything on-air. Why did you schedule him on Saturday night? Please see me."

I decided to work it through. "Got your note," I said, wandering into JC's office. "I heard what you heard."

"That commercial he butchered?" JC said. "Not once, twice, not three times. Every hour?"

"Blame me," I said. "I put the copy in the studio without reading it. Anyone would have stumbled over those lines."

"I disagree," JC shot back. "I don't hear that man being anything except an all-night jock on this station. I didn't like anything about his show."

I convinced him to let me work with Leo, insisting that his burning desire to make it would overcome any shortcomings. I made a copy of JC's note, and put the original in an envelope for Leo with a note attached: "Call me on this when you get a chance—don't call or see JC."

Leo called the next morning, asking, "Whattafuck is this? Why's he attacking me?"

"JC caught a bad moment," I said. "You have to show him you can do a better job. Meanwhile, let me handle the live copy problem. There's no way that copy should have gotten into the studio written that way. JC's giving me one more chance. He's letting me put you on this coming Saturday night."

Although JC continued to be his harshest critic for a while, he would eventually become one of Kid Leo's biggest supporters.

From then on I reviewed commercials for grammatical and vernacular errors, screening out cliches and words like "chicks" and "broads," which were common in those days. Jeff Kinzbach and Steve Lushbaugh developed production styles that made our in-house commercial work distinct. It took considerable time, effort, and imagination, in an antiquated studio where tape was spliced with razor blades and dated equipment ran tape at different speeds, but they did some incredible work. Under the stylistic influence of the Firesign Theatre, using bizarre humor and quick cuts, they produced some particular masterpieces for George Fitzpatrick's

Heights Art Theatre in Cleveland Heights and Westwood Theater in Lakewood, the cutting-edge houses that scheduled cult-favored Friday and Saturday "Midnight Movies." The ads made for some of the most entertaining sixty seconds on radio anywhere and rivaled or even surpassed the quality of agency-created national commercials. ·

When we had to run a commercial that didn't fit our sound, we devised a subtle but effective way to let listeners know we agreed with their complaints. From a Firesign Theatre album, Jeff and Steve lifted voice samples exclaiming "Barney!" and "Clem!" They were carefully and strategically added to offensive spots. Exceptionally wretched commercials were branded for three in a row, a triple Barney—"Barney! Barney! Barney!" It didn't take long for our most perceptive listeners to pick up that we were running those spots "under protest." It went on for months, until a competing station notified clients of the practice.

I pitched using our staff anytime we could, which was a win-win situation. Everyone on the airstaff was required to cut a certain number of spots, because of the need to have a variety of voices on the air. If a spot ran only on WMMS, there was no talent fee. Spots that ran elsewhere, however, brought the air talent extra money—sometimes hundreds of dollars more per commercial, to supplement their meager salaries. It also gave them and the station wider exposure. It quickly became common to hear Len Goldberg and Denny Sanders on stations in Youngstown and Canton, and eventually on competing stations in Cleveland. With his great pipes, Goldberg landed such high-profile local accounts as Audio Warehouse and Cleveland Tux. Since Len was both an on-air personality and the "voice of WMMS" for station IDs, hearing him made one think WMMS regardless of what station his voice was heard on.

We also had the advantage of running only eight minutes of commercials an hour, not counting public service announcements, while stations like WIXY ran double that number. To reduce clutter, we discouraged 30-second commercials by charging a rate that was 80 percent of the 60-second spots. We were so successful we had to go to nine minutes per hour, then ten—still nothing compared to radio today, where stations break for ten minutes at a time, not per hour.

WMMS was rapidly building a "new rock" identity, with exclusive airplay of the new Brian Auger album, the first Lynyrd Skynyrd album, and Mott the Hoople's *Mott*. Labels took notice. WMMS was selling product. The labels bought more advertising. Walt Tiburski was a happy man. We were exceeding revenue projections.

I contracted for syndicated programming including the *King Biscuit Flower Hour*, an hourlong weekly concert program, and renewed the *BBC Rock Hour*, which carried concerts recorded by the British Broadcasting Company (where reserved British audiences applauded rather than cheered). We instituted weekly press releases, writing them Monday afternoon and distributing them Tuesday morning. Everything was written out longhand, typed on old 1950s-style Smith-Corona typewriters and distributed by hand. Jane Scott at the *Plain Dealer* and Bruno Bornino and Harriet Peters at the *Cleveland Press* started mentioning WMMS programming and promotional events in their Friday entertainment supplements. The mysterious "decision maker" at *Scene* magazine maintained his grudge against the station, which we later learned was directed at Denny and me for being "outsiders," and continued to ignore us.

We pounded out proposals for just about every student union and concert promoter, in addition to Belkin, to co-sponsor concerts with us by lending our call letters to them. In return, we provided additional free promotional mentions for their shows on what we called our WMMS concert "laundry list." We struck a comparable deal for rock-oriented and jazz crossover bookings at Rodger Bohn's Smiling Dog Saloon, a former bowling alley in a high-crime section of West 25th Street that was an oasis for musicians and booked the top names in jazz, plus occasional rock acts. The deal included a clause allowing concerts sponsored by WMMS to be recorded and broadcast on Saturday nights at midnight.

We had one great concert after another. Stand-outs: Joe Walsh and Barnstorm, Halloween night at the Allen Theatre in Playhouse Square—Barnstorm ran the range from tight and precise to pure improvisation, and Walsh was outfitted in a chef's outfit, complete with tall white hat. Lynyrd Skynyrd at the Smiling Dog—the perfect setting—they were young, had plenty to prove, and made certain no one would regard them as Allman Brothers Lite. Neil Young and what was left of Crazy Horse with Nils Lofgren played the Music Hall downtown; it was the infamous *Time Fades Away* tour, and anyone anticipating more *Harvest* was rudely awakened. There was Blue Oyster Cult at the Agora, Brian Auger and Weather Report at Case Western Reserve University's Adelbert Gym, Robert Klein and Melissa Manchester at the Smiling Dog, Leon Russell at Cleveland Stadium, and the underrated Ellen McIllwaine at the Smiling Dog. All were memorable shows, and the best was yet to come.

We really wanted the Agora, the 800-seat venue (meaning you could cram in 1,200) on East 24th Street north of Chester Avenue, on our roster of venues for co-promoting shows. It was located within easy walking distance of Cleveland State, and its parking lot was directly off the Chester Avenue exit on I-90. Owned by Hank LoConti, it was the city's best rock club and had its own studio, Agency Recording. But it had a contract for co-sponsorships and live broadcasts with WNCR. The deal was negotiated during WNCR's progressive-rock days, but owner Nationwide Broadcasting did not cancel the association when the station changed formats. So here was this conservative, nearly unlistenable Top 40, breaking format for a live hour of Spooky Tooth or Blue Oyster Cult. But Denny and I tried numerous times and could not get a meeting with owner Hank LoConti. Bob Karr, the salesperson Walt Tiburski assigned to the Agora, also called the club daily. Hank finally agreed that he and the club's booker, Jim Mauk, would meet with me, Denny, Karr, and Walt. We came up with a contract making one notable change from the WNCR deal. The national act shows would continue on Mondays, but instead of carrying them live, we would record and remix them for Wednesday evening broadcast. The *WMMS Monday Night Out at the Agora* made its debut in January 1974. Cleveland's growing rock and roll community was taking shape. Photographers Janet Macoska, Anastasia Pantsios, and Fred Toedtman covered every show and event—and became regulars shooting visiting artists at WMMS. Anastasia also covered the local music scene extensively for a number of publications, local and national. Freelance writers Tim Joyce and Derek Van Pelt also covered the local scene, but with observations far more skeptical and negative. Another local character was the ubiquitous "Peanuts," who used only that name, keeping his real name a mystery. Peanuts started out as a writer with *Scene* but had a falling out with the publication, went freelance, and was always a major supporter of local talent. I've known Peanuts for over thirty years and I still don't know his real name.

A talent we strongly believed in was singer-songwriter Peter Laughner, whom we felt would take his material international. Another person I met in my early days at WMMS was Michael Stanley, who played me his second album, *Friends and Legends*. After hearing it, I promised him I'd make certain WMMS was solidly behind it. For the next thirteen years, his career and mine would be intertwined.

CHAPTER 4

"THAT'S MY STATION!"

Debbie Ullman was the first of the new Boston hires to arrive, and she settled quickly into both the Cleveland and WMMS grooves. She bought a monster of a mid-1950s automobile and rented a tiny house by a creek that fed into the Ladue Reservoir near Hiram, in a rural setting that bordered on Appalachian, with a wood stove, an electric toilet, and a garden.

Her musical preferences ranged from the anticipated softer edge of progressive rock to, unexpectedly, some balls-out rock and roll. Her on-air delivery was just the right shade of bohemia—not overwhelming, not too earthy. Best of all, she ran a tight board—no dead air. She so exceeded expectations that I began cross-promoting her show in other dayparts (the time segments that divide a radio or TV day for ad scheduling purposes) within two weeks of her debut, instead of the planned three months to give her time to grow into the format. JC, a harsh quibbler when it came to new talent, considered her "a real find."

Then came Donna Halper. I hired her over the phone, without a face-to-face meeting, admiring the fact that she accepted the offer at my word. She arrived one evening early in November, after a long drive from Boston through bad weather. Her first words: "Aren't you going to ask me how my drive was? OK, I will. Terrible. It rained the whole way." She barely paused to take a breath. Her mood didn't lighten when she inspected the music office library, where she immediately noticed a misfiled album. "This is it, huh? This is what I have to work with? I wonder how many more of these

I'll find. So—I'm not what you expect, am I? I bet you were expecting some Boston hippie chick. Well, that's not me and if that's what you expected, I'm truly sorry."

That was Donna. Combative, always on the defensive, almost always assuming the worst in others. As time went on, I learned her attitude was the defense mechanism, and sometimes self-fulfilling prophecy, of someone who was introverted, shy, and didn't feel she fit in. But she proved to be the music director WMMS needed.

Debbie Ullman stopped by after her show one morning. In addition to working morning drive, she was WMMS public service/public affairs director, with the off-air duty of compiling and scheduling public service announcements—those ten- to sixty-second community messages radio stations were once required to carry by the FCC. She also scheduled and hosted a weekly one-hour public affairs program, also demanded by the FCC, that we named *Jabberwocky* after a similar program on WCVB-TV in Boston. (Contrary to myth, the title had nothing to do with Lewis B. Carroll and *Alice In Wonderland*, though we never denied it.) We chatted a few minutes, and she asked my opinion of newswriter Ed Ferenc. I put it back on her—what did she think of his work? No problem, she said, she enjoyed working with him. He had some great ideas, and he wanted to do his own newscast. I suggested he should see me the next day, giving me time to run the idea past JC, and giving Ferenc time to make an audition tape.

JC agreed that someone other than the morning host should deliver the news, and that multiple voices create team spirit. I cued up the audition tape, gave Ferenc my spiel on sounding authoritative, and said we'd try him out.

"What about my name?" he said. "Want me to change it from Ferenc?"

"No," I said. "It's 'Ed' I have a problem with." He looked stunned. I explained that was supposed to be a joke. We shook hands. Deal.

A few days into his newscasts, Ullman proposed "Flash" for him, Flash Ferenc, the name coming off a current Kinks track, "Here

Comes Flash." I came back with a compromise, Ed "Flash" Ferenc. Deal.

Among Donna's assets were the Canadian contacts she made in Cambridge. WCAS once added an album by Canadian artist Bruce Cockburn to its folk rotation, which led other Canadian labels and managers to send releases, hoping the exposure might lead to deals with U.S. labels. Donna asked her sources to continue the Canadian album service when she moved to WMMS, and to broaden it to rock and pop.

One of those contacts, Bob Roper of A&M Records, sent her the debut album by Rush, which originally was released on Moon Records, a small independent label. Donna brought it up in one of our Monday afternoon meetings, where she'd weed though the week's new releases and resubmit previously released material that, for one reason or another, we had held off on adding. It was fresh power rock our nighttime audience couldn't get enough of. Donna wanted to do Bob Roper a favor. A&M had passed on Rush, but Roper was hoping to establish a stronger relationship with the band's Canadian managers, knowing they would eventually deliver an artist his superiors admired.

We added the album and decided to concentrate on a track called "Working Man" instead of the preferred priority track, "In the Mood." "Working Man" sounded like fist-punching blue-collar rock. It went into our new-release bin that night. Denny played it that evening. The phones went wild with immediate and unexpected reaction: "Where did you get that new Led Zeppelin track?"

Denny called me at home, amazed at the size of the reaction and that most callers were convinced Rush was Zeppelin. I had a flashback to spring 1967, when Boston's WRKO convinced listeners that "New York Mining Disaster" and "I Can't See Nobody" by the Bee Gees could be the Beatles under a pseudonym. WRKO never said they were the Beatles, they just didn't say they weren't.

Now we had Rush to ride out and get everyone talking. I briefed Donna the next morning on her success in unearthing the kind of album we were lusting for, one the Top 40 stations couldn't deal with. We were beginning to build our "exclusive to WMMS" arsenal. "Well, of course!" she said. "Why should you be surprised? Isn't that why you hired me? I would have done the same exact thing you did anyway."

Despite her nonchalance, Donna was thrilled. She immediately phoned Roper, who insisted she call Rush's management. They had to hear this report from the source, and to know they needed to ship Canadian stock to Cleveland record stores. Within two weeks, the Rush album became the city's fastest-selling import, and soon afterward the band played a date at the Allen Theatre. In the liner notes on the American version, they thanked Donna and WMMS.

On a visit to Boston, I heard a couple of songs on WVBF I hadn't heard before—live versions of "Rocky Mountain Way" by Joe Walsh and "Frankenstein" by Edgar Winter. Both songs had crossed over from album radio to Top 40 in studio versions. Having WVBF's would give us an edge. Back in Cleveland, I asked David Spero if he was aware of a live release. He wasn't. I then called WVBF and asked for this inspirational BLF character I'd heard in my car one night the year before, who had, without knowing it, persuaded me during a moment of doubt to pursue a career in radio. I hoped to work some kind of trade, though the list of rarities we'd accumulated wasn't long. Bonnie Raitt's "Blender Blues" and Van Morrison's "Just Like A Woman" were not precisely WVBF fare. WMMS once had a supposedly notable live Led Zeppelin BBC concert, but it got pilfered with a few other gems during the Metromedia to Malrite transfer, and was sold to a used record dealer by a former announcer in debt.

I introduced myself to BLF and defined my mission. "Don't know where they came from. They're just here," he said. "Gimme your number an' I'll pass it along." I sensed he suspected I was a fed. But something told me I would work with this character someday. I pictured a grizzled old prospector.

A few weeks later, I got a call from Charlie Kendall, an on-air personality at WVBF. We talked for an hour, comparing notes, stations, music, likes, and dislikes. We worked out a deal for the Walsh and Winter tapes, strictly between us. The tape arrived a few days later. Kendall even included the complete Joe Walsh concert on the reel, featuring a blistering live version of "Turn To Stone."

I decided to wait until Friday night, party night, to launch those tracks and another. A small station in the South had sent me a half-hour tape of Lynyrd Skynyrd from a studio in Memphis. The show was recorded a few months before the band recorded its debut album. It included a live, slightly different arrangement of "Freebird" that opened with Ronnie Van Zant saying, "We're gonna put some grease in the fryin' pan." If they all went over as I anticipated, there would be a big buzz by Monday.

The phones went wild. By the close of 1973, "Freebird" was the most requested track on WMMS, and having the alternate live version allowed us to play it frequently. And because "Freebird" was already exclusive to WMMS—its length made it incompatible with the formats on WNCR, WIXY and WGCL—we now had a track that was competing against itself on the same radio station. It didn't get much better than that. We were giving listeners something they couldn't get at home or buy at a store.

Denny was put in charge of procuring live concert performances and rare studio recordings—a collection that would enlarge to thousands of reels and come to be known as the celebrated WMMS Archives.

Adding to our musical evolution was a developing kinship with Peter Schliewen of Record Revolution. In weekly visits to his store, we would listen to the latest imports, compare notes on music trends, and wonder how both his store and the station could capitalize on them. WMMS began adding more British imports, giving us another edge over the Top 40s; they were still in the early stages of reacting to us by adding album tracks from our most-played artists. Suzi Quatro, whose "48 Crash" became a most-requested tune, Curved Air's "Metamorphosis," and even Bryan Ferry's solo album became WMMS exclusives, because the Top 40 music directors didn't know where to find those tracks. Many British acts wanted us to play their imports in spite of what their U.S. labels said. They had better royalty rates in Europe and made more money selling albums manufactured there.

The labels began to see WMMS as a station with increasing influence in the retail record markets of Cleveland, Akron, and even Canton. When new music was played on WMMS, it sold, regardless of whether it did in other parts of the country. Unexpectedly, albums by acts like Roxy Music, the Sensational Alex Harvey Band, Audience, Larry Norman, the New York Dolls, and Brian Auger sold briskly and in greater volume in Cleveland than such album rock artists of the time as Electric Light Orchestra, Johnny Winter, Joni Mitchell, Manfred Mann, Bachman-Turner Overdrive, and Emerson, Lake and Palmer. *Friends and Legends* by Michael Stanley was, by year's end, a top three album in Cleveland.

Our pride in the station was growing, in all departments. In spite of the antediluvian equipment, there was a confident new feeling. Sales people were getting responses from buyers, notably from those around the same age, and they built a positive and untypical bond with both the programming and production staffs. Request lines rang so insistently that we hired interns from area colleges to handle the load.

Blue-chip advertising accounts—the department stores, banks, and fast food franchises—remained skeptical and, for the most part, on the sidelines. But Walt Tiburski's FM sales staff was gradually and methodically breaking down resistance, and steadily writing orders from clients who had become converts to the format.

We were briskly advancing toward the sound and image I imagined, maintaining countercultural creditability without estranging the conventional suburban young adult—the audience we needed to win. It was the place where, in the course of an hour, one could hear acts as dissimilar as Suzi Quatro, Andy Pratt, Linda Ronstadt, and Steve Miller.

WMMS's success at breaking new music was not limited to harder rock. Singer-songwriter Phoebe Snow broke out of the

Cleveland market, and a live cover version of Carole King's "Goin' Back" by Nils Lofgren went to heavy airplay on WMMS, catching on with the rest of the country within weeks, which forced A&M to release a civilian version.

Patti Smith's first commercial radio airplay anywhere was on WMMS with her independently released single, a cover of "Hey Joe" backed with an original composition, "Piss Factory," which we received from Peter Laughner, who also had a knack for finding cutting-edge music for us. Other acts like Pittsburgh's David Werner, New York's Elliot Murphy, and Boston's Andy Pratt and Jamie Brockett had more success in Cleveland than in their home towns.

The audience was becoming attuned to our image as an irreverent station. When the City of Cleveland lobbied stations to run a New Year's greeting from Mayor Ralph Perk proclaiming Cleveland a city on the rise, we scheduled his recorded announcement once per hour—adding the sounds of gunfire, police sirens, crackling flames, a laugh track, and a "yeah, sure" after every sentence. The city never protested, presumably because no one in City Hall would ever contemplate listening to this nothing FM station. Our listeners, however, called to cheer.

Ratings are a program director's report card. We'd live or die based on numbers from ARB—the Audience Research Bureau, which became Arbitron—which were based on four-week surveys taken three times a year. The morning the fall ratings for October–November 1973 arrived at the station, early in 1974, I saw JC and Milton Maltz crammed into JC's tiny office, two doors from the FM control room, wearing glum, solemn expressions. JC was seated and hunched over the desk. Maltz stood over him, trying to look over his shoulder.

"JC, I don't understand," Maltz grumbled, pronouncing the last word so it sounded like two. "We put in all this money, had all these BILL-boards, did EXACTLY what that sonofabitch MIKE-all JOE-seff told us to do, and LOOK AT OUR NUMBERS! Where ARE they?" Both Maltz and JC anticipated the October–November book as the one that would finally show the positive results they expected for WHK's expensive "cover hits" format designed by consultant Mike Joseph. It didn't. Known as "cover shits" around the building, it was D.O.A.

"Here, here, JC—look at this," Maltz snarled, pointing to another station's numbers. "We should be doing THIS—going UP . . . Look, John. Look! This station DOUBLED—DOUBLED—its numbers from the last ARB!"

Suddenly, both Maltz and JC looked stunned.

"My GOD, John," Maltz bellowed, clutching his chest, feigning a heart attack. "That's MY station! That's the FM!"

I ducked before they saw me. There was no way I could have kept a straight face in those circumstances. Back in my office, I closed the door and pumped my fist in the air. We were on our way! It wasn't until the next day that JC acknowledged an uptrend on WMMS to me, and two days before I could review an ARB survey book of my own. Back then, doubling our audience meant moving from a 1.9 share to a 3.8 in total audience. Unknown to me, at that time, was that the numbers were WMMS's best ratings to date. Among eighteen- to twenty-four-year olds, we were closing in on the crown.

Days later, the latest WHK program director was axed.

CHAPTER 5

NUMBER ONE

My biggest obstacle was our engineering department, which still relegated us to second-class status. Seeing an opportunity in our ratings improvement, I sent Fisher and JC a memo noting that the airstaff had been having problems with two turntables for well over a week. The problems could be heard over the air. Engineering's solution was to shut down one of the turntables. Fisher and JC agreed, insisting that engineering chief Tom Bracanovich pay attention to the Find Me frequency and assign an engineer to WMMS as his primary duty. Bracanovich designated Gary Sharpe, who resembled an addled Ted Nugent with his long hair and goatee. Sharpe ingratiated himself to the airstaff with a ready stash of pot and hash—and one day left a batch of potent, pot-laden brownies in the production room.

Fisher, who stopped in to ask about a missing spot and had skipped lunch because of another Maltz offensive, noticed the brownies and took a couple back to his office for a snack, not knowing what was in them.

Harlyn "Hal" Fisher, whom Maltz picked from his stations in Rochester, New York, to manage WHK and "the FM," was something of a fish out of water at WMMS. He grew up and attended college in South Dakota, spoke in what sounded like a southern Ohio drawl, and called himself a "small-town guy." He'd started his radio career as a sports announcer in Youngstown, moved into programming and sales, and for a brief time hosted a kids' TV show in South

Bend, Indiana. A lay church leader, he was genuinely uncomfortable hearing profanity. I never heard him say as much as "hell" or "damn." He was also a Nixon Republican who'd met the president and had a photo on the wall to prove it.

Later that afternoon I had a brief meeting with Fisher to discuss moving the music library. He appeared confused, and he rummaged through his office and briefcase. "I can't find my appointment book," he said. "I have a favorite pen I've misplaced. And I know there is something important I have to do, and I can't remember what it is. Did you ever have a day where you just feel agitated? I just don't feel connected with my body today. Hope I'm not coming down with something."

Later, he was pacing the hall. "I forgot what I was going up the hall for," he said. Minutes before 6 p.m., I saw him in the hallway again. "I know there's something I was supposed to do," he said, putting on his overcoat and rubbers, "but I can't remember what it was . . . and I still can't find my appointment book or pen . . . I don't want to have another day like today. I'm going to get some rest and hope I feel better tomorrow."

Less than five minutes after he left, I heard the sound of a madman trying to break down a door with his fists. I left my office, turned the corner, and found Maltz pounding on Fisher's office door. "Hal, where the HELL are you? Hal! Hal!" He asked if I'd seen Fisher, and said they were supposed to have a meeting. This was years before pagers and cell phones. There was no way to reach Hal. I said he might have gone home—he wasn't feeling well and looked ill.

"I don't CARE! He's not DEAD, is he?" Maltz said. "You mean he went HOME? We had a MEET-ing!"

A brief item in the *Cleveland Press* in January of 1974 said that WNCR, a local Top 40 AM station, was getting a new general manager. The station had a "modified Top 40 format," the story said, and "expects to keep it that way." Whenever those words appear in reference to a radio format, expect the opposite. A month later, Nationwide announced that the "modified Top 40 format" was history. Starting March 6, WNCR's format would be "tight," "upbeat," and country. Country on FM was Maltz's original intent for WMMS, before those frigging hippies coerced him into keeping album rock. Curses, foiled again. Maybe.

WNCR launched the format as scheduled. In Nationwide's free-spending promotional style, half the billboards in Greater Cleveland seemed to carry the news. I felt we ducked a bullet because the company hadn't moved WGAR, its hot adult-contemporary "Musicradio," to FM.

Eighteen days after that, a headline in the *Plain Dealer* caught the staffs of WHK and WMMS, not to mention WNCR, by complete surprise: "WHK to go country." The story in the *Cleveland Press* noted that five WHK disc jockeys and two newsmen had been discharged. In fact, the jocks read about the format change and their firings in the paper before getting official termination notices.

I dropped by sales manager Dave DeCapua's office to discuss a sales promotion and found myself blindsided by Maltz, who sat in the corner of the office, about to light a cigar. I congratulated him on the format announcement, and asked how he was going to take on WNCR. He stood, removed the still unlit cigar from his mouth, and crushed it in his hands. "We are going to c-r-r-RUSH the competition!" he snarled, grinning and crushing his cigar into an ashtray on DeCapua's desk. "This is the FOR-mat I wanted to do from the beginning. I made the mis-TAKE of listening to that greasy-haired KNOW-it-all from New York, Mike Joseph. I'm a better PRO-gram director than any of those guys. We will OWN this town."

WHK introduced its country format twelve days later, and a story in the *Plain Dealer* gave Maltz the chance to crow about programming the station his way. "Where I usually had used my own intuition and research," he said, "I decided to call in a so-called expert consultant to give me what I had hoped to be an objective third-person opinion of the format. He suggested the softer side as opposed to hard rock, with a downgrading of personalities and the bringing of music almost totally upfront. It's obvious that AM radio still is personality—plus music. FM's forte is tons of music where the human voice is an intrusion."

Maltz, Fisher, JC, and the AM sales staff rejoiced in the WHK format announcement. The WMMS staff regarded the *Plain Dealer* story in a different light. One line, in particular, drew everyone's attention: "FM's forte is tons of music when the human voice is an intrusion."

"It's nice to know what that little cocksucker really thinks of us," said Len Goldberg. "We're the fucking genie he'd like to put back in the bottle."

As I saw it, Maltz and JC would be hellbent on developing WHK and making life miserable for WNCR—leaving us free and clear to direct WMMS without the shackles of Malrite corporate. Country? Yee-haw!

After our fall showing, I believed WMMS had a chance to dominate in two categories: teens, and adults ages eighteen to thirty-four, by the spring survey covering April and May.

I was wrong. We did it with the Winter ARB, for January and February. In our primary target audience of listeners ages eighteen to thirty-four, WMMS ranked first, ahead of WGAR, WGCL, and fourth-place WIXY. Among men in that target age group, our margin of victory was even wider. Amazingly, we also climbed to second place among women, just behind WGAR.

We were ecstatic. But the most astonishing results were outside our target audience. Among adults ages eighteen to forty-nine—the category traditionally known as radio's "money demographic"— WGAR ranked first, but WMMS had climbed to second. Third-place WGCL was far behind. For WMMS to have this kind of showing proved that our brand of music was quickly gaining mass appeal. We also ranked second with teenagers, the audience traditionally owned by Top 40, behind WGCL and ahead of WIXY. It was party time. Walt Tiburski was already calculating a rate increase. It was my first major ratings victory, and a quite unexpected one. I sprinted down the hall to JC's office, ARB book in hand. "JC, we did it! What do you think! We're number one, eighteen to thirty-four— ahead of schedule!"

Huddled in the corner, like a wolverine eager to pounce on its prey, was Milton Maltz. He was not smiling. He stood up. "JAWN GOR-MAN? Come in here! Now, WHAT do you THINK," he bellowed, before a long pause. "What do you THINK those RAY-tings mean?"

"That we can raise the rates," I said.

"That's what SALES managers are supposed to think," he said, pointing a finger at my chest. "Do you know—do you REALLY, RE-ALLY, REALLY KNOW, what a PRO-gram director should be concerned with? Do you?"

"No, sir—what?"

"JACKALS!" he snarled. "JACKALS! JACK-ALS! You know what a JACKAL is? Now that you have these NUM-bers! Those NUM-bers you are holding in your hand! All the other RAY-DEE-OH stations in town—every PRO-gram director in town—are going to be like jackals! JACKALS! READY TO BITE YOUR ASS! Their mouths are salivating! Their teeth are gnashing! Jackals! Jackals! READY TO BITE YOUR ASS!"

Maltz looked at JC. "Anything to add?"

"No, Milt," JC said, looking slightly embarrassed. "You said it all."

"GOOD!" Maltz chortled. "Now, get OUT there and pro-TECT my RAY-dee-oh station!"

Afternoon host David Spero was becoming odd man out in terms of the station's musical direction. A staunch proponent of country-tinged and folk rock, he felt increasingly uncomfortable with the expanding airplay given British pop, glitter, reggae, and rhythm and blues. While other staffers were embracing new varieties of music, he confronted the transformation vigorously and openly. He told *Scene* magazine that 1973 "wasn't a really big year for music," when David Bowie "didn't happen big like he was supposed to," and little happened beyond the Eagles, Linda Ronstadt, and Joe Walsh.

It was not the collective opinion of the staff. But Spero had his own plans, which didn't include WMMS, and he resigned unexpectedly in March. "It's not to another radio station," he said. "Don't worry about that. I'm leaving radio altogether. I'm leaving to manage Michael—Michael Stanley. We're putting a band together, and he's gonna go on the road to support his album." They'd only known each other about a year. Stanley's father, Stan Gee, was a salesman at WHK who told Spero he had a kid who wrote songs and was friends with Joe Walsh—who had just done an album with Stanley. Spero listened to it, and loved it. He set up a *Coffee Break Concert* where Stanley played the entire album acoustically, and arranged a $250 appearance at Record Theater when Stanley's *Friends and Legends* album was released. Stanley, at the time, was working at Disc Records. The Record Theater appearance cost him the job, and he told Spero, "I guess it's just you and me."

Spero made the right decision. His experience and industry connections went back a decade to his teens, when he worked on *Upbeat*, the weekly music show that ran from 1964 to 1971 and was produced by his father, Herman, and syndicated nationally from WEWS-TV. He could provide Stanley the break he deserved, and *Friends and Legends* was the stuff of great albums. I also recognized their challenge. Though Stanley was a local artist, he didn't yet meet the cliquish standards of *Scene* magazine, the only local publication of any real circulation that supported local bands. "Originally a Cleveland boy," *Scene* said, when listing Stanley in its music calendar, "he became a buddy of the Colorado clan headed by Joe Walsh and Steve Stills." We assumed it was just another opportunity for the rag to slam WMMS and any artist—even local—connected to it.

I chose Kid Leo as Spero's replacement. His style of music was exactly what we needed in the afternoons. He wouldn't mind playing the Eagles and Ronstadt, or BTO or the Doobie Brothers or other stuff we needed to play, and he'd expose new music he believed in. The only stumbling block was clearing it with JC, and I scheduled a meeting for the next morning. I was armed, dangerous and ready to campaign. I told him of Spero's resignation, which was a nonevent because he wasn't going to a rival station and would be managing an act we were committed to. But my suggestion of Kid

Leo for afternoon drive met silence. I pushed. Leo had personality, and the potential of being great. He "got it" regarding our musical diversity, and he was a conversationalist who enjoyed talking with musicians. He would be able to interview Brian Eno one day, Neil Young the next, and Becker and Fagan from Steely Dan the day after that. He loved the music and the lifestyle. He was comfortable in the settings of concerts, clubs, or parties.

The expression on JC's face made one fact clear—he wasn't buying it. Finally, I showed him a list of what he would call "Kid Leo Music." A signficant number of titles had crossed into the mainstream from overnight airplay. I also produced a list of the top-selling albums in Cleveland, which had a fair amount of "Kid Leo Music" in the top thirty. I cited the successful Winter ARB.

"I know you feel highly about Leo," JC said. "I do not believe that man is ready for afternoon drive and certainly not the replacement for David Spero. I just don't know where this man's head is. You should replace David Spero with someone similar in style—not someone who is going to take that shift 180 degrees in a different direction. Who's that part-timer I heard filling in for Len Goldberg a few weeks back?"

"Matt the Cat? Wouldn't you have a problem with giving an afternoon drive shift to someone who is part-time, while Leo, who is full-time, remains on the all-night shift?"

"No, not at all," JC said. "A situation came up where you needed a milder mannered disc jockey, and Matt's your man. Leo's too out there for afternoon drive. I really can't let you do that."

I had no problem with Matt the Cat assuming the shift, but it violated an unofficial pecking order where dues were paid by gradual improvement in airshifts. Leo was already full time and it would be a logical choice to make him our new afternoon drive announcer.

It was a rare disagreement. I knew, from conversations with program directors in other markets, I had far more autonomy in programming than most. It was time to know my close. "I'll try Matt the Cat," I said, and called Matt with the news. He didn't even ask what the job paid. Leo called later, wondering if the plans for afternoon drive included him. I told him the truth, and told him not to worry—his time would come, and eventually I would get what I wanted.

Spero moved into music management, booking the Michael Stanley Band for its live performance debut at a heavily publicized *WMMS Monday Night Out at the Agora*. John Bassette, a popular African-American folk singer who was also Len Goldberg's neighbor, opened the show with a set spotlighting his WMMS hits, "Weed and Wine" and "Hessler Street." Jonah Koslen and Dan Pecchio, who had built his own following as a member of Phil Keaggy's famed Glass Harp, accompanied Stanley. But the moment everyone would remember was Kid Leo shoving a cream pie in Spero's face on stage. A slapstick farewell from WMMS.

Bryan Ferry of Roxy Music had scheduled a local promotional stop to boost interest in the band's first Cleveland performance, which was booked for May 26 at the Allen Theatre. Belkin Productions was anxious about the show, because they had booked Mott the Hoople, a more entrenched "new rock" band, for two shows the preceding night at the same venue. Complicating matters, a rival concert promoter, American, booked two shows at the Allen the night before, with the Eagles, another act receiving substantial airplay on WMMS. How far could the concert dollar stretch in Cleveland when the past thirty days had seen shows by the J. Geils Band, Mountain, Foghat, the Marshall Tucker Band, the Greg Allman Band, Steve Miller with Boz Scaggs and James Cotton, and two sold-out Genesis concerts? And when James Taylor, Brian Auger's Oblivion Express, Procol Harum and Golden Earring, King Crimson, and Jesse Colin Young were scheduled before the Mott the Hoople and Roxy Music shows?

Atlantic, Roxy's U.S. label, and EG, their management company and European label, chose Cleveland for the band's "breakout" market. The national music press and radio programmers were watching the Roxy Music phenomenon in Cleveland, and questioning if it was real. In Cleveland, Kid Leo was the champion of Bryan Ferry and Roxy Music. That brought him the privilege of introducing Ferry to the city. Arrangements were made for Ferry to spend an hour with Leo on his 6 p.m. to midnight Saturday show.

If listeners had been able to watch, they would have seen Kid Leo continuing his transformation from hard-rock street punk to sophisticated rocker. Having recently shaved his beard and updated his wardrobe, he wore a light-colored three-piece suit, doffing the jacket for the interview. His long, straight hair still fell well below his shoulders, but for the last time in a professional appearance. He made an appointment with a barber the following Monday and adopted the contemporary pompadour hairstyle he would be known for throughout his WMMS career.

The date of the interview, May 4, was the fourth anniversary of the Kent State University shootings where the Ohio National Guard killed four students. Jane Fonda, then derided as "Hanoi Jane" for her opposition to U.S. involvement in Vietnam and her visit to Hanoi, was one of the speakers at the annual memorial on campus. I sent Flash Ferenc to cover it. He was in the production studio as Leo's show opened, editing and preparing a special feature on the event, frantic to air it before Ferry's scheduled time of 7 p.m. He dashed into the FM control room to begin a report that lasted more than five minutes. Leo, tense and fidgety, silently rehearsed his conversation with Ferry and chain-smoked cigarettes in the back of the tiny studio. Predictably, Ferry and his entourage arrived one minute into Flash's report. Leo's nervous energy began veering into ire. He wanted the report to wrap fast. When Flash seemed finished, Leo threw him out of the studio without a closing, and segued immediately into the interview.

Ferry proved to be a consummate entertainer, an engaging conversationalist, and a discriminating guest disc jockey whose personal selections ran that evening from Bob Dylan to sixties rhythm and blues. Unlike many of the British acts of that era, Ferry was debonair, humorous, gregarious, and sharp. Listeners heard an extraordinary two hours of music and conversation—and the direction in which WMMS was leading both radio and musical tastes.

•   •   •

Then there was Lou Reed, who hit Cleveland in late September, 1974, to promote his fifth solo album, *Sally Can't Dance*. He was in his Orbitrol and Desoxyn drug period.

Billy Bass, the former WMMS personality and manager who was now working for RCA in New York, used his market knowledge to schedule a full day. He approached *Exit* magazine for a cover story on Reed, and Peter Laughner, the singer-songwriter-journalist-poet, drew the assignment. Denny and I rode in the limo with photographer Mike Mellen to meet Reed's flight at Cleveland Hopkins Airport.

It arrived around 11 a.m. Reed was first off the plane, wearing dark shades, a suede hat, and a leather jacket with its collar turned up, concealing the lower half of his face. On his arm was Barbara Falk, his publicist. He greeted us by spitting on the floor. Following dead-fish handshakes, he removed his hat, revealing close-cropped, peroxide-blond hair, and slipped into his drugged-out persona. Real or acted, it was difficult to tell. We piled into the limo to drive to Nighttown in Cleveland Heights, for a lunch including Jane Scott of the *Plain Dealer*, Peter Schliewen of Record Revolution, and miscellaneous WMMS staffers. There would be drinks in a private room, lunch, the interview with Leo at the station, and an in-store visit at Record Revolution.

Reed made two comments in the car. To Denny: "I hate your beard. You should shave it off." Then he asked if anyone was holding his drugs. Laughner opened a film canister he pulled from his jacket and handed Reed two black beauties, which he put in his pocket, ostensibly for later use. Reed was literally carried into the Nighttown, either as part of the act or out of the need for speed. Either way, it was a grand entrance. He was propped up against a wall inside the restaurant at a corner table.

Debbie Ullman, who knew him from the days when the Velvet Underground used to play the old Boston Tea Party club, approached him to reminisce, mentioning a mutual friend who'd lost a successful career in music to heroin addiction. "He's off smack," she said. "He's into yoga and doing really well."

"Fuck that," Reed said. "Chemicals do the same thing as yoga and meditation, and they do them faster."

Seeing a number of bearded people in the restaurant, including the waiter, Reed looked at Denny, snapped his fingers, and said, "Hey, you—you, you," until someone tapped Denny on the shoulder to get his attention. "Why does everyone have a fucking beard in this fucking city? What is this, beards-town?"

"Hey, Lou," Bass called from across the table. "Talk to Kid Leo here. You're gonna be on his show later." He motioned Leo to an empty seat next to Reed. Leo, developing into a skilled pro at interviewing the boorish British bands of the seventies, still looked apprehensive about meeting someone he saw as a true icon of rock. "Follow baseball?" he asked, searching for common ground. Reed nodded. "What do you think the Yankees' chances are in the Series?"

Reed lowered his shades for eye contact. "What league are they in?" he said.

"Why dontcha give me odds on the game?" Leo said. "When you come back next month we can settle the bet."

"I could bet you—but I won't keep my word," Reed said. "And I could sign something, but you wouldn't be able to read it, and if I lost the bet I wouldn't pay it off anyway."

An hour later, they were on the air. Leo did his best with Reed's one-word answers. Any attempt to converse was met with silence. Leo played a few tracks from the new album, promoted the Record Revolution appearance, and tried to close the interview on an absurdist note. "One more thing, Lou—is it true blonds have more fun?"

Reed replied, "Is it true you're an asshole?"

That ended the interview. I was irritated more at Leo than Reed, for not defending himself and getting in the final word, but recognized it wasn't worth pursuing. Reed was quickly escorted out of the station for his appearance at Record Revolution. The radio was on WMMS, and Leo was playing "Street Life."

"Who's that?" Reed asked me. "That's sweet."

"Roxy Music," I said. "It's from their *Stranded* album. I think they have a new one coming out in England next month."

"Fuck Roxy Music," he said. "I don't like them. I don't like their music. Bryan Ferry, right? I like his solo stuff better."

I decided to quit while I was ahead. At Record Revolution, Reed stood behind a counter, dancing, signing autographs—taking in the scene with apparent delight.

CHAPTER 6

IT'S STILL A BUSINESS

In May of 1974, Flash asked me to check out a tape from a Betty Bezkorovan, who was his girlfriend at the time. She sounded promising. I called to set up a meeting and listened to the tape again, realizing she'd already abridged her name to Korvan. We'd end up calling her Babz for short, and Krash whenever she had an accident in her battered Gremlin.

That was Betty Korvan—a petite and reticent exterior containing a mouse that roared. She was a Lourdes Academy graduate who was studying philosophy at Cleveland State when a friend who thought she had a nice voice talked her into doing news on WCSB. Betty got hooked on radio, met Flash, and followed the exodus to WMMS. She worked nights typing invoices at a West Side trucking company, and she turned out to be the biggest Led Zeppelin fan I ever met. I told her our two most important rules—"Don't fuck up," and "Don't make the same mistake twice"—and hired her for Saturday nights and vacation fill-ins.

We still needed one or two part-timers with commercial radio experience who would broaden our base beyond the Cleveland State station and my penchant for hiring Bostonians. Starting the search, I asked Denny for airchecks of the rejects as well as the prospects he had screened. He delivered a ratty box stuffed with tapes in their original envelopes.

I listened to one from a Jimmy Perdue, and was intrigued. His limited experience included part-time work on WABQ, one of Cleveland's two stations aimed at the black community. His tapes showed he was a little raw and lacked polish, but I liked him. I also liked the idea of a young African-American announcer on what was perceived as a white rock station since Billy Bass's departure in 1972. It could be another unique WMMS dichotomy. I set up a meeting with Perdue, liked him immediately, and signed him up. He resembled a young David Ruffin. Rather than put him on the air immediately, I gave him a month of off-air work to learn the music and cultivate his on-air sound by recording "test" shows—feeling gratified that WMMS had reached the point where we had a certain standard to live up to.

Advertising stretched us, too. Walt Tiburski had to add more people in sales to cover growing demand. Kid Leo, whose original off-air duty was writing ad copy for clients, couldn't keep up with the volume, even when I pitched in. I set up a schedule using the whole staff, with Denny and Matt the Cat as chief copywriters.

Volume wasn't the worst worry from advertising, however. WMMS was often the target of demonstrations, both pro and con, about our public service announcements and commercials for abortion referral services. I took a frightful measure of crap from Bible-thumping zealots. But when I barred the PSAs of one abortion referral service with a history of unethical practices, the service demanded to buy time, and said it was willing to pay "top of the rate card." I didn't oppose selling time to referral services or clinics, but I believed we had the right to require their services be genuine. To keep this disreputable group off the air, I told Hal Fisher, JC, and the sales department that we shouldn't run any paid spots for abortion referral services. After more discussion, and undeniable evidence of unethical practices by this particular service, we agreed not to carry their spots.

That would have been the end of the matter—except for Denny, who read a scheduled PSA for an approved, nonprofit abortion referral group, inadvertantly followed with "Since I Lost My Baby," by the Temptations. Though the incident took on urban legend status, it was an honest error. Of course, when Denny opened his show on Easter Sunday with Mott the Hoople's "Roll Away the Stone," that was a different story, and it caused a number of devout Christians to complain of his insensitivity.

Who would have thought we'd have that many devout Christians listening to WMMS on the way home from church?

An unusual tension spread through the building that spring. One reason, oddly, was that Milton Maltz had become lower key and less given to yelling and stomping tirades. Something was about to happen, but no one knew what. Then a tall young man was whisked up the stairs to the Malrite corporate loft. Maltz came to my office at the end of their meeting and asked if anyone could drive his guest to the airport. Jeff Kinzbach volunteered.

"Something's up," Kinzbach said the next day. "This guy, his name is Carl Hirsch, asked too many questions about WMMS. He was asking the kind of questions someone would if they were considering about coming to work here. He asked about you, about the airstaff. He wanted to know what we thought of Hal Fisher and Maltz, and he even asked about Dave DeCapua and Tiburski, and said he was flying back to Philadelphia."

A few weeks later, Malrite put out a memo welcoming Carl Hirsch as the new vice president and general manager of WMMS and WHK. He was a Cleveland native and a graduate of Shaker Heights High and Kent State University, and he started in radio as an intern answering phones for Cleveland radio legend Bill Randle on WERE. He sold advertising in Florida after college, at two Miami stations, before returning to Northeast Ohio. He worked at WKNT in Kent before getting hired as sales manager at WCUE—where he ended up as vice president and general manager, and added programming to his duties when the PD quit and there was no money in the budget to replace him. He was coming back to Cleveland from Philadelphia, where he was general manager of WRCP-AM and FM.

Carl was anything but subtle. A few days after he arrived, we had a new slogan: "We don't go to work. We go to war."

He had clearly defined goals for WMMS and WHK. He detested that Maltz ran the stations like small-market Wisconsin properties. He envisioned WMMS and WHK as major-market stations and would manage them as such. What he did best was keep Maltz at bay. Unlike Fisher, who became a constant target for Maltz's abuse, Hirsch did not take anything from anyone. He was not always the easiest manager to work for, but there was a method behind the madness. He was brilliant. He had no tolerance for office politics or internal conflict.

"When I first came to WMMS, I looked at it as a diamond in the rough," he said later. "One of the first problems I saw was unprofessionalism and a looseness that didn't have to be there . . . I came to Malrite here with the authority to do whatever was necessary, whether it be format changes or whatever. I had to evaluate the entire situation. With WMMS, I had to make it more professional." He looked at the books, said we were losing a fortune, and concluded that Malrite really needed to invest more money. "We liked the musical format just as it was," he said, "but to continue to do it, we'd have to realize some financial or commercial success, so that we could support paying everybody. Because it's still a business, it isn't only a club. And there was a club mentality that prevailed around here, like, 'This is an in thing and you don't understand.' I said, 'I do understand, but we have got to sacrifice a little something to pay for it.' I think if I brought anything to the station, I brought a business sense to it, but at the same time not losing any of the show business flair and the flair for what we really had—a creative product."

He got it. With Carl, I knew we could reach our goal of being the best rock station in the country.

But his first focus was WHK. Carl took its country format a step further by turning it into a combination talk and country station, and hiring Gary Dee—the city's most controversial and top-rated talk host—to do morning drive. Joe Finan moved to middays, giving WHK a one-two punch of well-known personalities. Fueled by Dee starting the day, WHK rose to the top of the ratings in a matter of months.

Carl didn't miss a thing. I learned that because of Archie Rothman, whose *Time Machine* was a program I inherited on Sunday nights. It was a jumble of old radio shows, comedy, and show tunes that had nothing to do with our audience, but apparently drew some regular listeners. Personally, I couldn't listen to it. Rothman had a head of hair he dyed bright red, and seemed to have a vast knowledge of show business esoterica and erotica from early in the century. But he was a handful.

Hal Fisher worried because Rothman invariably brought teenage boys he called "interns" with him when he taped his show on Wednesday or Thursday evenings. Suspecting they were underage, and concerned about the station's potential liability, I had to tell him no guests were allowed. Carl was listening on a Sunday night in early June when Rothman, doing a show on ragtime music, played the "Fuck Cheer" version of Country Joe and the Fish's "I-Feel-Like-I'm-Fixin'-to-Die Rag." When I arrived at the station the next morning, a note was already taped to my door: "See me at once." I did, and a furious Carl let me have it.

I suspected Rothman was testing the waters. It was not unusual to detect blatant, often gay, double entendres sprinkled through his programs, which were sloppily edited anyway. He pleaded ignorance when I called him, claiming the only reason the "Fuck Cheer" aired was that he did not have the original studio album with the "Fish Cheer," and was unaware that the *Woodstock* album version was different. I asked Denny to check the last few *Time Machine* shows, for anything from bad edits through double entendres to material Rothman might have used when his show was carried on WXEN and WNCR. Denny reviewed four shows, heard numerous double entendres, found all four had material from WNCR, and even heard one mention WXEN. Rothman was recycling old shows into new ones, but his sloppy editing gave him away.

"It gets worse," he said. "You know, I like the guy, he's an eccentric old soul. But the quality of his edits is terrible. It's clear that some of the material was taped from television, probably on a hand-held mic held up to the speaker, because you can hear shuffling in the background. The levels are all over the place. And he's giving free plugs to restaurants and gay bars in Lakewood, to antique stores along Lorain, and he mentions this book store on the West Side in every single show. I know these are not logged as commercials." For example, there was Rothman's visit to the Cleveland

Public Library, "which is only seven blocks away from Lordburger [a fast-food chain], where I had a delicious, juicy hamburger."

"I'm going to call Archie and read him the riot act," I said. "Don't tell Carl about this other stuff."

"You just did." Carl was standing behind us and heard everything. "I want you to call Rothman and tell him, in no uncertain terms, if he violates any further rules with this progam, it will be canceled immediately."

Carl's secretary delivered a memo to me confirming our conversation and his point. I shot a memo to Rothman. It asked why a show supposedly focused on the year 1916 included the Woodstock cut, which could jeopardize our license; told him production was unsatisfactory and that programs needed to feature new material; banned promotions, giveaways, and contests, and banned him from the control room and record library, from which he'd borrowed and not returned material. As a courtesy, I phoned to read him both Carl's memo and mine.

"Why? Why? Why? I feel like I'm being singled out and persecuted like some outcast," he cried. "I can't do a fresh show for this Sunday. Why didn't anyone bring it up before? Why is it an issue now? Why, why, why?" He said he would come in to redo the next show to make it completely original, and asked if he could bring friends to help—"a couple of high school kids I'm teaching the ropes to, fine boys."

"Archie," I said, "take my advice. Quit while you're ahead."

He redid the show, and Carl was mollified. But problems continued. I had to review the show in advance every week. The beginning of the end came when I needed somebody to take over hosting the public affairs interview show *Jabberwocky*. Rothman volunteered, noting he had connections with the arts community. Recycling or pirating material wouldn't be possible, so we gave him a shot. Then a guest on the show criticized the way gay people were labeled in the media, saying, "A man fellates one penis and he's branded a cocksucker for the rest of his life."

When that went out over the air, Rothman ran out of second chances.

.   .   .

Sales manager Dave DeCapua, who had hired most of the WMMS sales staff, resigned and moved into television. The odd choice to replace him was John Gil Rosenwald, an ex-Marine who went by his middle name. He sold time in the early days of WMMS, in the late 1960s, and frequently talked about deserving a Purple Heart for a few years he spent with Procter & Gamble. The sales staff labeled him "The Big Plain," after the McDonald's hamburger with nothing on it. Plain was not our style.

In the hallway, after Rosenwald's appointment was announced, Carl asked Murray Saul what he thought of Gil's appointment. Murray replied loudly, "He doesn't inspire me" and Gil overheard the comment.

Len Goldberg was miffed about getting no response when he asked about negotiating a raise. He could walk out as a free agent, because he had no contract, and his commercial spots had given him some recognition. Dramatizing an air-conditioning problem that engineering had ignored, leaving the studio almost unbearably hot, he did his entire show wearing nothing but bikini briefs—and, for effect, remained that way off the air. A few weeks later, Boom resigned to concentrate on commercial voiceover work.

I moved Matt the Cat from afternoon drive to middays, feeling he had the style to replace Goldberg's distinct voice and personality. To replace Matt, I got JC's reluctant agreement to move Kid Leo to afternoon drive in thirty-day trial periods. JC wanted to meet with Carl about loosening the purse strings to hire what he called a "real" afternoon drive talent, so Leo could return to overnights, "where he belongs." I played along, planning to stall the proposal indefinitely while alerting Leo. "I ain't gonna let anyone take this away from me," Leo said. "No JC, no Hirsch, no nobody. I'll show those motherfuckers I'll be the best damned fucking afternoon drive jock they ever had." Jimmy Perdue, my recent hire, replaced Leo in the overnight slot.

Nothing in radio is permanent, but the schedule was more temporary than anyone imagined. Boom called a few weeks later, saying he wanted to return. JC agreed to it, and we created one of the most unsual lineups in station history. Debbie Ullman did morning drive, from 6 a.m.–9 a.m.; Len Goldberg came on from 9 a.m.–noon; Matt the Cat went from noon to 4 p.m.; Leo did afternoon drive from 4 p.m. to 7 p.m.; Denny followed from 7 p.m. to 10 p.m.; Steve Lushbaugh was on from 10 p.m. to 1 a.m., and Perdue held the shift from 1 a.m. to 6 a.m.

I left at the end of July for a week's vacation on Cape Cod. Denny was acting PD. He called expressing concern about Perdue, who hadn't been the same since attending a WMMS-sponsored concert with the New York Dolls at Chippewa Lake amusement park in Medina County the previous weekend. Perdue was breaking format and speaking gibberish. I asked Denny if we could ride out the week and deal with it the following Monday. He said he'd try.

Driving back to Cleveland late Sunday night, I reached signal range of WMMS after crossing the Ohio border from Pennsylvania. Donna Halper was wrapping up her *Prisoner Request Show* and sounded distressed. It was only 1:45 a.m., fifteen minutes early, and it wasn't like her to cut out early on a show that was her pet project. Perdue was up next. I heard three consecutive cuts tracked from Funkadelic's *Free Your Mind . . . and Your Ass Will Follow*, followed by silence. Perdue opened the mic and recited the lyrics to the three tunes he had just played. Uh-oh. Perdue, who brought his dog to work with him, tried to get it to speak. "Speak, puppy. Puppy, speak. Speak, puppy, come on. Speak. Puppy, speak. Come on, puppy—speak." Twenty minutes of that.

I rushed into the station at seven the next morning and was met immediately by a worried-looking Debbie Ullman. "He's in bad shape," she said. "Someone slipped him PCP in a joint at the Dolls concert, and he never came down." Moments later, a glassy-eyed Perdue, in conversation with himself, came down the hallway. One could not converse or reason with him. Within an hour, he was sitting lotus-style on Prospect Avenue, just outside the station parking lot, intending to commit suicide by getting run over.

I called the police and Perdue's parents. Marion Bow, a Hessler Street neighbor of Len Goldberg and occasional date of Murray Saul who was working in the station reception area, helped me talk Perdue back inside, convincing him there were better options than ending it all. Despite therapy and professional care, however, too much damage had been done. It would not be best for Perdue to return to active duty on WMMS. Betty Korvan moved to nights as a full-timer. Months later, we learned the identity of the scoundrel who fed Perdue the PCP: Members of New York Dolls' road crew were supplementing their income by selling large quantities of PCP and other hard drugs to local dealers.

CHAPTER 7

HATCHING THE BUZZARD

Over the decades, you might have read and heard many variations on how this bird of prey emerged as the WMMS mascot and logo. Contrary to myth, it was in no way inspired by the annual return of the buzzards to Hinckley, Ohio. I was not even aware of Hinckley until 1975. And it wasn't filched from another station or similar mascot. But I can thank the long-gone *National Lampoon Radio Hour* for unintentionally giving us both the need and the means to create the Buzzard.

The original WMMS logo displayed the call letters beneath a half-rainbow. A corporate design shared by all Metromedia album-rock stations, it was Madison Avenue's version of psychedelia—straight out of the late 1960s, complete with lettering that went out of fashion with *Laugh-In*. It was briefly updated, in the early seventies, by adding a tongue logo like that used by the Rolling Stones. If the Stones didn't sue Metromedia, they should have.

Because Metromedia owned the rainbow design, Malrite needed a new logo after it assumed ownership of WMMS in December 1972. The first effort, unveiled in January 1973, used the call letters as an acronym for the slogan "Where Music Means Something." It was crudely drawn on a sickening yellow background for an early poster, using a lettering font nearly identical to one adopted several years later by competitor WWWM-FM, "M105." Unfortunately, the slogan begged to be abused. Any product that has been around for a while, including a radio station, is best known for what it once was. The best WMMS, up to that point, was the station of Billy Bass,

Martin Perlich, and "Queen Bitch" Shauna Zurbrugg; the WMMS of January 1973 was a muddle that showed the glory days of FM radio were over. Wherever the poster was hung, it became standard practice to revise it to "Where Music MeanT Something."

Walt Tiburski wanted a new logo to replace it from the time he joined WMMS, soon after it was adopted. He asked his sister, Judy, a graphic artist, to create a design depicting WMMS as a mainstream progressive-rock station. She delivered "The Mushroom." It looked phallic, and it was supposed to—and to ensure that no one missed the sex, drugs, and rock and roll message, an elf or leprechaun was added, tokin' a joint next to the mushroom stem. Judy also cleaned up the lettering. For that moment in time, it was the perfect logo. WMMS had no real marketing budget, but Tiburski somehow managed to come up with a few hundred bumper stickers and T-shirts.

The Mushroom logo was in use in July 1973, when I became music director and returned a call to Robert Michaelson, Jr., who was entering the radio syndication business with a radio version of *National Lampoon* magazine. I was interested, listened to a demo, and liked it. *The National Lampoon Radio Hour*, mainstream comedy for the Baby Boom generation, debuted Sunday night, September 16, 1973. Response was immediate, in Cleveland and across the country. Michaelson had a hit—a home run.

A few weeks later, we signed our first trade contract, trading on-air commercial time for print ad space, with *Zeppelin* magazine, an alernative biweekly based in Cuyahoga Falls. Our first ad was scheduled for their debut issue in January, 1974. Denny thought up a full-page ad depicting a radio tower shooting lightning bolts, under the headline "Tower of Power." When the slogan turned out to be the copyrighted name of a syndicated religious program, we came up with "Soundwaves Bounce Back." We wanted the ad to look like a comic book cover, with caricatures of our airstaff in individual circles surrounding the tower.

Judy Tiburski was busy with other projects, so Walt suggested using a staff artist from Tokyo Shapiro, a local chain of audio stores whose odd name came from having Jewish owners selling mostly Japanese-made equipment. Walt had a strong relationship with the chain. He kept some of the women in its Euclid headquarters supplied with concert tickets, albums, and tight, thin Mushroom T-shirts, which they wore braless to WMMS events. He nicknamed them the Tokes. I gave their artist, Greg Souchik, a stick-figure sketch of our proposed ad and publicity photos of our staff. A week later, he brought us the finished product. We paid him in albums and concert tickets. It was our first full-page ad.

Denny and I were satisfied with the caricatures, but not the "Soundwaves Bounce Back" slogan—or the Mushroom. It communicated sex and drugs, but not rock and roll. It had a static, generic quality, and you couldn't animate it. We decided to work on something new, looking ahead to March and the advance promotion, or "roll up," for the spring ratings period that started in April. We discussed logos we knew. I mentioned a study in Boston that gave top honors to the Indian bust design of Shawmut Bank as the region's most recognized symbol. A staggering level of respondents, close to eight of ten, associated the logo with the bank. We also talked about well-known radio logos and agreed that our favorite was the stencil-style lettering of WBZ and the Westinghouse stations—in part because it stayed consistent regardless of format or promotion changes. We reviewed sports logos such as Chief Wahoo, the mascot of the Cleveland Indians. Why couldn't a radio station have a mascot like a sports team? We met with JC, who suggested we adopt the slogan "Air Aces" from WABX in Detroit. But we didn't want to do a blatant steal from another station, and Cleveland's WKYC had used a similar slogan, "The Greatest Air Show on Earth," in the sixties. Then I flashed back on an earlier idea.

Driving home one evening, in early December 1973, I pulled out of the parking out and passed underdressed hookers shivering under umbrellas on Prospect Avenue. Turning onto East 55th Street and heading east on Euclid Avenue, I saw a faded, disintegrating sign next to an abandoned building that read, "Mayor Perk's Model Cities Program." Denny was playing "Desolation Row," from Bob Dylan's *Highway 61 Revisited* album. I couldn't have asked for a better soundtrack to the drive along the dark, dreary potholed route. I was living in an apartment on Euclid and Cliffview Road in

East Cleveland. A few nights earlier, I heard what I thought was the sound of firecrackers; it was a shooting that left three people in critical condition. Once past University Circle, I was driving through neighborhoods that resembled a war zone.

I thought of the popular poster I had on my office wall, depicting two buzzards sitting on a branch, one saying to the other, "Patience, my ass. I'm gonna kill something." It captured the attitude of the time. The discussion Denny and I had about a logo was fresh on my mind. When I reached home, I stick-figure sketched a smirking buzzard, perched on a tombstone overlooking a graveyard. A bird of doom for a dying city whose centerpiece was a crumbling building with the name Terminal Tower.

I completed the sketch. The despicable looking Buzzard licked its chops over a gravestone marking the burial site of WIXY. Other stones in this mushroom-covered radio necropolis belonged to WNCR and WGCL. I didn't bother with WLYT. Few knew of that station, dead or alive. A streamer at the top of the page, in the horror style of E.C. Comics, read "THE WRATH OF THE BUZZARD!" I decided to sketch a second version, slightly tamer, in case *Zeppelin* took offense to the call letters on the slabs. This one had the same Buzzard, in a field of mushrooms, but perched on an immense mushroom instead of a gravestone, holding two ARB diaries in its saliva-dripping beak. One book for WIXY, the other for WGCL. If this second version was also rejected, I figured we could easily erase the other stations' call letters and replace them with the word "ratings." An abundance of mushrooms in the print ads would make a smooth transition to the Buzzard.

I showed Denny the sketches the next day and began to define the Buzzard. He got it immediately, and compared the Buzzard to Fritz the Cat, R. Crumb's Zap Comics character. I sent copies of the stick-figure sketches to Souchik at Tokyo Shapiro and asked him to call back for specific information. But he felt the WMMS work would take too much of his time. We never heard from him again.

Around the same time, Robert Michaelson called to let us know he was cutting his *National Lampoon Radio Hour* to a half-hour on December 9. Its national sponsor, 7UP, had withdrawn after the

Nixon impeachment show, which they found offensive. We agreed to carry the shortened version, and we filled the second half hour with *Untitled*, which was hosted every week by a different air personality given total freedom to program it however they wanted.

The day after the show, I walked into the station lobby and a visibly stressed Verdelle Warren, our usually unflappable receptionist, handed me a stack of phone messages. All were complaints. I asked her to put through to me the next complaint call that came in. I barely reached my office before the phone rang. "You motherfucking asshole! WMMS fucking censorship! Where the fuck do you get off, man? You guys suck."

I asked what the problem was. "You fucking are. You censored the fucking *National Lampoon* show." I said we didn't censor anything. "Fuck, yeah—you fuckin' cut the second half hour." I said we were notified in advance that the show was being cut. Why else would we have a new show ready to go on after it? "You fucking liar. They fucking said so at the end of the show. They said you censored the show."

I asked for the caller's number and promised to call back, then went to production and asked Jeff Kinzbach to fast-forward to the end of the show. It ended with the announcement, "This radio station is censoring the second half of the *National Lampoon Radio Hour*." It was a prank, by the Radio Hour, on the stations carrying it. I returned to my office and returned the listener's call, telling him they fooled us, too. "You're a fucking liar. I heard what they said." I started to clarify. He hung up.

The calls continued, followed by letters—including two well-packaged, larger-than-average envelopes that arrived the morning of December 12. The first contained a comic strip. Its first panel was a crude drawing of a frog sitting on a lily pad, smoking a joint and listening to the *National Lampoon Radio Hour* on headphones. The second panel has the frog kicking the WMMS mushroom violently out of the pond. A complaint in the form of a comic strip? I loved it. The artist had a return address on West Boulevard. His name was Mark Spangler.

The second envelope held a neater, three-panel strip showing a long-haired hippie toking a joint, leaning against an immense transistor radio tuned to WMMS for the *National Lampoon Radio Hour*. The second panel had a giant mushroom crashing down on the radio, cutting short the Lampoon broadcast. In the third panel, the listener said, "You people have the best FM I've ever heard, but whatdya mean cuttin' the hour in half!!" The artist's signature on the strip was "Dave." The return address was "Dave, W.Blvd."

I showed it to Denny and said we had our artist. Now we had to find him. Denny got on the case. It took a few weeks, but he followed a trail that led to American Greetings and Helton's girlfriend, who passed on the message that "a John Gorman from WMMS called and wants you to do some work for him."

David Helton, the "Dave" from the second comic strip, and Mark Spangler turned out to be roommates who had migrated to Cleveland from Chattanooga, Tennessee, for entry-level jobs drawing cards at American Greetings. Helton was a fan of WMMS, and he was ecstatic over our interest in him. Since he worked full time at the greeting card sweatshop, he could only meet with us in the evening. I wasn't available on a night that he was, but I suggested he come to the station and meet with Denny, who gave him the stick-figure drawings and explained the image we were looking for. It was a thrill for Helton just to meet Denny, whom he listened to nightly on his favorite station. He called in early April when the artwork was completed. I gave Denny twenty dollars out of my pocket to cover it—figuring I'd be reimbursed and that concert tickets and albums would supplement it. Denny and David agreed to meet at West 50th and Detroit Avenue, neither of them realizing there was no such place. Fortunately, on one of those windy, sleeting April days that feel like February in Cleveland, they both went to the nearest intersection, West 48th Street.

Denny unveiled the artwork. Helton's finished product, the first Buzzard, blended the classic cartoon style of the 1930s and the E.C. horror-comic style of the 1950s. It was the meanest, most bad-ass Buzzard imaginable, complete with an evil eye and smug smirk, under the headline "Wrath of the Buzzard." Perfect. We showed it around. The airstaff loved it. Malrite and the WMMS sales department opposed changing the Mushroom logo. Denny and I propped the art against the wall in my office and stared at it for a while. "I say go with it," I said. "Me, too," Denny said.

The Buzzard made its debut on April 16, 1974, in *Zeppelin*. They had no problem with the gravestone references to other stations. In fact, they said they admired our "feisty spunk." After *Zeppelin* folded, we quickly made a trade deal to put Buzzard ads in another new alternative weekly, *Exit*. Writer Tim Joyce wrote, "It's a perfect image for rock and roll suiciders pushing thirty and stuck in jobs that they hate in a city that Gorman seems to be symbolizing in a rotting cadaver." Pure poetry. And even though they were wrong, we did not dispute the listeners who insisted the real meaning of the mascot was the "buzz" in Buzzard. "Yeah, man, I get it, man— the Buzzard's got a buzz on, man."

We could put the Buzzard in typical "listener" roles: in the shower, cruising down the highway in a spiffy convertible, on a boat, on roller skates. The character became more defined. Naturally, there were also in-house, not-for-publication versions that showed the Buzzard enjoying a fuller array of activities covered by sex, drugs, and rock and roll.

Still, the Buzzard was not the official WMMS logo. The Mushroom was. Judy Tiburski's original design was morphed by our printer into a slick "psychedelic" (read "dated") version that appeared on all official stationary. The Buzzard was still an outcast in his own home. And the twenty dollars I fronted for the art? When I put in for reimbursement it was rejected, because I didn't have prior authorization.

It was time for some guerrilla marketing. One front opened thanks to an act named Lucifer's Friend—a powerhouse hard rock band from Germany. Their album had cracked the top twenty in Cleveland, and only Cleveland, thanks to concentrated airplay on WMMS. Their American rights were held by Billingsgate, a tiny independent label in Chicago. One of its principals, Ralph Cox, also managed a silkscreen business, Fountainhead International, which he ran out of his garage. He pledged to print a couple hundred T-shirts for us with Lucifer's Friend on the back and the Buzzard logo on the front.

Around the same time, Billingsgate released an album by another German band, Epitaph. I cut a deal for Cox to print an equal number of Epitaph/Buzzard T-shirts, but Billingsgate substituted the band Neu, an experimental electronic act they needed help with. No problem. I just wanted the Buzzard visible, and on the front.

Waiting for the T-shirts, I found a second roost for the Buzzard—the movies. Thanks to a trade deal Walt Tiburski set up through Academy Advertising, a slide of the horrendous "Where Music Means Something" poster appeared onscreen during previews at Loew's theaters in Greater Cleveland. Helton designed a new slide that had the Buzzard welcoming moviegoers, and reminding them to listen to WMMS after the show.

Biggest of all, literally, was the deal we cut with Shelly Turk, owner of the Music Grotto record store on Euclid Avenue across from Cleveland State University, which put a larger-than-life Buzzard on the side of the building. Record labels took turns leasing the Grotto's west-facing side wall to paint building-size reproductions of current album covers. Because WMMS was the only station in town regularly programming their product, I proposed that they include and pay for the Buzzard art as well.

The deal provided the character, perched on a mushroom, a permanent roosting place, and gave WMMS its first billboard—a prominent one. The Buzzard shared space with David Bowie's *Diamond Dogs* cover, Gary Wright's first solo album, and the Sensational Alex Harvey Band's *Next*, among many others. The Buzzard roosted on the Music Grotto wall until the building was torn down in the early 1980s.

Billingsgate printed 500 Buzzard T-shirts, one hundred more than expected. We distributed the shirts to everyone on the airstaff and support staff, including interns, engineers, and office help—even WHK staffers sympathetic to the cause. When an air personality made a personal appearance or hosted an Agora or Smiling Dog

"Night Out," wearing the Buzzard T-shirt was mandatory. We gave a number away at personal appearances. In May, I wrote a memo to the staff: "It's voting time again. What would you prefer for the next batch of WMMS shirts and stickers—the original mushroom design or the new David Helton creation, the WMMS Buzzard? I need feedback. Meanwhile, check out the Music Grotto wall."

Slowly, the sales department gave in to the Buzzard. Carl Hirsch listened to my long justification for the character and vision for its marketing. I believe he was already sold, and he approved making it our official logo. The only part he didn't know was that the *Lucifer's Friend* album cover on the T-shirt—depicting a tall young man in a trench coat next to a wizened geezer with a hook for an arm—was unofficially recognized by everyone at WMMS and WHK as "the Hirsch and Maltz portrait." Copies hung on nearly every office wall and remained an inside joke for years.

Helton was ready. We joked about the Buzzard becoming Cleveland's Mickey Mouse—leading to a Buzzard Land amusement park filled with sex, drugs, and rock and roll themes—which led us to consider the irreverence of Rocky and Bullwinkle, and how the Buzzard needed to symbolize lampoonery and double entendres.

Helton brought up Looney Tunes, with Porky Pig saying, "Tha-tha-tha-that's all, folks" at the end of a cartoon, and sketched the Buzzard in a Looney Tunes–style target. But it resembled a dartboard—ammunition for our rivals. He drafted more conceptions, first drawing the Buzzard's head, then sketching a backdrop. He tried circles, triangles, and finally the "Star Buzzard" logo, the most familiar of all Buzzard designs. We never used consultants, outside agencies, staff meetings, focus groups, or test marketing for it or any Buzzard campaign.

With the Buzzard our official logo, we coveted the idea of going where no station had gone before. How we could exploit the identity, how could we make WMMS greater than the combined respective peaks of WIXY, KYW, and WHK? How could we build the Buzzard into the most recognized logo in Cleveland since Chief Wahoo? Going beyond the obvious T-shirts and sweatshirts, I felt we could market key chains, belt buckles, roach clips, even Buzzard comic books, and we did. Denny warned against letting the logo become too corporate, and he had a point. One of the most difficult things was knowing where to stop. Even though the Buzzard was created for promotional, commercial purposes, I wanted to keep it as a sort of icon and avoid crossing a vague line into exploitation.

JC wanted someone to dress up in a Buzzard suit. Sports teams from high school to pro were being overrun by costumed mascots inspired by the San Diego Chicken—which originally was the KGB Radio Chicken but outgrew the station. I resisted. When WMMS had a "Buzzard event," the Buzzard should be there, as the symbol of the station, on banners and signs. But our personalities should represent the station. How would somebody in a Buzzard costume present himself? I won that one, but had a close call when somebody showed up at a station event wearing a Buzzard costume— homemade but very impressive, and very close to the official logo. He had gone to a great deal of trouble, and he was there to say he could be the Buzzard. "You better take that off right away," I told him. "The copyright laws and lawyers are way beyond us. You've got to get rid of it. You could be in big trouble." I never saw the costume again.

I wanted the Buzzard to have a mystique. The character could be depicted in all sorts of ways—in print, in animation, on clothing, on inflatables—and doing all sorts of things. But if somebody dressed up as the Buzzard, the character would lose its "theater of the mind" quality. As long as he kept that quality, the Buzzard could be as iconic and intimate, and as real and illusory, as radio itself.

Our one real problem with the Buzzard came, ironically, when we tried a partnership with Hinckley—the Medina County township that officially observed the annual return of its buzzards, which are actually turkey vultures, with Buzzard Day. Since the late 1950s, it's been a folksy event featuring a pancake breakfast sponsored by the chamber of commerce at the local elementary school. Some see it as a first sign of spring, and it seemed like a natural for us. We decided to become an official sponsor in 1976, contributing on-air promotion. We didn't make a big deal of it, but we tried to find a place in the Cleveland Metroparks' Hinckley Reservation for an appropriate musical performance, something acoustic and folk oriented. We didn't succeed in that, but Hinckley was excited about our participation. Neither we nor they had any idea what it would bring to a typically gray March day.

It literally became a victim of its own success. An unprecedented crowd arrived, and Hinckley came to a gridlocked standstill. The park was jammed. To the regulars, it was invasion. So many gave up trying to get into the all-day pancake breakfast that it did less business than usual. It was like Woodstock had come to town, complete with long-haired pot smokers. Rumors spread that folk singer John Bassette would perform with Alex Bevan, or that a rock festival was taking place somewhere in the park. I saw it as a huge success. Hinckley was furious. We had to send our marketing and promotion director, Dan Garfinkel, to a town meeting a week later, armed with an apology and a $5,000 check for the Chamber of Commerce. He barely escaped with his life.

The next year, the Buzzard had no part in Buzzard Day. At Hinckley Elementary School, where drawing a buzzard was an annual assignment, a parent told me kids were warned that anyone drawing the WMMS Buzzard would get an automatic D.

CHAPTER 8

THE WORLD SERIES OF ROCK

Early in 1974, an opening act for Wishbone Ash, at the Allen Theatre, went unnoticed except for a small review in *Scene*: "Opening the concert was Bruce Springsteen, heralded as 'the next Dylan.' Well, judging from his performance, Springsteen is about as much the 'new Dylan' as Archie Bunker is a commie." Springsteen returned to Cleveland two weeks later, in late February, this time to headline a *WMMS Monday Night Out at the Agora*. Backed by a seven-piece, pre–E Street band, he delivered a blistering performance to a house less than half full.

Springsteen notwithstanding, we were packing most of the Agora Nights Out—no easy feat considering that Monday is the quintessential "dead" night for the average club. Jules Belkin was enjoying near-sellouts of any concert we co-sponsored with an album rock artist.

Live shows and concerts had become part of our success. We had a well-oiled machine supporting them. Radio formats and playlists in other cities were tightening up, but we moved in the opposite direction. We started approaching virtually anybody doing a concert in town, pitching free plugs for "co-sponsorship" and the right to say "WMMS Presents." If the music in any way resembled something we were putting on the air, we would sponsor it. Artists benefited from daily on-air mentions. The station benefited because of the connection between an act and the station "presenting" it. WMMS sponsorship became a seal of approval, which made negotiations easy on our end.

The real winners were listeners, whose support was making Cleveland America's rock capital. Concerts sponsored by WMMS were among the few things that drew people downtown in the 1970s, and something was happening every night of the week. Cleveland was a place where one could follow an act's career from the beginning. Many would start by playing the Agora on a Monday or Tuesday night. They'd move to a larger venue for their second appearance, playing the Allen Theatre or Cleveland Music Hall. Public Hall was the next stage, and finally the Coliseum in Richfield or Blossom Music Center—and later, the WMMS World Series of Rock.

Some acts didn't make all the stages, skipping a beat or falling back a rung, but those who did made it a virtual trade route. U2 started in Cleveland playing a show at the Agora in 1981, followed by dates at the Music Hall, the Coliseum, and Cleveland Municipal Stadium.

Kiss played the route, despite a brush with disaster along the way. They first played Cleveland at the Agora in January 1974, as the mismatched opening act for guitarist Rory Gallagher. Even in their early days, they wore makeup and superhero costumes, in a stage show that used a lot of lighting and a smoke machine. Near the end of the show, drummer Peter Criss was on a moving riser that got stuck near the ceiling. The drumming suddenly stopped. Criss was unconscious, nearly asphyxiated from the stage show smoke. Hank LoConti pulled him down, and he was taken by ambulance to St. Vincent Charity Hospital. It was the only time I saw something go radically wrong on stage, and the band vowed never to play another club with low ceilings.

Their next date in town, in June, was at the Allen, opening for the New York Dolls—a unique bill that no other city could claim. Kiss, suffering no lasting ill effects from their Agora show, won over the Dolls crowd. It was not difficult to that conclude they would be headlining their next appearance in town. The Dolls kicked off their show with the vigor of the young Rolling Stones, but ran out of steam midway through their performance. One could see the toll a steady diet of liquor and drugs was taking on some members of the band, which was showing early signs of self-destruction. The drug business their crew ran on the side didn't help.

A true indication of WMMS's musical influence and concert power came the weekend before Memorial Day 1974. On Friday, the Eagles played two sold-out shows at the Allen Theatre. Michael Stanley landed a brief but prominent appearance as opening act, his best exposure to date. On Saturday, Kid Leo emceed two Mott the Hoople concerts, both shows selling out well in advance, a significant achievement for a band heard on only one radio station in town. Aware of performing in their best market, Ian Hunter and the boys surpassed even expectations raised by advance hype. Hunter also served as a gracious host afterward, inviting a few WMMS staffers to a post-show party at the Keg and Quarter. I asked him why he paid such strong homage to Bob Dylan. He said, "You are what you steal—so you steal from the best."

The weekend closed with one more sold-out show, by Bryan Ferry and Roxy Music, which again surpassed expectations and was hosted by Kid Leo. It had to be the only show on their American tour where the audience responded loudly and positively to every song they performed. Cleveland knew its Roxy Music.

It also knew its WMMS. I realized in amazement that night that our announcers were not drawing the boos and jeers that typically greet radio personalities hosting rock concerts. Leo was welcomed with cheers and hollers—not bad for a "Find Me" FM air personality whose lone exposure outside of overnights was a six-hour Saturday evening shift.

On Monday, Denny, Walt Tiburski, and I met with Jules Belkin and Wendy Stein from Belkin Productions to move ahead with a recent idea: an all-day, multi-act concert at Cleveland Municipal Stadium.

Outdoor rock festivals were difficult to produce because of problems with crowd control. Instead, promoters put mini-festivals on tour, featuring a couple of big headliners and several supporting acts. A stadium concert looked to be different and bigger. Belkin knew the risks but thought it feasible because of his relationship with Browns owner Art Modell, who had just signed a twenty-five-year lease with the city to operate Municipal Stadium.

The previous year, Belkin staged an outdoor concert at Tiger Stadium in Massillon, with Moot the Hoople and Dr. Hook. Five people were injured when a riot broke out, which cost Belkin his permission to stage a Leon Russell concert outdoors at Cloverleaf Speedway in Valley View. Belkin hooked up with Modell instead, in what became a lucrative deal for both. Seating was limited to 20,000, primarily around the bleachers. The show didn't sell out, but it was successful and went without incident, helped by the mellower crowd Russell attracted.

For our show, Belkin contacted the Beach Boys, who were in their "progressive" phase and had not yet devolved to an oldies act. They were touring as a package with Chicago. Belkin also planned to add local favorites Joe Walsh and Barnstorm, Lynyrd Skynyrd, and the then-unknown REO Speedwagon. WMMS was the obvious station to sponsor it because of our relationship with Belkin, growing status as the concert station, and wide musical variety. Unlike most album rock stations, we played the Beach Boys, old and new.

The date was set for Sunday, June 23. It would be far larger than the Leon Russell concert the preceding summer.

Jules Belkin repositioned the stage to face the field and stands, allowing for a capacity near 90,000. Belkin expected a crowd of 40,000 to 50,000. He was concerned, as always, wondering how many concert dollars were out there. I expected 60,000, and privately wondered how we could parlay it into bigger ratings for WMMS. Walt Tiburski, who was friendly with Mike Love, the Beach Boys' management, and Joe Walsh, wanted it to be successful beyond all estimates. He brought in the audio dealer Tokyo Shapiro as a sponsor to further entice concertgoers with the chance to win sound equipment. The *Cleveland Press* also agreed to sponsorship.

We threw around a few ideas for a name, none memorable. I tossed out "The Super Bowl of Rock & Roll." But that was a little too hard and heavy for the Beach Boys and Chicago, and the NFL would cease-and-desist us for using "Super Bowl." My next idea, "World Series of Rock," met mixed reaction, but nothing better came up. The name then caught on fast, and it became the backdrop to all the other Cleveland Stadium concerts of those years.

When you have that many people in one place, crowds can get rowdy. I asked Flash to write a station editorial with a "whole world's watching" take. The concert's success would be the opening for other rock-oriented events. He wrote:

A lot has happened with concerts in Cleveland. A lot more could happen. But it only takes a few for it not to. One year ago, Cleveland, as a music center, almost became a thing of the past. Why? Because rock concerts became synonymous with violence. But, once again, we think a lot has happened since that time. Now, performers are coming back to Cleveland. They get a good reception and, above all, they want to come back. In many cities, you would be fortunate if there would be two or three rock concerts a month. Here in Cleveland, we have concerts three, four, maybe five times a week. And we're still growing. We still have to test that growth. Our first test will come this Sunday, June 23rd, at Cleveland's lakefront stadium. This test will certainly be a tough one. It will be a long day—and a lot of people will be there. To pass the test, WMMS HAS to WIN the World Series. All you need is one rock, one bottle, and the air for them to fly in—and then we lose. And if we lose, the players, who want to come back, also lose. And above all, when that happens, you lose, too. This is Ed Ferenc speaking on behalf of the staff of WMMS.

Flash delivered the piece. I scheduled it to run on Friday at 7 p.m. and 11 p.m. and Saturday at 8 a.m., noon, 4 p.m., and 8 p.m. I can't say that the commentary made the difference, but more than 60,000 people attended the WMMS World Series of Rock, without incidents worse than an occasional drunk, stoned, or bad-tripping patron. No fingers were blown off, no eyes blinded.

We sat in the press box, looking over the entire stadium. The concert became our greatest exposure to date. Our air staff emceed the show. Minutes before the Beach Boys took the stage, Jules Belkin pulled Tiburski and me aside. Grinning ear to ear, he said, "There'll be more. Lots more."

The following Monday, Jules called with our next missions. The second World Series of Rock, scheduled for Sunday evening, August 4, starring Emerson, Lake, and Palmer, the Climax Blues Band, and the James Gang. And Crosby, Stills, and Nash . . . *and* Neil Young . . . and The Band . . . and others . . . for Labor Day weekend.

Based on my own listening habits, I always believed, "Own the holiday weekend, own the months preceding the next one." I aimed for programming to overachieve during long holiday weekends. While other stations went on autopilot with top 500 countdowns, I would do the opposite—present normal programming, to superserve the audience. Rather than have part-timers—or no talent at all, merely recorded programming or board operators cueing records—I wanted to showcase the A-team all weekend. Give listeners the best, and pump our adversaries full of lead. I believe the station providing the best holiday soundtrack automatically becomes the station of choice.

Labor Day weekend 1974 put us in the rock and roll history books. We knew it the day of the concert, when the banner headline atop the front page of the *Cleveland Press* said, "ROCK FANS JAM STADIUM." Beneath the subhead, "88,000 rock fans win Modell's praise." Reporter Bruno Bornino wrote,

It's a beautiful crowd. I'm proud of these youngsters. We've had rowdier fans at Browns-Steelers games.

Art Modell, owner of the Browns, wore a big grin as he talked about THE concert everyone is talking about: Saturday's "World Series of Rock," which attracted 88,000 fans to the Stadium.

The rock fans were there for a concert which began at 2:30 p.m. with Jesse Colin Young. The show went on with music by

Santana and the Band and finally ended at 11:30 p.m. with the headlining act—Crosby, Stills, Nash and Young—on stage, and with the fans screaming for more.

"The fans always want more," said a weary Jules Belkin. Belkin, who sponsored the show with radio station WMMS, had been at the Stadium since 7 Saturday morning.

"We sold 82,648 tickets," said Belkin. "But I think there were closer to 88,000 fans here. "No matter which attendance figures you use, this is still the largest enclosed concert ever staged in the United States. It's also the largest gross for a single concert."

At the crack of dawn Monday morning, Walt Tiburski was armed with sales "hype sheets" for his staff to send to all WMMS accounts, current and proposed. Each sheet was a copy of the the *Press* front page with an overline: "Nearly $1 million grossed in one day proves WMMS radio gets results!" Tiburski never missed a chance to tout the benefits of buying time on WMMS. It wasn't an easy mission. Despite rising ratings and undeniable influence, America was still divided by generation. To most people over thirty, WMMS was still that hippie, underground radio station. The big department stores—Higbee's, Halle's and May Company—could not be persuaded to buy time. But Tiburski, like a pit bull in contact with flesh, would not let go until WMMS had the respect and money of the blue chips and the agencies.

A few weeks after the World Series of Rock, WIXY attempted a listener appreciation day at Pineway Trails park. Only 800 showed—and Rare Earth, the band scheduled to perform, didn't.

Other artists who performed in Cleveland at WMMS World Series of Rock concerts over the years included Pink Floyd; Crosby, Stills, Nash, and Young; Emerson, Lake, and Palmer; The Band; Santana; Rod Stewart and The Faces; J. Geils Band; Uriah Heep; Aerosmith; Blue Oyster Cult; Mahogany Rush; Yes; Ted Nugent; Journey; ELO; Foreigner; Thin Lizzy; AC/DC; and, in their first American dates, Def Leppard and the Scorpions.

The relationship between WMMS and Jules Belkin was special. I doubt there was another like it between a concert promoter and a radio station. Occasionally, we'd have out squabbles, and it wasn't an exclusive relationship, since we also, depending on circumstances, would work with other promoters, and Jules with other radio stations. But Jules was a class act all the way. His shows ran like clockwork and he truly cared about the audience experience. And acts respected him. The end result was that Cleveland had the best rock and roll concerts in America.

CHAPTER 9

GOT-TA GOT-TA GET DOWN!

"... and I smoke dope," Murray Saul told Dave DeCapua in his interview for a WMMS sales job. That assertion, Murray believed, convinced DeCapua he could sell the format in spite of being twenty-eight years older than the median age of the typical WMMS listener.

By then, he had already led quite a life. Born in Cleveland on May 14, 1928, Murray Saul was an only child whose father was a cutter in the men's clothing business. His mother was a housewife. He grew up on Brackland Avenue, in the largely Jewish neighborhood off Eddy Road on Cleveland's East Side. He attended the Cleveland public schools and recalled skipping out occasionally for big band concerts at the Palace Theater downtown. By 1946, he was in the U.S. Army, stationed in occupied Japan. In his recollection, it was a party.

After the service, he attended Ohio State University on and off, until he joined a friend and became a carnival pitchman in the summer of 1949. He traveled as far as Phoenix, and he smoked his first joint. Wearying of the carnie life, he returned to Cleveland in 1950 and landed a job as driver for a prosperous traveling salesman. By 1954, Murray was a traveling salesman himself. In 1957, with a little help from his family, he bought a men's clothing store near Collinwood High School, then the city's largest, in Five Points, calling it Murray's Men's Wear. The store flopped, and he sold commercial real estate. He listened to jazz for entertainment, and in 1962 he moved to New York City. He sold clothes in the Bronx, manned a check-cashing booth in Trenton, New Jersey, and finally worked a jewelry stand at Macy's. He found jobs in between with street fairs, where he met a woman who enjoyed smoking dope. After thirteen years, Murray was reunited with the joys of cannabis.

He returned to Cleveland in 1965 and went back on the road as a traveling salesman. He met a woman named Barbara. They hit it off and got married. Three years later, he got involved in politics and the Carl Stokes mayoral campaign, switched jobs, and began selling calculators. He had his rebirth in 1971. He split with his wife in an amicable separation and began spending time in Kent with people half his age and younger. He made friends who remain close to him. And he began listening to progressive rock music. WMMS became his radio station of choice. He called Martin Perlich on the air one day to tell him, "I'm your closest friend." In late 1973, something motivated him to apply for a sales position at the station. He looked like an interesting character. Even at WMMS, he was hard not to notice—as old as most staffers' fathers, bald on top, with a wild outgrowth of hair on the sides and a muttonchops down to his chin.

"I just hired him," DeCapua told me smoothly. "He may not be the same age as you guys, but he'll probably get respect some of the others can't with some of our potential clients."

"But what does he know about the format?" I asked. "Does he understand what WMMS is about?"

"I think you'll be surprised," DeCapua replied. "I certainly was."

Every time I heard Murray converse, I knew I needed to find a way to get him on the air—especially after the day I heard him on the phone with his aunt, Anna Singer. The only surviving family member of her generation, she was a childless widow who had made a living running an East Side dry goods store with her husband. Now she was very hard of hearing and living alone in public housing near East 105th Street and Hough Avenue. Murray, her only living relative, would often visit and attend to her needs. "I'll be over on Tuesday," he said loudly into the phone one afternoon while calling to confirm a visit. She said, "Friday?" He said, "No,

TUESDAY!" "Thursday?" "TUESDAY!" "Monday?" "No, TUESDAY!"
"Wednesday?" Frustrated, Murray shouted into the phone, "TUES-
DAY! TUESDAY! TUESDAY! TUESDAY!"

I could hear him from my office, well up the hall from the sales
office where he sat bellowing. I knew there was something I could
use from that, but didn't know exactly what for.

Then Kid Leo and I conspired to play a practical joke on Denny
before Thanksgiving 1974. Leo, who usually had immediate after-
work plans, was constantly provoked by Denny's practice of waiting until the last moment to enter the studio for his air shift. In
some magazine or newspaper, I'd found a definition of "turkey."
Leo and I modified it to stretch to a minute-long script that ended
with, "Now, WMMS presents the biggest turkey of them all—Denny
Sanders!" We asked Murray to cut the track, and Leo used it in
place of the regular top-of-the-hour ID as he closed his show on
Thanksgiving eve. A couple of weeks later, Murray and his roommates threw a wild party at their apartment on Euclid Heights Boulevard in Cleveland Heights. Walt Tiburski started playing air guitar
and dancing to a hard rock tune on the radio. Fueled by the frenzy
of music, dancing, and Tiburski's gyrations, Murray shouted, "Get
down, Walter! Walter, get down! Get down! Get down, dammit!" It
inspired me to ask Murray back to the production studio to cut another opener for Denny's show—yelling, "Rock and roll! Dammit,
get DOWN!"

Denny enjoyed it, and Leo liked it so much he wrote another. It
was a rhyming, kick-off-the-weekend piece, barely a minute long,
that again featured Murray. Aired at 6 p.m., it served as a close for
Leo and an open for Denny. We called it the "Weekend Salute."

Now we had something. Murray and I went to lunch at Jim's
Steakhouse in the Flats the following week and started to sketch
out another piece, adding different elements. Murray's shouted
refrain of "Tuesday!" to his nearly deaf aunt turned into "Friday!
Friday! Friday! Friday!" His injunction to "Get down, dammit!" became a signature closing. An increasingly frenzied Murray told listeners it was time to cork the smokestacks for the weekend. Time
to grab your honey, speak some Spanish, twist a few tunahs, turn

your rack into something wonderful and enjoy the easy life. Yayza yowza bowza wowza! The "Get Down," as it became known, had a language of its own, but our listeners figured it out. A rack was a bed. Tuna was pot, and tunahs were joints. Speaking Spanish was a Kent State-ism for how one spoke after doing a few quaaludes. The "Yayza-Yowza" break was Murray's nod to speaking Spanish. It lasted two minutes, then three, then a regular five or six as it became a weekly fixture at 6 p.m., after Leo closed his show by playing Bruce Springsteen's "Born to Run."

The feature developed quickly. Though we wanted it to sound spontaneous and ad libbed, it wasn't. Murray and I would try to do lunch on Thursday and Friday, to sketch out ideas and then write the script. Because the first part was "serious" and usually built around something in the news—local or national politics, the state of the city, schools, the economy—he'd usually bring the *New York Times* and local papers we would reference. We'd eat in a different part of town every week, looking for fresh perspective. We might see a factory or business being closed, and use that as our starting point. Ideas could come from anywhere, including the station. Milton Maltz was the inspiration for "The Slavedriver," the otherwise nameless Everyboss of all wage slaves, who became a regular target.

The sermon was chorused by, "It's Friday! Friday! Friday!" to launch the weekend:

> We're outta that manure hacienda!
> It got pretty hectic this week!
> The whole week was one long insanity ! . . .
> You should've seen the meetings they had!

All those tight-assed Slavedrivers glidin' around, hardly touchin' the ground!

At one session, they all went out to the Slavedriver's Slavedriver's Slavedriver's favorite restaurant—The Pewter Whip!

Instead of music, they had an endless tape of our moans and cries, providing a familiar background to all those Slavedrivers!

After Bloody Murrays they ordered the specialty of the house.

For appetizers there was minced Slave meat cocktail, delicately garnished with broken finger nails, blisters, and calluses!

Oh, he liberally splashed that cocktail with a seasoning consisting of our blood, our sweat, and our tears!

After a salad of money greens on a bed of used adding machine tapes, he ordered the main course . . . Cannibal Stew!

Ah, tender young lambs, aged quickly, par roasted, and then dried out!

They offer a sauce of stale ideas, worn out traditions, and greed!

And they serve it up with a side dish of boredom and stupidity!

Well, let them choke on their meanness, we're outta their stew pot,

Because it's Friday! Friday! Friday! Friday!

We'd always work in the "Yayza-Yowza":

We're not lookin' for tunahs with good taste . . .

We're lookin' for tunahs that taste good and make ya feel good!

Yayza! Yowza! Bowza! Wowza!

Oob-La-Doo, Oob-La-Dee, Oob La Dah!

Arrrrrrggggggggh!

And every week we'd come up with a new close:

Turn your rack into a basketball court this weekend!

The object of the game is to get the highest (pause) score—and a fast break'll get you down closer to the goal!

Make sure your passes are bringin' the ball right up there to the basket—getting' ready!

Arrrrrrggggggggh!

The hook shot!

That'll do it!

Get that basketball honey of yours in there and just have the
best party of 'em all!

Oh, we're gonna visit Mom over the weekend!

And everyobody's got ta—Got-ta, Got-ta, Got-ta, Got-ta,
Got-ta, Got-ta, Got-ta

Gotta, Gotta, Gotta, Gotta, Gotta, Gotta, Gotta, Gotta, Gotta,
Gotta, Gotta

Gottagottagottagottagotta—GET DOWN, DAMMIT!

Sometimes, the Get Downs dealt out social commentary, such
as in the opening to this weekend salute delivered on the last day
of the school year:

We're outta that solitary confinement!

It's rough in there!

They handcuff our souls and arrest our brains—which brings
me to the topic of the evening—school is out for almost everybody—and what a long year it's been!

The biggest baby sitting service in the world—school!

They prepare you for yesterday!

They talk about a world that never was and never will be!

And they talk about, talk about it, talk about it—but they
aren't even close!

They don't care if you learn—as long as you keep still!

They don't care what sense it makes—as long as you say it
right!

They don't care if it's true—as long as the text book says it
that way!

They take the bite out of life and they even take the life out
of bite! . . .

And to all you graduates—it'll be fun to look back and savor
those irreplaceable memories!

But let it be known!

The best is still comin'!

But it's gonna be different!

•   •   •

By early 1975, Murray was a big on-air presence at WMMS. In addition to the Get Down, he hosted two shows that helped meet our FCC mandate to provide two hours and fifteen minutes of public affairs programming each week. One was *We the People*, which ran in five-minute segments at 3:25 p.m. Monday, Wednesday, and Friday. For Murray, it was a dream forum that showcased him in a completely different context. The five-minute shows were edited from interviews that might last close to an hour with politicians, civic leaders, and business people. Fueled by his passion for a city in which his roots ran deep, Murray asked direct questions in a conversational and sometimes irreverent style. "How long is the Queen planning to stay in Cleveland?" he asked a corporate flack when British Petroleum took over Standard Oil of Ohio. His other show was *Jabberwocky*, the 8 a.m. Sunday hour previously hosted by Debbie Ullman.

Murray performed his Get Downs solo, but there was one very memorable time when he was joined in the booth by Dennis Wilson of the Beach Boys.

Over the years, Murray and I had gotten to know Dennis, who was truly an ungrounded wire. You never knew which Dennis was going to show up.

In 1976 the Beach Boys were in town and Dennis agreed to do a Get Down with Murray. He also agreed we could film it for a future TV spot. Dennis showed up at the station slightly drunk, carrying a gallon jug of scotch, which he kept pouring into a plastic cup.

Dennis went over the Get Down script with Murray and me and everything seemed fine. But when it began, and Murray launched into "Dennis Wilson, you're a Beach Boy, how do you 'Get Down' in California?" Dennis looked at him and suddenly broke into tears. He said, "My father's name was Murry . . . and he used to beat us . . . and Carl wet the bed . . ." and then he drifted off into gibberish.

Dennis's handlers went mad. Ted Cohen, a former Clevelander who was national promoter for the label, demanded the filming stop. I told him he had no right to stop it. Walt Tiburski, hearing the disturbance, ordered it stopped (because of his friendship with Mike Love). He also was angry that Dennis got into trouble every time he showed up at WMMS—and most of the time it was with me. I grabbed Dennis by his shoulders, threw him into my office, and slammed the door to get him out of the fray. As soon as I closed the door, Dennis's muscle-bound handler, whom we knew only as Damian, pounded loudly and tried to bust it open. I heard Tiburski shouting to open up, so I did. Damian ushered out Dennis, who at that point couldn't decide whether he should laugh or cry. I realized that such incidents must have been fairly common with him.

Tiburski and Cohen insisted that the separately recorded audio and video be turned over to Cohen. Cohen also tried to seize a camera from photographer Janet Macoska, who was shooting stills. Tiburski insisted, but Janet refused. Cohen told her if the photos ever saw the light of day she'd never work in rock and roll again. He was serious.

After that incident, I had little interest in seeing Dennis again—and couldn't wait to hear about Mike Love's complaint to Walt.

Len Goldberg had a different take on the incident, however. He said Dennis told him he was taking a method-acting class with Lee Strasberg in L.A. He already appeared in one forgettable movie, *Two-Lane Blacktop*. Len believed that what Dennis did was an act. It looked real to me. Whatever the case, Dennis spent his adult life getting bailed out from problems he created.

The Get Down wasn't followed on-air by anything in particular until July 1975, when KC & the Sunshine Band released "Get Down Tonight"—an appropriate choice. We soon replaced that with Earthquake's powerful live version of the Easybeats' "Friday on My Mind." Years later Ian Hunter released "Cleveland Rocks," and Columbia label head Steve Popovich gave us a prerelease tape of it. That song moved "Friday on My Mind" to third place in what was now a familiar trilogy.

•　　　•　　　•

As the Get Down evolved and found its rhythm, one of the lines that worked well had to do with calling Cleveland the "capital" of something. Slush capital, party capital, and so forth. One Friday, before a World Series of Rock concert, we came up with "The Rock and Roll Capital of the World." It was purely by accident, and almost got edited due to the Get Down's length that day. After hearing Murray deliver it live, I called Boom on Monday morning and told him we needed to cut a new top-of-the-hour ID. I thought it was a good line, and wanted to establish it on WMMS before a competitor stole it. We were expanding the top of the hour from the "Wrath of the Buzzard" to broader messages, including "Serving two countries, three states, and you," "The Thundering Buzzard," "Your concert connection," and "Cleveland Rocks on WMMS." Within a few months, the "Rock and Roll Capital of the World" line was being picked up more widely. Though we service-marked new slogans to protect them, this one gained popularity quickly and was picked up by labels, TV stations, and newspapers. We thought it was a great slogan that gave the city pride. We kept using it heavily on the air, to establish it as another "when you hear it you think of WMMS" slogan.

Ultimately, this weekend-launcher that began as one minute with Murray became a twenty-minute production. At 5:55 p.m., Leo announced it was time to "Wash up, punch out, and put the wraps on what we call the afternoon session on WMMS," and played "Born to Run." At 6 p.m., Murray delivered the Get Down. Then Denny played "Cleveland Rocks" and "Friday on My Mind." The weekend was officially kicked off.

CHAPTER 10

"WE DON'T GO TO WORK; WE GO TO WAR"

We had no direct competition in our format. *Cleveland* magazine, in an article about WMMS in January 1975, hinted that this helped explain why we were "the number one radio station in Northeastern Ohio" and "indisputably the rock station in Cleveland."

Competition improves product, and we were about to get some. The first hint was a baffling in-house campaign against Nick Mileti and his young partners, brothers Tom and Jim Embrescia, owners of WWWE-AM and WWWM-FM. Comments, jokes, and potshots, all originating from Maltz's office, flew through the halls and circulated in meetings: "You know what WWWE stands for? Why Worry, Who's Embrescia?" "You know what WWWM stands for? Why Worry, Who's Mileti?" After three weeks of this, Maltz walked into my office, sat down, pointed a finger in my face and growled, "Did you EVER meet Nick Mileti?" I hadn't.

"Well, let me just WARN you about him," Maltz said. "His EMpire is built on CREAM cheese. He has no found-DAY-shun. You know what that MEANS?"

I said I didn't know much about Mileti, except that he owned the Richfield Coliseum, brought the NBA to Cleveland with the Cavaliers, and bought the Indians when they threatened to move to New Orleans.

"He owns NOTHING. Nothing! He spends other people's money! He has no money of his own invested in his projects! You say you never ever talked to Mileti? How about your staff? Has anyone on your staff ever talked to Mileti? How about those Embrescia brothers? Have you or ANYONE on your staff talked to either one of THEM?"

"No, I doubt it, Mr. Maltz," I said. "I'll be honest. I've never met them. I don't even know what they look like."

"STOP! DOUBT IT? You said DOUBT IT? You don't KNOW?" He slammed my office door shut. "YOU don't KNOW for CERTAIN?" He sat down. "As a PRO-gramming director, you should KNOW who your staff is TALKING to! At ALL TIMES!" He lowered his voice to a whisper. "Tell me, John. Who is of Eye-talian descent on your staff?"

"Italian? Denny and Leo."

"What are their last names? REAL names?"

"Denny's is Cefalo." This was before he changed his name legally to Sanders.

"How is that spelled?"

I spelled it out.

"What about the other one?"

"Leo? It's pronounced Trav-al-yan-tay—T-r-a-v-a-g-l-i-a-n-t-e. The G is silent."

"How do YOU know how to pronounce those names so well?" he asked. I said I had a lot of friends who are Italian.

He leaned over my desk. "Did you ever hear the term 'guinea'? GINN-EE?"

"Yeah," I said. "It's derogatory."

"You're WRONG," he said. "A GINN-ee is an Italian that just cares about himself and his immediate family! Mil-ET-i, the Em-BRAY-za brothers, they don't care about anyone but themSELVES. They're guineas! And you must ORDER your staff not to talk to them. If you LEARN of ANYONE talking to them, I want YOU to inform ME! Immediately! Immediately! Understand?"

He stood, opened, the door and stomped out. I took a few minutes to decompress, closed the door, and took a deep breath, wondering what that was about. Apparently, he believed that an Italian radio station owner would hire Italian DJs.

Later, a clerk from Record Revolution called. "You should know this," he said. "There's a new progressive rock station coming in a month or so. We got a pitch from a salesman representing them. They're supposed to go up against your station. The call letters even sound similiar to WMMS."

"Is it WWWM?" I asked. It was, and it was inevitable that our success would lead to direct competition and another Cleveland FM challenging us. WWWM, which competed with WDOK, WQAL, and WDBN with "easy listening," was the logical candidate. Carl Hirsch called a meeting away from the station, unheard of in the past, to discuss coordination among departments. The singular good news accompanying a new challenger was that Carl persuaded Maltz to part with a few dollars to increase our budget and clean up loose ends.

We needed new studio and production equipment. The WMMS signal had deteriorated. Metromedia had let maintenance slide, and Malrite had budgeted too little money to correct the problems. We got calls from Mentor to Bay Village, from east suburbs, and from Akron and Canton about the signal problems. East Side Tokyo Shapiro stores stopped using WMMS to sell audio equipment. The signal also suffered from sibilance, creating a splashing sound effect on any word containing an *S*. All three turntables in the studio were dropping channels. Announcers couldn't put telephone calls on the air because lines had not been wired to the board properly. They had to listen to the studio board, instead of monitoring the station's signal, because classical WCLV would override WMMS on the studio's poor receiver. One Saturday afternoon, a listener called Matt the Cat to inform him we were off the air. Now, it all would be fixed.

Preparing for competition, I extended on-air giveaways, expanding them from morning drive and weekends to twenty-four hours, seven days a week. I promoted "forward motion" delivery, urging everyone to sound exuberant, continually moving forward, promoting coming artists and new music, promoting giveaways in advance, using the best elements of high-gloss Top 40 minus the speed-rap shrieking. I also pushed for word economy—the fewer words used, the more important each word becomes. I quoted Carl Hirsch's credo: "We don't go to work, we go to war."

My main concern was Malrite's willingness to head off an attack. The Buzzard logo, though quickly evolving into everyone's favored icon, was still struggling to win official sanction. All promotion and marketing came from initiating our own trade deals. The sole outdoor billboard was the Buzzard mural on the Music Grotto, furnished by support of record labels. We had bumper stickers, but the stock was well behind demand. I doubted a new station would try a format broader than ours. More likely, they would aim at our vulnerabilities, such as our practice of playing multiple tracks, not just hits, off current albums.

On Tuesday, March 4, 1975, WWWM went album rock. Changing its name to "M105," it made its debut at 7 p.m., with Emerson, Lake, and Palmer's "Fanfare of the Common Man." War had begun.

WMMS was at an immediate disadvantage. Mileti and the Embrescia brothers were known and respected in the Cleveland advertising community. Minority partner Bob Zingale had been a partner with Norman Wain and Bob Weiss at WIXY. Carl Hirsch, whose prior experience in the region was at WCUE, did not have their local and regional connections. Neither did Walt Tiburski. My counterpart was Eric Stevens, a formidable opponent. Son of a respected independent record promoter, Perry Stevens, he was music director of WIXY before he was twenty, and he was very tight with WEA, the Warner-Elektra-Atlantic distribution company. He also produced music before joining M105, including "Smokin' In the Boys Room" by Brownsville Station, and a Cleveland group, Damnation of Adam's Blessing, whose 1970 song, "Take Me Back to the River," still received occasional airplay on WMMS.

Stevens, operating from his own Top 40 background, understood WMMS. We were working to be the soundtrack for everyone in our target demo, playing everything but blatantly bubblegum Top 40. Stevens took our playlist, trimmed it dramatically, and kept the music flowing. The formula had worked elsewhere. Incumbent album rock stations were falling as new, tight-listed stations entered their markets. The older stations became too hip for the room. Wanting to avoid that, we had to take fewer liberties than we once could, while still breaking new music and taking a chance on a Labelle or Isley Brothers, moves that other album-rock stations wouldn't make. I learned how shrewd Stevens was after we played "Who Loves You," by the Four Seasons, a disco-tinged record right on the edge of our format. It wasn't album rock, but it turned out to be popular for us. Within a week I heard M105 playing it.

Air personalities were secondary on M105. The jocks, not allowed to talk or do interviews like the WMMS staff, read from liner cards and stressed that M105 was the "home of continuous music." WMMS carried eight to nine minutes of commercial spots per hour. M105, with fewer spots, ran all-music, commercial-free weekends and frequent three-hour "continuous music sweeps." It provided opportunities for M105 to lure listeners, and they did a good job of parroting WMMS. They'd have to play something godawful for us to get those listeners back. M105 was the station that gave us the kick in the ass to make it, and make it on our terms.

One rule was constant: If it ain't broke, break it and fix it better. When Murray Saul had a birthday, he celebrated on Charlie Kendall's show, bringing music that was popular when he was growing up and mixing it with current tunes. That couldn't happen on any other station. We put listeners on the air, taking calls to sound as live and plugged-in as possible.

M105's format did not allow for calls. Their jocks were "announcers." When they tried to compete on personality, it was by hiring Wyn Rosenberg, a journeyman Top 40 jock who'd worked in Cleveland and other markets under various names, to do mornings. They renamed him "Mudcliffe," which inevitably became Mud. Their billboard campaign asked, "Is Mud dirty?," and on-air questions for listeners ran to the level of "How old were you when you did it?" It was juvenile stuff, and tame by today's standards, but it was an early manifestation of the "If you can't beat 'em, out-gross 'em" school. Wyn was far too talented to be pigeonholed as a teen-appeal shock jock.

We had proof of how strong our voice was when Len Goldberg quit, as he did periodically in those years. Mostly out of spite and his seething dislike of Maltz, Boom went over to M105. We had to pull most of our IDs and promos, because he was the voice of WMMS, but he only lasted one weekend. He was the voice of WMMS, and he couldn't fit into M105's rigid mold. Those hearing him thought they were listening to WMMS. Boom came back to WMMS, as a weekend host and part-timer, and stayed.

Being associated with up-and-coming acts was a tremendous asset for WMMS. We listened to virtually every album release, and we didn't limit our listening to what promo guys were hyping. Nor did we follow the standard progressive-rock album route. We had a funk quota, and we played pop crossovers. One example was the Raspberries' "Side 3." WMMS had never played the Raspberries, since they were regarded as anti-album rock, but it was a standout power pop rock album. We broadened our audience by broadening our playlist. One of our earliest slogans was "Playing the widest variety of rock and roll," and it was true.

Whenever an artist came to the station for an interview or promotional stop, we always had them cut an ID. The standard one was, "I'm So-and-So. Whenever I'm in town, I listen to WMMS."

The idea came from Top 40. It always stuck in my mind that Boston's WMEX had Eric Burdon of the Animals do one. When I was fourteen, I thought the Animals were cool, and WMEX was cool for having the Animals say the station was.

We had the only Bruce Springsteen ID on the planet, and it was one of our best: "I'm Bruce Springsteen. I don't have a radio, but Miami Steve does—and he lets me listen to WMMS." U2's Bono heard it on a visit to the station a few years later, and cut one in a similar style: "I'm the singer, he (Edge) is the guitarist, and we both listen to WMMS."

Artists who became superstars sometimes stopped cutting IDs. But Sting did one: "I'm Sting of the Police, and I get a buzz out of the Buzzard." When he left the group and no longer did radio interviews or station IDs, we edited out "of the Police." When Joe Walsh joined the Eagles, we had IDs from his days with Barnstorm in the early seventies. When Walsh heard them years later, he recut about a half dozen new ones, along with one announcing his candidacy for president. Rush proclaimed us the best station in the nation. Suzi Quatro did a TV spot for free, just to promote the first station in America to play her music. We had the Isley Brothers, Lattimore, Labelle, and other rhythm and blues and dance music acts cutting personality IDs.

Other album rock stations picked up on their impact and street credibility. By the eighties, syndicated shows like *Rockline* would offer IDs for their affiliates. Locally, M105 and WGCL complained to labels about acts endorsing WMMS. Some were sympathetic, and I'd have to settle for "I'm So-and-So, and you're listening to WMMS"—just short of an official endorsement. We'd get everybody and anybody who came into the station and was any kind of celebrity, including Ted Koppel, Lillian Carter, and Rodney Dangerfield. Even if they were out of the format, like Mel Torme, or Slim Whitman, or Boxcar Willie.

We ran at least three an hour, sometimes more. They were especially useful when we wanted to insert the call letters during sets of music we didn't want to interrupt. It made us sound like an entertainment capital, and it contributed to the illusion that WMMS was the place where stars hung out, though it wasn't entirely illusion. Acts enjoyed us because we were passionate about the music.

Bruce Springsteen, David Bowie, Southside Johnny, and Mott the Hoople were strongly identified with WMMS. M105 reacted by identifying with a Canadian band, Klaatu, named after the alien who comes to warn against war and nuclear arms in the movie *The Day the Earth Stood Still*. The station started a rumor that the Beatles were back together as Klaatu, and even created a supporting documentary. Some sales people felt we'd better jump on it or M105 would finally have one on us. My feeling was, let them. How long is the life span of a Klaatu versus a Springsteen? And why associate our station with a rumor we knew to be false?

The biggest problem M105 created was a problem of their own that they turned to advantage—unsold commercial time. It enabled them to bill themselves as the "home of continuous music," and to boast, "While they're talkin', we're rockin'." We eventually had to respond with our own commercial-free hours, and played on our call letters to proclaim "We're your Music Marathon Station." Tonnage worked better than time. Playing "another twenty songs commercial-free on your music marathon station, WMMS" had more impact than measuring by the hour.

It helped that we had the cool places and the biggest concert venues locked up. M105 went after small rock clubs, which wasn't a bad grassroots way to get out their call letters, but small clubs were notorious for paying their bills late, if at all. Playing, promoting, and sponsoring live music gave us a tremendous edge. A familiar song recorded months earlier might blossom into something greater onstage. A moment's inspiration or distraction can produce something memorable, whether it's magical or messy. Fleetwood Mac's live "Rhiannon" was far more powerful than the soft rock studio version. The live version of "Southern Man," by Crosby, Stills, Nash & Young, transformed the song into a massive dueling guitar jam between Neil Young and Stephen Stills.

Top 40 radio didn't play live tracks. WMMS did, and also started playing alternative versions of familiar songs, old and new. Few listeners, for example, knew that "The House of the Rising Sun," by the Animals, was edited for U.S. release from the longest hit single in British history. The hit version of "I Saw Her Again," by The Mamas & The Papas, was also shortened from the original recording, as was "Laugh Laugh" by the Beau Brummels. We'd try to find the never-heard or seldom-heard versions, tracking down overseas releases to get albums nobody else had. They became image "exclusives."

We built an image that we had an archive—a huge library filled with live performances, unreleased material, bootleg tapes, rarities, and oddities. Through a variety of sources—an engineer, a concert promoter, a friend of a friend—we acquired a library of alternative takes and basement tapes. Denny introduced unusual cuts by announcing he was going into the archive in a manner that suggested a visit to Jack Benny's vault or the Great Library of Alexandria. Denny was a master of the theater of the mind. The archives grew rapidly. Every interview, every live concert we broadcast—including every *Coffee Break Concert* and every Agora and Smiling Dog WMMS Night Out—was archived along with material from the BBC and the *King Biscuit Flower Hour*. Every piece of production, random airchecks of our talent, and masters of all of our celebrity IDs were also locked in this real-world vault—which was actually a small, nondescript closet.

CHAPTER 11

CONTINUOUS PARTY

Debbie Ullman lived nearly fifty miles from downtown, and her drive to WMMS took more than an hour, much of it on two-lane country roads. Even after late-running concerts or parties, she always declined invitations to spend the night closer to the city.

On November 15, 1974, she was in the final stretch of her drive home when an oncoming car cut in front of her to turn into a driveway. Ullman hit it broadside. Slammed into the metal dashboard, she was knocked unconscious, broke her jaw, and lost three teeth. Her left side was paralyzed. She was hospitalized for more than three weeks, with the first week in intensive care. Her recovery was steady but slow. She regained complete use of her side after two weeks, but her mouth was wired shut. Clearly, she would not be returning to the air soon—and during her convalescence, she decided not to return to WMMS. Blaming the long hours and lifestyle for inattentiveness that contributed to her accident, she also felt the station was moving away from the brand of laid-back, post-hippie radio she favored.

I didn't want to see her go. She was one of the founders of the new WMMS and she had deep roots in the format's past. But she knew her close. It was time to move on. On the air, for the first few days, it was announcer-of-the-day. I suggested using the sound of a roulette wheel as the opening of the morning show. I moved Betty Korvan to mornings as the permanent fill-in, with a more music-intensive format. I enlisted Music Grotto manager Larry Bole to work part-time and fill-in shifts and host our weekly import album program. We were short-staffed, with no budget to work with.

Driving to work one morning, it hit me. I'd been talking for several months with Charlie Kendall at WVBF in Boston. Its glory days as a kick-ass, Rock'n Top 40 were over. Kendall, a real rocker at heart, was getting fed up with its devolution into constant format alterations imposed by a committee of alleged programming experts. He might be just what we needed—that big set of pipes, super-serving the rockers with a high-energy style in morning drive. Kendall would be a true upgrade, giving WMMS a shot at parity with WGAR by siphoning off the younger end of the audience from morning leader John Lanigan.

Kendall was intrigued. "If this place is half as good as you say it is, and if I can get paid a decent wage—even if a lot of it is incentive—I'd seriously consider it." He named a figure. It was more, far more, than anyone earned at WMMS, but it was the starting wage at WHK. I thought the price was reasonable, even a bargain considering Kendall would be leaving one of the country's most vibrant regions for what was then Scorched Earth Cleveland. I took the figure to JC, who immediately shot it down.

I wasn't ready to concede. By the following month, Kendall's growing unhappiness at WVBF and our battle with M105 left room for compromise on both sides. I could get JC to come up with more money, and agree to a five-day work week, if Kendall would take fewer dollars and accept the job of music director in addition to morning drive. Donna Halper was leaving for a job with the Mercury label that she was offered after the success of Rush (Mercury had signed Rush to a U.S. distribution deal).

Kendall made his debut on WMMS in early June. He had a deep baritone, a tight, smooth delivery, and a Top 40 background that taught him how to "walk up" tunes, sounding excited and keeping his show in forward motion. His style was infectious, adding to the diversity of our personalities, which became a strength competition couldn't match.

Matt the Cat found his style as an effective midday guy, smooth and companionable. Leo refined his Kid Leo character into a unique and bracing voice for afternoon drive. Denny's relaxed passion was a perfect fit for evenings, and Betty Korvan brought a solid bundle of sultry energy to overnights.

For Kendall, coming from Boston, Cleveland's sole attraction was the promise of a cool radio station. But his visit for a job interview coincided with a big party being thrown by Murray Saul, his roommates, and Dan Garfinkel at Murray's apartment on Euclid Heights Boulevard in Coventry. I brought Kendall, who met the group, partied heartily thanks to an ample supply of Columbian red bud, and said to me as he left, "I'm here."

That neighborhood, and especially the apartment, was a home away from home for WMMS. Garfinkel lived in a huge apartment next door, two buildings from the Heights Art Theatre. I lived on Lancashire, close enough to see Murray's window. Denny Sanders lived on the street, as did Matt the Cat. Irv's Deli on Coventry was a hangout where many ideas were hatched, and its characters provided constant entertainment. Also nearby was Record Revolution, where Peter Schliewen kept turning us on to new European music. It was a continuous party.

The Beach Boys got a full taste of the lifestyle when they played a WMMS World Series of Rock show with Chicago on Memorial Day weekend in 1975. The tone was set when Murray, Walt Tiburski, and I met them at the airport, the night before the Saturday show, and Carl Wilson of the band rode back with us in the limo. Murray, quite comfortable in the limo, lit up a joint and said in loud satisfaction, "You know—we deserve this!"

I wanted to get one of the Beach Boys on WMMS that night. To some of our audience, the group was no longer cool, but they still had a mystique and a lot of fans. I invited Carl Wilson to be a guest disc jockey, and told him he could play whatever he wanted—chances were we had it. Maybe because he was intrigued, he said yes.

He showed up with a couple of assistants during Steve Lushbaugh's show, asked to see the WMMS library, and bet me we wouldn't have Shelby Flint's "Angel on My Shoulder," a minor hit from 1961. He was pleasantly surprised, even shocked, we had the entire album, and he was like a kid in a candy store going through titles. It was the first time I heard about the Wrecking Crew, the famed studio musicians who provided the backing to most of the hits coming out of L.A., including the Beach Boys. Carl said the Monkees had gotten a bad rap for not playing their own instruments, and he cited his own band, along with the Byrds and Paul Revere and the Raiders as acts that didn't play their own instruments on their records. The Wrecking Crew provided Phil Spector his "wall of sound," and backed everyone from Frank Sinatra to Barry McGuire and Sonny & Cher.

Lushbaugh was nervous because he knew little about the Beach Boys, so I ended up going on the air and doing the cross-talk with Carl. Someone lit a joint and passed it around. Carl refused, citing his no-drugs commitment to transcendental meditation. "Come on, just one toke." He ended up taking quite a few. It was one of those once-in-a-lifetime on-the-air magic moments. Sadly, it wasn't taped—the machine was down for repair.

Carl's brother Dennis also stopped by. He was too drunk to go on the air but did have a few hits from the joint—and wound up at the Apollo Lounge next to the station, pounding down vodka shots with Howard Shanker, a friend of Walt Tiburski who owned an entertainment supply company.

We had to be backstage at Municipal Stadium the next morning, hours before the show. When I arrived, Tiburski was already there and livid, demanding to know what I'd done to Carl and Dennis Wilson. Tiburski and singer Mike Love were friends, and Love was furious. Dennis had gotten so drunk he couldn't hold his head up, and Carl was so stoned he had told Love to take his TM and shove it. The show did go off, in part because the Beach Boys had a back-up drummer to augment Dennis—which led me to believe this wasn't the first time he'd had a hangover on the day of show.

Dennis's troubles continued that evening when Karen Lamm, his new wife, flew into town to meet him and join the tour. What made it unusual was that she was the ex of Robert Lamm of Chicago, who was on the same tour. Wilson was so drunk when Karen showed up, he physically threw her out of their room at Swingos and had to be restrained.

I watched their show from the stadium press box—deserted of press because they were in an outdoor area closer to the stage—with Kid Leo, Murray, and a few other people. One was Sam the Bam, a person Leo knew from the old neighborhood. He became a good friend. Like me, he was a huge Brian Wilson and Beach Boys fan. He was also an extraordinary sailor, who could maneuver a boat under any weather conditions. He also on occasion had access to nearly pure cocaine. Sam was in the press box with us watching the Beach Boys concert. Suddenly he pulled out a spoon and vial and started putting spoon after spoon after spoon of this primo cocaine up everyone's nose. At one point, Murray asked me, "How much of this stuff can we possibly do?" When Murray cut his "Get Down" the following Friday, he talked about the show and mentioned "Sam the Bam with his shovels" who "kept shoveling up my nose."

The Beach Boys' World Series of Rock show opened a summer that propelled Murray to cult status. We saw it most clearly on Labor Day weekend, on the odd occasion when the Regional Transit Authority held a rally on downtown Mall C to celebrate its creation from the merger of the Cleveland Transit System, Shaker Rapid Transit, and five suburban bus lines.

Because WMMS was trying to get an ad buy from RTA, Carl Hirsch asked if I could get a band for the rally. It was short notice, but Dr. Hook & the Medicine Show agreed to appear because they were in town playing the WMMS Freakers Ball at the Smiling Dog Saloon. It was advance publicity. I suggested we also have a live Get Down. Murray didn't want to do it, because RTA wanted him to announce all the cities they would serve. I told him we needed it, it would take only part of his Get Down, and he could do it his way. But none of us knew what to expect.

The fact that he could draw a crowd surprised everyone, including Murray. It was his first interaction with a live audience. He went through the cities—"Bay Village! Beachwood!"—and drew moderate applause for each. Then, "East Side! Are you with us?" That got a big cheer. "West Side! Are you with us?" A bigger cheer. "We're here to celebrate something else, too! We're celebrating the first year of Nixon being in exile!" That drew the biggest cheer of all. Energized, Murray started running down his Ten Commandments of the Easy Life, including "Honor thy Colombian and thy Gold!" He shocked us at the end by jumping into the crowd to continue his "Gotta-gotta-gotta-gottas." At one point, he lost his mic, which was quickly picked up by a fan who yelled into the mic, "Eat your pussy for the weekend."

Back at the station, part-timer Shelley Stile was running the board and handling production of the broadcast. Her original outcue was "Get down, dammit!" and applause. But she knew how to read Murray, and kept the lines open to Mall C. It ended with Dr. Hook and Charlie Kendall bringing Murray back on stage, with Dr. Hook's eye-patched Ray Sawyer saying, "Murray got down, but he couldn't get up."

The performance took Murray from a cult following to a mass audience. *Exit* magazine did a feature story about him the following week.

"Saul on the Mall" took us into fall. Murray's fame was further recognized when *Radio & Records* asked for him to do a Get Down at its annual convention in Houston. We were becoming recognized on the industry convention circuit, and Murray wanted to do it, but the request was turned down. The decision went all the way up to Milt Maltz, who feared the appearance would either make Murray a national star, sending him to a larger market, or would get him busted for smoking pot on the streets of Houston and make Malrite look bad. I felt the opposite, but read the room and didn't argue the issue.

We saw more proof of Murray's popularity at Kent State University, at a Jethro Tull concert co-sponsored with WMMS a week before Halloween. The band's label chartered a bus to make the long drive from the station, and Murray boarded with a younger woman he'd invited as his date. She told him during the ride that she wasn't interested in sex with him, which soured his mood.

We arrived at Kent in time for the opening act, UFO. Dan Garfinkel, who had recently become our marketing and promotion manager, checked arrangements with Wendy Stein from Belkin. Dan, known as the Duck, was a Brandeis graduate we met when he worked with Ray Shepardson's group to save and revive Playhouse Square, and we were trying to tie in with its long-running revue, *Jacques Brel is Alive and Well and Living in Paris*. He filled a need that was becoming urgent, one that Denny and I could no longer handle ourselves, and he was Murray's neighbor in the Coventry area. When Wendy said she needed someone from WMMS to emcee and introduce Tull, Garfinkel immediately suggested Murray as a natural choice. It was a Friday night.

Murray, who was glad to have an excuse to get away from his date, got his instructions from Garfinkel and walked backstage. As he later described it, "A side of beef stops me and says, 'What are you doing here?' I say, 'I'm going to bring on Jethro Tull.' He says, 'Jethro Tull requires no emcee. If you don't have a pass, leave!'"

Garfinkel, figuring his work was done, dropped some acid and found his seat. Murray stormed down the aisle. I heard shouting from the station's section of seats. It was a highly animated Murray, looming over Garfinkel and berating him furiously: "Don't ever subject me to that again! I will not allow that!" Garfinkel was gripping his seat, probably thinking he was having a bad trip. Murray went on and on, at the top of his lungs. People in front and in back stood on seats to see. People finding seats stopped to watch. The tirade probably lasted five minutes, but it seemed like an hour. Murray, still angry and shouting, finally sat down.

Huge applause broke out. In front, from behind, from the rafters. I told Murray to stand up. The applause swelled and quieted. Murray, suddenly inspired, shouted, "Got-ta, got-ta, got-ta, get DOWN!" Now there was cheering. Murray climbed onto his chair and stretched out his arms like the pope. He began turning slowly in acknowledgment, and he was showered with joints. Jethro Tull did not get crowd reaction even close to Murray's that night.

I wish we'd had someone filming him everywhere he went. Listeners liked meeting personalities, but there was something surreal and magical about the reaction to Murray. At World Series of Rock shows, most of us would be careful about venturing into the crowd because of the difficulty of getting around. Not Murray. He'd decide to meet the people, leave the press box or loge, and a path opened in the crowd, like the Red Sea parting, as he walked along. Everybody knew who he was. They'd hand him things he put in his pockets as he walked all the way to the stage, accepting greetings. The seas would part again as he returned. Back in the press box, he'd empty his pockets of joints, pills, pipes, and paraphernalia, picking through it like a kid examining trick-or-treat loot on Halloween, deciding what could and couldn't be trusted.

Halloween itself brought a WMMS party that became the stuff of legend, mostly for the wrong reasons. Its host was actually Rodger Bohn, who owned the Smiling Dog Saloon, a bar on a seedy stretch of West 25th Street that is best remembered as an oasis for local and touring jazz musicians. Bohn, who looked like a biker with his leathers and long ponytail, supplemented jazz with everything from rock and reggae to comedy. The Dog was one of the first joints Lynyrd Skynyrd played "up North," a few weeks after their first album was released. (Bohn closed the club in 1975, later opened a jewelry store on Clifton Boulevard, where he died in May 1996 of injuries suffered in a beating during a robbery.)

We broadcast Smiling Dog concerts on Saturdays at midnight, recorded by Dick Whittington, who was best known for his band, Dick Whittington's Cats. Bohn wanted to throw the Halloween party in appreciation, for WMMS, his friends, and his Smiling Dog employees. It was a private party, not a public show, and he rented the WHK Auditorium, which was dirty and musty but in the same building that housed WMMS. Despite the name, Malrite did not own it. Bohn greeted everybody at the door with a tank of nitrous oxide—laughing gas—for a cheap high and to get everyone in the mood. Some people came in costume.

Headlining the entertainment, he had Sun Ra and his Arkestra, who were on an extended tour of the Midwest and playing the Dog the following night. Getting Sun Ra, an innovative and eccentric jazz musician who maintained he was of an "Angel Race" from Saturn, was a real coup. The chance to see him in such intimate surroundings, a crowd of about a hundred, was exciting.

To open, Bohn found a band he said was something of a side project for a group of guys who worked in advertising agencies around Akron. They were called Devo, and Bohn said they were really weird but good, a perfect fit. Devo lived up to his billing. They came out and did a bizarre set like nothing we'd seen before. The crowd loved them—until they wouldn't stop playing and kept repeating their set over and over.

Sun Ra was becoming impatient. Devo's unending performance was preventing him from taking the stage, and he wouldn't play if he didn't go on at a certain set time. The crowd, which first supported Devo, shouted for them to get off the stage, demanding Sun Ra. They refused. Sun Ra never performed.

I've read about the party in newspapers and magazines over the years, always in distorted and exaggerated form. Members of Devo invariably recall it with self-serving spin, saying they knew they were going to make it when they were booed off the stage at a WMMS Halloween Party. They've said the crowd had trouble dealing with their humor and "wanted a local version of Led Zeppelin." The real story was that Sun Ra was the headliner, and he never got to perform because of Devo. That's why the crowd was mad. It had nothing to do with Devo being too sophisticated for the room. Devo was good, but they violated one of the cardinal rules of show business: They didn't know their close.

We closed out the year with a project that became one of our crowning achievements, a contemporary version of *A Christmas*

Carol—something that has been done many times since then but was another oddity for an album rock radio station of the seventies.

Denny Sanders and Dan Garfinkel scripted the adaptation from Dickens. Murray was Iggy Scrooge, and he played it to the hilt. David Spero was his ghostly partner, steel magnate David Marley. Kid Leo was Little Leo, Matt the Cat played Matt the Cratchit, and Shelley Stile was Mrs. Cratchit, with Betty Korvan as daughter Martha. The three spirits, of Christmas past, present, and to come, were Len Goldberg, Charlie Kendall, and Steve Lushbaugh. Verdelle Warren played Scrooge's fiancee. Denny, Lushbaugh, Jeff Kinzbach, and Ed Ferenc were various men about town. Guests from outside the staff included Michael Stanley and Alex Bevan.

Murray led a special Christmas Get Down when it ended. We were proud of the entire production, which was broadcast on Christmas Eve and billed as the "Buzzard Theater of the Air." Reaction was enormously positive, and listeners mentioned it for years afterward. Its broadcast became a Christmas Eve tradition.

But we needed to know our limitations too. The following spring, the "Buzzard Theater of the Air" tried an adaptation of *The War of the Worlds*. It was a case of trying too hard. The script used the bizarre premise that an alien death ray turned people into household appliances, and it probably would have made a better video. Sound effects were the key to making it work on radio, and it challenged even the considerable skills and imagination of Denny, Kinzbach, and Lushbaugh. *Christmas Carol* had taken a week to put together, but they were still assembling the second half of *War of the Worlds* while the first fifteen minutes were on the air.

It was a disaster. When the program failed to generate the response we had for *Christmas Carol*, it soured everyone—especially Kinzbach and Lushbaugh, who had worked nonstop doing intricate production work with primitive equipment. "Buzzard Theater of the Air" went on nearly permanent hiatus—although we did a series of Saturday night Halloween specials in the eighties starring Boom (Len Goldberg). Denny flashed on the name of an old and long-forgotten villain from *Colonel Bleep*, a fifties children's

TV cartoon—Dr. Destructo. The show opened with the legend of our Dr. Destructo. Every Halloween, mild-mannered Len "Boom Boom" Goldberg turned into an alternate personality when a black cat crossed his path or he accidentally walked under a ladder. He became Dr. Destructo, with his kettle of heavy metal.

Every break was scripted. One had Dr. Destructo unleashing his rabid Dobermans on Bonnie Tyler to eat her alive—complete with screams and chomping sounds. In another, Dr. Destructo poured hot lead down John McEnroe's throat. He even ate a kitten—complete with predictable double entendres.

Tom O'Brien's production fed Boom's bellowing voice through harmonizers and reverb with a background of eerie sounds. Denny and I wrote the material, including a phony commercial that had Dr. Destructo presenting a major outdoor concert starring every heavy metal band we could name, and promising it would close with a nuclear explosion.

For the next week, WMMS and Belkin fielded calls asking where the concert would be held and how to get tickets.

CHAPTER 12

THE SWITCH

We gave listeners something they couldn't get elsewhere: true exclusives—new music that other stations didn't yet have.

Denny and I recalled exclusives from Top 40 radio of the 1960s, when stations would scramble to be first with a new single by the Beatles, the Rolling Stones, or the Beach Boys. The winner would milk it for all it was worth, building anticipation by tracking the progress of a record from the airport to the station, playing it with great fanfare, and grandly releasing it to other stations, which they'd claim were taping. It was great radio.

Exclusives went out as record labels built more sophisticated marketing campaigns, which they called "set ups." Album rock stations didn't play the exclusive card because it smacked of Top 40. We knew better. Exclusives added to the station's excitement and image, and they became part of our ongoing battle with M105. On rare occasion, they beat us. (Eric Stevens had some connections we didn't, because of his history with WIXY and relationships he established in the music industry over the years.) Mostly we beat them. One Rod Stewart album came to us, two months before release, from the general manager of Malrite's station in Milwaukee. One of his jocks was friends with a member of Stewart's band, who gave him a tape.

Exclusives also came from a secret weapon: The Switch—a small toggle switch under the desk in my office.

Frank Foti, our engineering wizard, installed the on-off switch and connected it to a tape machine set up next door to my office, in the production studio, which recorded from the turntable in my office. When a record promoter came in to preview an album that wouldn't be released for weeks or months, I'd flip The Switch as soon as he put it on. While we were listening, tape was rolling next door. I recorded dozens of exclusives that way, and we were careful how we used them. Timing was everything. Playing cuts immediately or too soon might tip our hand. Playing a record that wouldn't be released for three months made little sense. But we'd have it on hand to play a few weeks before anyone else had it.

Most labels hated exclusives. They wanted airplay, which has always amounted to free advertising for their product, but they had elaborate marketing and sales campaigns worked out. Advance exclusives muddied their plans and brought complaints from other stations wanting exclusives or favors of their own.

To limit their ability to block us, we often premiered our exclusives on Friday night, after the local label and distribution offices closed for the weekend. If one of them called the studio, or sent a cease-and-desist telegram or fax, I was the only person authorized to respond, and I would make myself impossible to reach. This wasn't paranoia. There were occasions when I recognized the cars of record promoters parked outside my home, hoping to hand-deliver me a cease-and-desist letter. I'd always come in late on Monday, during the last hour of the morning show, and Charlie Kendall or Jeff Kinzbach would announce we'd received a warning and couldn't play the exclusive anymore. But we'd had the whole weekend and Monday's morning drive to play it, and the labels looked like bad guys spoiling the party.

The leak of a Rod Stewart album, which came from Malrite's station in Milwaukee, so upset Russ Thyret, the head of Warner Records, that he stopped service of all Warner product to WMMS. The embargo ended after a few days, when he made a rare trip from L.A. to meet with us. We refused to reveal our source but agreed to be more considerate. At least for a while.

The same company was furious at WMMS when we broke Fleetwood Mac's *Tusk* album as an exclusive, early in the fall of 1979. That one came on cassette, from a friend in New York. To ensure its delivery, I had to buy a seat for it on a commercial flight. I was a nervous wreck waiting for it at the airport—once again on a Friday night—and drove it to WMMS, where Denny Sanders immediately put it on the air. We played one cut every half hour, inserting "WMMS exclusive" in case anyone tried to tape it. Warner was upset because Fleetwood Mac was their most important act at that time, and they worried about *Tusk* being a somewhat experimental double album which sounded nothing like its predecessor, the multi-platinum *Rumours*.

My favorite was when Henry Droz—president of the Warner-Elektra-Atlantic music group, the umbrella distributors of those labels and their affiliates—flew in for a dinner meeting at Swingos with WEA's regional representatives. Dave Lucas, the local marketing manager, was called away during dinner for an important phone call. The interruption wasn't welcome. He returned with color drained from his face. Twenty minutes later, he was called away again, and again returned white as a sheet. When the waiter called him to the phone a third time, and Lucas returned visibly upset, Droz, impatient and tired of the interruptions, demanded to know what was going on.

Lucas told him WMMS was playing the new Jackson Browne album, *Hold Out*. Now Droz was upset. He was known as "the architect of modern music distribution" and this wasn't the way he liked things done. It's worse, Lucas said—WMMS also has the new Queen album, *The Game*. Droz asked how it could happen. Didn't the label have control?

They have another one, too, Lucas said—the Rolling Stones' *Emotional Rescue*. Droz erupted. My answering machine filled with messages from Lucas and others from the WEA staff. "Please, please, you don't know how serious this is."

For us, it was a hat trick, a triple crown. But it did fuel the suspicion that we were taping, though the Browne and Queen albums came from an independent promoter, who knew Droz would be in town and wanted to make trouble for WEA. He used me, and I used him.

The Stones album did come via The Switch, from Paul Goldberg, the local Atlantic representative. I got him to play the entire album for me by showing interest and having staffers stop in—on cue—to hear the tracks. Weeks after we went on the air with it, he asked if I had a way to tape from turntable. Instead of answering directly, I told him that Carl Hirsch had a Learjet at Burke Lakefront Airport. Whenever there was an exclusive available, I would use it to pick up our copy. I said that *Emotional Rescue* came from a secret source in Toronto, and that I'd flown there, had dinner at my favorite restaurant, and flew back in time to world-premiere it on WMMS.

I don't know if Goldberg believed it, but he and Larry Bole, the local Warner representative, came to my office to catch me soon afterward. Bole put an advance copy of Fleetwood Mac's *Live* on the turntable. While he and I listened, Goldberg walked into the production studio and started talking with engineer Tom O'Brien—looking around inquisitively and hoping O'Brien would somehow give himself away. Bole lifted the needle from *Live* to break up the track.

By then, however, we had moved the tape machine into a different studio and hidden it where it couldn't be seen from production or the on-air studio. Tape was rolling. Because Bole had lifted the needle, it took O'Brien an hour of editing to reassemble the tracks we had, and to fake a couple of edits by playing parts of songs twice. We figured it would go unnoticed by an untrained ear that hadn't heard the material before. We had our exclusive. Bole rush-delivered the album to all radio stations in the region after he heard us world-premiering it and wrote off the rumors that my turntable was the source.

We had exclusives every week by the mid-1980s. The Switch was never the prime source of them, but it qualified as a sort of WMMS exclusive itself. Years later, the record guys weren't really surprised when I finally told them how I did.

CHAPTER 13

THE VOICE OF ROCK AND ROLL

Fleetwood Mac was an act we had jumped on early, right out of the box. There was something timeless about their music. Their self-titled 1975 album, the first with the line-up including Lindsay Buckingham and Stevie Nicks, received strong reaction that was made stronger when we scored live versions of some tracks. We gave them considerable airplay, and "Rhiannon" instantly became our most requested and played track. We were the only station with the live version, which was far more powerful than the softer version on the album.

Music director Shelley Stile pulled off a daylong exclusive with *Rumours*, released in February 1977, the same month WMMS moved to the Plaza Hotel. The immediate reaction gave little clue of how huge the album would be. But we knew it was something unique and special—product that would cause more defection from AM to FM, and from other stations to WMMS. We cemented our relationship with the band, getting to know everyone in it and connected to it. What gave us a solid edge with the band was our airplay of their pet projects—Fleetwood Mac spin-offs. They were all good and received well in Cleveland, but were usually neglected in other markets.

Walter Egan, formerly of the cult surf band the Malibooz, had one hit record nationally, "Magnet and Steel," off the *Not Shy* album coproduced by close friends Buckingham and Nicks, who also played on it; in Cleveland, he was a superstar, with a half-dozen tracks receiving airplay. Buckingham and Nicks also played on John Stewart's album *Bombs Away Dream Babies*, with the hit single "Gold," which was huge in Cleveland months before it broke nationally. Rob Grill, former lead singer of the Grassroots, was a fishing buddy of John McVie, who produced his one solo album, *Uprooted*—with guest appearances by Buckingham and Mick Fleetwood—which wasn't played much in any other market but had a big hit in Cleveland with "Rock Sugar." Most successful of all was Bob Welch, a close friend of Fleetwood, who scored three hit singles off his 1977 album, *French Kiss*.

We also dug into our library and played the *Buckingham-Nicks* album, which was recorded in 1973 before the two joined Fleetwood Mac. The music was similar to what Fleetwood Mac's would evolve toward, and many believed we were playing rare and unreleased Fleetwood Mac. The catalog album started to sell and it was the prime reason for Polydor to rerelease the album. Solo projects by Fleetwood Mac members also did well, with most of them debuting on WMMS as "World Premiere Exclusives."

By the time Fleetwood Mac played the Coliseum in September 1977, the band had actually sold a million copies of *Rumours* from the Cleveland WEA branch alone. We launched what we called the "WMMS Fleetwood Mac Attack," and took full ownership of what had become the biggest rock band in the country. We landed exclusive interviews, becoming the exception to the rule that they were no longer doing radio interviews, and we had them cut station IDs. The day after Stevie Nicks flubbed on stage and accidentally thanked Cincinnati instead of Cleveland, she cut a humorous ID, which said, "When I'm not in Cincinnati, I'm in Cleveland, and listening to WMMS."

We played it to the hilt that their logo was a penguin and ours the Buzzard, even tying in with Fleetwood Mac to donate a penguin to the Cleveland Metroparks Zoo. We also outfitted the band with all Buzzard merchandise and paraphernalia. For months to come, it wasn't unusual to see a band member or associate of Fleetwood Mac sporting a WMMS item on national TV.

Backstage at a World Series of Rock concert at Cleveland Stadium a year later, we presented the band with personalized, hand-painted mirrors individually created by David Helton. By that time, they were consuming massive quantities of cocaine, and it was rumored their annual consumption cost them more than $200,000 a year. Christine McVie, who got the first mirror, commented, "I'm afraid we'll scrape the mirror down to the paint."

My hunch that I would someday work with "BLF," the gravel-voiced character I had first heard on my car radio in Boston back in 1972, turned out to be accurate. He arrived at WMMS through a chain of events that started with the departure of his former WVBF co-worker, Charlie Kendall.

Kendall had moved to Cleveland with his wife, son, dog, and cat, but he and his wife separated soon afterward. He was a smooth and witty Mississippian with a line for everything. He wasn't naturally a morning person, but he was a great morning guy once he made it into the studio. He wasn't afraid to get behind new music he liked, which is unusual for a morning show host, and he deserves credit for putting Southside Johnny and the Tubes on WMMS. He also partied hard, in a work environment that could seem like being on permanent tour, and was linked romantically with several women at the station. It never got in the way of their work, but his intense relationship with Shelley Stile was briefly the hottest item at the station, and their breakup made it easier for him to leave in 1976 to become a program director in Dallas.

Not inappropriately, Stile replaced him as music director. It was her first full-time slot at the station, and she never did have a full-time air shift. But she was already enough of a presence to have her own fan club, and as her name implied, she had style. She was a twenty-three-year-old magna cum laude graduate of Kent State University, working at WCUE in Akron, when I first met with her, and I knew within five minutes she belonged at WMMS. Vacation relief, regular weekend shifts, personal appearances, and a brief Saturday night disco show gave her a high profile. Rock and radio were still overwhelmingly male-dominated industries. But Shelly, like Betty Korvan, was up to it. She was a bundle of energy who lived at the station and was plugged into popular culture.

Kendall's morning drive program went to Jeff Kinzbach, and we created a greater role for Flash Ferenc, who became a full-fledged sidekick, and the billing became official in December 1976: Jeff & Flash. Soon afterward, Steve Lushbaugh, who had been passed over for the morning program, left, and Betty Korvan took his former shift, 10 p.m.–2 a.m., opening up the overnight show. I immediately thought of BLF—the high-energy guy on WVBF who had first connected me to Kendall.

His name was William Lionel Freeman. BLF stood for Bill Lionel Freeman, because he didn't like William, and his show was the Bash. But his way of referring to "the Bash" and "BLF Bash" led listeners to believe that was his name. Eventually, inevitably, people started calling him Bash, and he went along with it.

He had visited Cleveland once since we met over the phone. On vacation from WVBF, he stopped in Cleveland on the way to drop off someone's hot-air balloon in Fargo, North Dakota. He timed the trip to make the WMMS World Series of Rock with the Rolling Stones—he was a huge Stones fan—and it gave him the opportunity to check out Cleveland. I got him tickets for the show, and we had dinner at Mexican Village and talked. He was an interesting person. Somehow, I had to hire him.

Now we had an opening, and Bash was ready. WVBF had abandoned his brand of rock and roll for disco, in a format so tight he was reduced to reading liner cards. In my mind, he was already hired, but, being cautious, he wanted to return to Cleveland and see WMMS on a regular workday. We were going to fly him in, but he insisted on taking a Greyhound bus. When I met him at the bus station, he was carrying only a tote bag. I asked if he had any luggage, and he said, "This is it." He unzipped it. It was a six-pack.

The radio station normally makes the rules. Bash had his own. Number one, only I could have his phone number, and only I could know his address. He moved into a house eventually, but only after a few years living at Marty's Motel in Strongsville. They changed the sheets for him—that was his line—and there was a liquor store across the street. Because he never wanted to act bigger than the music, he didn't give interviews and only reluctantly had his picture taken. He didn't want to make personal appearances, which only added to his mystique.

Hiring him was one of the best moves I ever made. Disk jockeys seldom stay long in one place, because they're always trying to move to a larger market, and Bash had a rap sheet of call letters on his resume. Like Kendall, he came from Top 40, where the rap on DJ's was that they double-parked their cars and left the motor running when they arrived in a new market. But Bash found home when hit Cleveland, and WMMS was the perfect station for him. I consider him the best all-night guy of all time, anywhere, because he knew how to deliver for a third-shift audience that was awake and anything but mellow. Because of his night-owl habits, which went back to when he was a baker in the U.S. Navy, he knew what the all-night audience needed.

He rarely watched television but was well read, politically savvy, and always spoke his mind, which I encouraged. On one of his first shows he described driving his VW bus from Strongsville up Interstate 71, which had not been plowed hours after a snowstorm. He said he was new to town but guessed people in Cleveland didn't pay taxes. "If you do, you're getting screwed," he said, going on a rampage about how bad the unplowed roads were.

The FCC required us to carry a certain amount of news and public affairs programming, and we had a large news commitment in morning drivetime. But because I felt much of the day should be music-intensive, I scheduled four newscasts with Bash, telling him to rip and read the Associated Press wire, no big deal. Though he didn't have time to rewrite, he revised the news as he was reading it. A few days after Mount St. Helens erupted in 1980 he said, "Y'know, that thing up there is formin' dis here lava dome, ya see, an' that's sorta like puttin' a cork on da thing." He made political statements in his own subtle way, if only by delivering a politician's name in a monotone. I'd get comments from listeners who "really liked what Bash said about so-and-so," but it was implied through inflection. Much later in his career, when WMMS was programmed by people who had no interest in the station's history, he went public with political views, especially during the Persian Gulf War, which he opposed. At one point, he told his audience he was leaving WMMS to go to the Mideast and do radio under the name Ali Baba Bash.

He became a major personality, an amazing feat given his overnight shift. His show had regular features, and you could set a clock by his adherence to them. I left the choice of music mostly to him. He played incredible variety, and he listened to everything that came out, staking out the production room before the day's work started. He would leave me notes—"Hey, check this"—referring to a musical find, and he was always right. He could've been a music director.

His signature came every Sunday morning, just before 1:30, when he marked "last call" by playing "Maggot Brain"—Funkadelic's ten-minute psychedelic guitar masterpiece that told listeners that if they were still awake, they were going to be up the rest of the night. Everybody in town seemed to know about it, and we never received a single complaint about the track's spoken word intro: "Mother Earth is pregnant for the third time/For y'all have knocked her up/I have tasted the maggots in the mind of the universe/I was not offended/For I knew I had to rise above it all/Or drown in my own shit." Bash juggled seamlessly from rhythm and blues to hard rock to an oldie. He signed off on Friday morning with a live version of Creedence Clearwater Revival's "Keep On Chooglin."

To Bash, a sunny day in the forecast was always a "bright blue beauty." He smoked cigarettes, a habit he said he picked up after leaving his birthplace of Burbank, California, to "equalize" his own atmosphere so he'd still feel like he was breathing Burbank's smog. The biggest risk with the rules was alcohol. It wasn't allowed in the studio, or even permitted in the station, because we never knew when FCC field enforcement people might show up. But Bash needed to go through a six-pack to do the show, and I looked the other way because I knew it was the fuel he needed. It never impaired his performance, and he never fell asleep. He enjoyed being up all night.

It made him a good match with Doc Lemon, the all-night jock

down the hall on WHK. WMMS and WHK staffers usually had little contact, but Bash and Doc had a great relationship. Doc also sounded like an old prospector and shared Bash's taste for Mexican food and beer, and they'd make burritos or chiles rellenos on a smuggled-in hot plate. Bash periodically checked on Doc, who would nod off from time to time. Doc was another ideal overnight guy, and probably the best all-night country jock at the time when Bash was the best overnighter in contemporary rock.

At the end of the summer, music director Shelley Stile saw opportunity in New York and felt it was time for her to move on, which she did. Leo replaced her on an interim basis. I wanted to give him the job permanently. Again, John Chaffee and general manager Gil Rosenwald felt his musical tastes were limited, that he wouldn't be able to deal with mainstream music, and that the labels would eat him for lunch. It took me more than a few weeks to convince them it would be a wise move. Leo finally and officially became music director in November. Though announced as official, initially it was on a trail basis. He eventually passed, and JC and Gil agreed to create a permanent budget item for Leo as music director.

The other departure was that of Murray Saul, whose position at the station was more a state of being than anything that could be pinned down by a job description. The beginning of his end at WMMS came when he marched in a Labor Day parade at Kamm's Corners on the West Side. A preteen boy yelled, "Get down!," which Murray took to mean that the Get Down was too popular. The next week he said he didn't want to do it anymore. "It's time to end—I don't want to be Dy-no-mite," he said, referring to TV actor Jimmie Walker. "I don't want to be pigeon-holed like that's the only thing I did in my life." He insisted on replacing "Get down" with "Let it be known" as the close of the weekend salute. It was lackluster compared to the original.

Still popular, but not reading the room, he demanded a contract from Gil Rosenwald, claiming that his face was a billboard for WMMS. It would have been an outrageous demand from anybody else, but I understood what Murray was saying. When he walked down the street, whether he liked it or not, he represented WMMS. But Rosenwald was the general manager, and he looked for excuses to terminate Murray. He finally had one and fired him on the spot. After his firing, Rosenwald walked into my office and said, "I hope that asshole is inspired now," a reference to the comment Murray had made about him to Carl Hirsch in 1974.

Murray, who was able to land a promotional job for Elektra Records, had sabotaged himself before. When there was an opportunity to syndicate and cash in on the Get Down, he refused on the grounds that it was his "gift to the world." Years later, he realized he had been bootlegged at radio stations all over the world, most notably WBCN in Boston. Fortunately, in its earliest days and before its popularity kicked in, Rosenwald had agreed that the Get Down would be owned by a corporation, Taurus Productions, not Malrite, giving Murray the rights to the original recordings. He agreed to put out a "Best of" CD, which was released in 1999 and has been a steady seller since.

When Led Zeppelin played a couple of shows at the Coliseum in April 1977, they stayed at Swingos and called Betty Korvan to make requests. The band was in shock because we had in our library anything they asked for—and it was an amazing moment for Betty, the station's biggest Led Zeppelin fan. They didn't want to do interviews—band policy—but she did manage to put them on the air as they called in their requests.

The concert was another chance for WMMS to make an impression. We bought time on the video screens, before the show started, for promotional spots animated by David Helton. The crowd cheered each one, and monitors at food stands, in bathrooms, and other locations made them inescapable. Between video, the screens flashed lists of upcoming WMMS-Belkin shows at the Coliseum, complete with the Buzzard logo. And one of the loges was draped with a huge banner reading "Led Zeppelin–WMMS," visible from every seat. Chairman Mao would've been proud of our exposure.

"The Buzzard Voice of Rock & Roll" was still another way we kept up the active presence of acts on WMMS. I viewed round-the-clock contests and giveaways as vital, as a way to offer listeners something beyond music and to create opportunities for audience participation. Prizes—tickets, albums, T-shirts—didn't have to be expensive. We wanted tonnage, which would allow more participants to win more often and encourage passive listeners to become active.

We assembled an all-star cast of rock stars and assorted personalities to provide three clues—their choice—to their identity. We ran three clues a day during morning, midday, and late afternoon drive. The contest went on for two weeks—and participants sent in their entries, with the grand prize winner receiving a fully loaded, state-of-the-art-for-1985 entertainment center. It was one of my favorite and most popular contests—and one that could not easily be duplicated since we had the actual rock and roll superstars providing clues to their identity. For one thing, we service marked the contest to prevent unauthorized use. We were getting clues from Bono and the Edge of U2, Peter Wolf of the J. Geils Band, Southside Johnny, Carlos Santana, and dozens more. My personal favorite was Debbie Harry of Blondie, who gave a clue with a New Jersey accent, saying, "I'm from Joisey. You from Joisey?" Even with bizarre clues like that, a good quarter of the entries had identified all artists correctly.

At the same time, we did another contest where the winner would get a chance to ask Mick Jagger a question live on WMMS. Jagger was promoting his *She's the Boss* solo album—and knowing he was serious about wanting the album to sell, we played hardball to lock up the promotion. Jagger's label, Columbia, ended up doing a similar promotion at other stations in major markets following the success of ours.

Later in the year, we had our first major promotion for Jeff and Flash, "Go Back to Bed." Listeners sent letters telling us where they worked, who the boss was, what the business phone was, and the time they woke up for work every day. The contest winner would get a day off, with pay. It was an ambitious idea that took a lot of work, but it was worth it.

We picked names a week in advance and contacted the employers. When we found businesses that would cooperate—and most did, for the on-air mentions—we'd call winners at their normal wake-up time and tell them, "Go back to bed!" We even set up a deal with a temp agency for substitutes. The promotion brought us massive press and TV coverage.

More evidence of success came later during the promotion, when Jeff and Flash hosted an "election night party" at the Dixie Electric Club in Parma, at the same State Road complex as Peaches, the record store chain that was making significant inroads in Cleveland. We expected 1,000 people, and 2,000 showed. Fortunately, the fire marshal didn't take notice. Downtown the same night, WMMS sold out the Agora for a *Night Out* with Crawler, a popular British rock band of the time.

On the first night of the fall Arbitron survey period, Thursday, October 20, 1977, after much internal debate, we debuted a weekly countdown show. Countdowns were acceptable for Top 40 but definitely a departure for an album rock station—even using an album list. Because John Chaffee doubted its success in our format, it took three solid months of convincing, plus an agreement from me that we would play the most popular track on each album.

The chart was very accurate for its time. Rhonda Kiefer, who had joined WMMS as an intern and become my valuable assistant programmer, set up a system to call dozens of retailers in Cleveland, Akron, and Canton each week for their current music sales. Questionable reports were filtered out, which was fairly easy to do. Store clerks admitted that some labels sweetened the pot for retailers by giving them the free albums known as "cleans" for reporting their products as the top sellers. The labels didn't realize we were wise to their scheme, and the retailers enjoyed getting a half dozen to a dozen "free" albums to sell, though artists affected by their practice never received royalties for the bonus albums sold.

The countdown show went on without any problems and sounded better than we expected. About three-quarters of the way through, however, we received a news bulletin that a plane carrying the band Lynyrd Skynyrd had crashed. There were no further details. Ray Hoffman, WHK's night newsman, rushed the bulletin to Denny, who immediately put it on the air and called to fill me in. After a short discussion, we decided to play nothing but Skynyrd; if someone tuned in, they would stay with WMMS to find out what was wrong. We knew the crash would not be a major story for conventional media. We would be the place where fans of the band would go for updates. This became a test of our staff's ingenuity and ability to go well beyond the call of duty. After Denny left the air and Betty Korvan took over, he spent the next three hours contacting FAA and the sheriff's office nearest the crash site for updates and actualities. M105 didn't hit the air with the news until 10:15 p.m.—thirty to forty minutes after WMMS—and kept reading the same wire reports, which weren't updated, while we were running actualities from the crash site.

We also located spokespeople from MCA, Skynyrd's label, and Peter Rudge, who managed the band. We were the first to report that there were casualties, and had a list on the air by 2 a.m. of who was killed and of the various injuries to other band members, most of them critical with back injuries. Rudge was so impressed that he gave our hotline number to everyone connected with Skynyrd to provide us with updates. By morning, Jeff and Flash had dozens of actualities and updates to work from. With Denny and Betty, who stayed on after her shift, we had the best coverage of any radio station. Though the crash occurred in Mississippi, other album rock stations around the country took their reports from us—as long as they credited "WMMS, Cleveland." Later in the day, MCA and Rudge thanked us for providing the most in-depth, tasteful coverage of the tragedy.

CHAPTER 14

MOVING ON UP

Bash nicknamed his show *The After Hours Joint*. He and Doc Lemon sounded like they were broadcasting from a combination truckstop and after-hours joint in a converted factory. It wasn't far from reality. The building at 5000 Euclid Avenue was old, seedy, cramped, and windowless. It fit the decay of the neighborhood. Cars were stolen every week from our lot on Prospect, and the street was a hooker haven day and night. Despite the thefts, Maltz refused to hire security until someone tried to steal the tires from his car—even though he was the only person with access to a small garage attached to the building.

Office space was inadequate, and Maltz had to share his bathroom with the common help, which irked him no end. Studio equipment hadn't been replaced since WHK installed it in 1949. The building had a history and funkiness we loved—it was a place where anyone could go out to the parking lot and smoke a joint during the day—but the station had outgrown it.

One plan was to move to the transmitter site in Seven Hills. It was equally close to both east and west sides, but actually inconvenient because Interstate 480 was a decade from completion. The I-271 corridor in Beachwood also came up as a possibility. But something about being in downtown Cleveland seemed to make sense. It would make us part of the city, accessible to all areas, and minutes away from most of the downtown clubs.

The search ended with the Cleveland Plaza, on Euclid Avenue at East 12th Street, a few blocks from the back-from-the-dead Playhouse Square. It had hustle and bustle and real traffic, and it was one of the few spots in Cleveland that, with imagination, looked like a real downtown. Halle's department store was still in business, and there were at least a dozen restaurants within walking distance. The Plaza itself was interesting, too. Previously the Statler and then Statler-Hilton Hotel, it once was home to WGAR and WNCR, was in its last days as a sort of fleabag hotel, and it had some business tenants including the David & Lee modeling agency; sports and talent agent Ed Keating, who had some of the city's most prominent broadcasters and sports figures as clients; and Nationwide Advertising, owned by Ted Stepien.

The move was relatively easy, considering the 15,000 albums and thousands of tapes involved. With everyone pitching in, we did it over a weekend, and our final broadcast from 5000 Euclid ended just before midnight Sunday. The only glitch was that we were supposed to be off the air from midnight to 6 a.m. Something went wrong when we signed off. Anyone still listening could hear us giving good riddance to the old facility until a listener called to tell us we were on the air. The night before, we'd had to sign off air at 3 a.m. for some move-related maintenance. The engineers randomly picked a track to test the microwave setup at the Plaza—"Dreamweaver," by Gary Wright. They played it over and over and over to fine-tune the signal and audio processing. Within an hour, Cleveland police were getting calls from listeners who thought something was wrong.

Wasting no opportunity for promotion, we played up the move on air, calling it our move from the eighteenth century to the twentieth. Jeff and Flash opened the new studios on February 14, 1977, by playing the live-at-the-Agora version of "Havin' A Party" by Southside Johnny & the Asbury Jukes. We never looked back.

The studios were not state of the art, but they were a welcome improvement. We now had space enough to accommodate our huge library and an entire band for interviews. Instead of a cubbyhole shared with office supplies, we had a walk-in closet for our growing archives. We also had two production studios, allowing us to record interviews and performances for later broadcast.

Another benefit of the new location was that it allowed us to do live remotes without worrying about phone lines. At 5000 Euclid, we had no line of sight to our transmitter, which prevented us from doing wireless microwave transmission from the station and the transmitter. We were one of the very few stations that had to run phone lines from the station to transmitter—one for WHK and two for WMMS stereo. When the lines went down, as they often did, we'd go off the air.

The move cost an estimated $2 million, including the new equipment. We had half of the twelfth floor—a total of forty-one rooms serving Malrite, WMMS, and WHK. WMMS had eleven of those rooms, which we outgrew quickly. A glass door separated the radio station savages from the corporate civilization. It wasn't long before the glass doors were the metaphor for corporate interference with WMMS: "We don't want anyone coming through the glass doors." The corporate side was silent and unsmiling. Our side had music blasting everywhere and people hanging out in the halls. It was always an upbeat party atmosphere.

Gil Rosenwald, who had recently been made general manager while Carl Hirsch was promoted to executive vice president of Malrite, had his office built with two entrances—one on the radio side, the other on the corporate side, to emphasize he was our connection to corporate. The glass doors represented an unspoken warning for radio people to stay out of the corporate side. Which didn't work because of the bathroom issue.

The corporate side had two restrooms, men's and women's, with multiple stalls. The radio side also had two, each with a toilet and a sink, both unisex. One bathroom outside the WHK studio had an intercom playing WHK. The other was around the corner from the WMMS studios and had WMMS on its intercom.

The problems were immediate. Time was critical at both stations. Jocks adhered to formats with required commercial breaks at specific time and had to deal with song length. Since the two bathrooms were supposed to serve every WHK and WMMS employee, a jock needing a quick pitstop might find the bathroom door closed. Leo would pound on it, yelling, "Get the fuck outta the bathroom—

that's for the jocks!" After another jock in the same situation used
WHK's bathroom, making it unavailable for a WHK announcer who
needed it, Rosenwald issued a somewhat ridiculous memo stress-
ing that jocks always had top bathroom priority. How to enforce
that rule was never explained.

The radio commoners began using the larger and better-
equipped corporate bathrooms, which did not sit well with Maltz.
If you were unfortunate enough to be in the bathroom when he
was, you'd get a third-degree—just to make you think twice about
coming back. A WMMS salesman using the bathroom was once so
spooked when Maltz walked in that he bolted without washing his
hands—leading Milt to comment frequently about him afterward,
"He doesn't wash his hands."

Joan Jett will forever be known for her unwitting contribution to
the best-known WMMS bathroom anecdote. Kid Leo, a couple of
record promoters, and I had lunch at the New York Spaghetti House
with Joan and her manager, Kenny Laguna. Joan was dressed in her
trademark black, skintight leather pants. She had a long history with
WMMS going back to the Runaways. In 1976, her "I Love Rock &
Roll" anthem broke out of Cleveland, and we had production manager Tom O'Brien make an extended mix we called the "WMMS
version." This was before extended mixes became commonplace.
Joan came back to the station after lunch to do an interview with
Jane Scott of the *Plain Dealer*, go on-air with Leo, and cut some IDs
for us. She was comfortable at the station, had some time to kill,
and asked where the restrooms were. Knowing what reaction she
might get on the corporate side with her spiked hair and leather, I
pointed her to ours. She took a shit that became legendary. Since
the bathroom had no ventilation, there was only one place odor
could go—the hallway, which it permeated for hours.

There was little mingling between WMMS and WHK, even
though staffers worked almost side by side. One reason was that
the WHK people, generally older, couldn't figure out WMMS. Another was the friction surrounding a vote on AFTRA, the American

Federation of Television and Radio Artists. WHK's well-paid staff wanted to vote the union out; the WMMS staff, paid less, wanted to keep it. In the end, AFTRA stayed.

Former Cleveland radio personality Don Imus had been fired from WNBC in New York for excessive drinking and drug use. Even after kicking his bad habits, he couldn't find work. Carl Hirsch took notice and hired Imus for afternoon drive on WHK—a brilliant move since it brought a strong marquee name back to Cleveland radio. Imus had handled morning drive for WGAR prior to his move to New York. While at WHK he was aloof and would not acknowledge anyone from WMMS, including myself. Despite his fall from grace, he still considered himself a star.

Imus hated Cleveland, and once an opportunity to return to New York opened up, he did so, and immediately cut a TV spot for WNBC, which had rehired him, in which he begged people to listen to him so he "wouldn't be sent back to Cleveland."

Corporate expected outside-the-lines behavior from WMMS, but most of it came from WHK, and often involved Gary Dee. He brought embarrassing headlines with his wildness and with his stormy marriage to Liz Richards, the *Morning Exchange* cohost on WEWS-TV. WHK newsman John Webster once went after him with a fire extinguisher during an on-air argument that resulted from Dee, on the air, calling Webster's wife a whore.

Dee was the most highly paid staffer. He was forty when he joined WHK from WERE in July 1975 for what was then a whopping $75,000. The average WMMS on-air personality was making less than $14,000 a year, and I was making a little more than $15,000 as program director. But Dee's ratings were worth the money, until the shock-jock persona took him over. He'd emerge from the studio at 10 a.m., thermos in hand, and make the transformation from the on-air Gary Dee to Gary D. Gilbert. He'd stand with his back against the wall in the hallway, head down and eyes closed, take deep breaths, and in one or two minutes come out of character. His problems came when he didn't come all the way out of that character.

●　　　●　　　●

The Cleveland Plaza evolved into entertainment central. David & Lee models would collide with pro athletes represented by Ed Keating, and with celebrities visiting WMMS. The building had two restaurants, plus Ted Stepien's Competitor's Club in the basement, featuring waitresses in short, toga-style dresses. Stepien hired foxy women, and he let them sunbathe on the roof in bikinis, with an option to go topless, within view of his office on the fourteenth floor. The roof of the Plaza and adjacent garage also became the new home for pot breaks. We later learned that the offices of one business in the building were a cocaine center where mirrors of the powder were set out for the clientele.

The Plaza was one of the last buildings to have elevator operators, some of whom were characters always ready to dispense "if the walls could talk" history. We learned that some of Cleveland's top politicians and business leaders booked rooms for trysts. Since it was a combination hotel and office building, it was easy to figure out who was doing whom. One married WHK manager took advantage of the situation to bed two of his salesgirls simultaneously, managing to keep it under wraps despite a few close calls. The rooms came in handy for us during blizzards that paralyzed the city during years it lacked the budget to deal with them.

As the building started converting to solely office use and was renamed the Statler Office Tower, old mattresses were stored one floor above us. One summer evening in 1980, they caught on fire. The building filled with smoke, creating a surreal scene. I could barely see Denny through the haze, doing his show, and he refused to leave the studio unless he could keep the station on the air. He said he'd go when he saw flames, like a captain going down with the ship.

The fire department finally ordered everybody out. WHK signed off, but Denny raced into the archives and grabbed the first tape he could find—a Joe Perry Project concert at the Agora—strung it up, and left. He couldn't have made a better choice. When we were finally allowed back into the building, the tape was just ending. We never had any dead air. Denny returned to the studio after the fire was brought under control, turned on the mic, and interviewed the firefighters. It ended up being the lead story on TV newscasts that night, and a story in the *Plain Dealer* the following day. Everything was opportunity for us. The fire, which caused $50,000 worth of damage, was ruled arson by the fire department—which suggested that maybe, just maybe, it was set by another radio station fearful of the Buzzard's dominance.

1. The pre-Buzzard WMMS mushroom logo, designed by Judy Tiburski, sister of then-sales manager Walt Tiburski. This was the station's official logo in 1973 through early 1974.

2. Everyone's hair was long when I arrived at WMMS in 1973. This is my first photo with fellow staffers, taken with the all-female band Birtha. *Left to Right:* Rosemary Butler (Birtha), Kid Leo, Steve Lushbaugh, Shele Pinizzotto and Sherry Hagler (Birtha), Jeff Kinzbach, me, Olivia "Liver" Favela (Birtha). Kid Leo's beard would be shaved a month later and the hair cut the following spring. Singer Rosemary Butler is best known as Jackson Browne's back-up singer. *(Fred Toedtman)*

3. My office in the early seventies. Denny Sanders, standing, is barely inside the door. The office was only large enough for two people. *(Fred Toedtman)*

4. Len "Boom" Goldberg, backstage at the first WMMS World Series of Rock, Cleveland Stadium, 1974. WMMS personalities brought the acts on stage and did between-sets announcements, which gave them and WMMS major exposure. *(John Gorman)*

5. Murray Saul at Norwalk Raceway, Norwalk, Ohio, 1977. The popularity of the Friday "Get Down" weekend salute made Murray a much-in-demand personality for public appearances. *(author's collection)*

6. Without a promotion budget, we had to use our wits. When RCA Victor bought the side wall of the Music Grotto, I convinced the label and Shelly Turk, the store owner, to add the WMMS Buzzard logo. *L to R:* Matt the Cat, Betty Korvan, Joel Frensdorf, Jeff Kinzbach, Denny Sanders, Kid Leo, Bob Zurich (RCA Victor records). *(Fred Toedtman)*

7. Matt the Cat in the WMMS studio doing his imitation of "Captain" Kenny Clean. *(Anastasia Pantsios)*

8. Kid Leo on the air in the WMMS studios reading over a list of what songs had been played earlier in the day. *(Anastasia Pantsios)*

9. Roxy Music were stars in Cleveland long before their national success, and Brian Ferry was a frequent visitor to WMMS. *L to R:* Kid Leo, Bryan Ferry (Roxy Music), Hal Kaplan (Atlantic Records), Mark Fenwick (EG Records, London), me. *(Dan Keefe)*

10. The Isley Brothers at WMMS, 1975. Few rock stations played their music, but at WMMS their songs were among the most requested. This was the first time the Isleys visited a rock-format station. *L to R:* Rudolph Isley, Chuck Schwartz (Epic Records), Chris Jasper, Ernie Isley, Kid Leo, Marvin Isley, me, Denny Sanders, Jeff Kinzbach. *(Fred Toedtman)*

11. Murray Saul and Shelley Stile opening the WMMS World Series of Rock in 1975. Murray's "Get Down" at the concert was filmed for an early WMMS television spot. *(Dan Keefe)*

12. The side stage at a WMMS World Series of Rock. The concerts provided us unmatched visibility, with crowds of 80,000 and more. *(John Gorman)*

13. We reprinted this 1978 *Cleveland Press* headline on one of our WMMS sales department "hype sheets," which was sent to potential local advertisers and national advertising agencies, promoting the success of a WMMS World Series of Rock concert at Cleveland Stadium.

Cleveland Press

Serving Its Readers for 100 Years

Saturday Final

No. 25725   Saturday, July 1, 1978

City becomes Rocktown as 86,000 fans roll in

By BRUNO BORNINO and SANDY BANKS

More than 86,000 music lovers insured with "a piece of the rock" — a $12.50 ticket to see Mick Jagger and the Rolling Stones — invaded downtown.

day, some camping at the gates in hopes of getting ringside seats to gaze at the legendary Stones.

And although many of them were mere babes when the Rolling Stones first burst into prominence on the

The scene outside the Stadium resembled a street fair. The scent of marijuana wafted through the air, mixing with the music of the Rolling Stones that poured from speakers on top of cars and vans parked in the Stadium lot. Many radios were

parking normally costs $2.25 for Indians games.

One enterprising young man was selling beers for $1 a piece from his cooler to the Stadium crowd at 5:30 a.m. Another young man was doing a brisk business with a tattoo

14. April 6, 1976. Bruce Springsteen's only visit to WMMS, which took place the day before he and the E Street Band played the Allen Theatre. *Back row, L to R:* Miami Steve Van Zandt, Charlie Kendall, me, Jeff Kinzbach, Steve Lushbaugh, Matt the Cat, Denny Sanders. *Front row:* Kid Leo, Bruce Springsteen, Shelly Stile, Dan Garfinkel. *(Dan Keefe)*

15. A strange incident never revealed until now. Dennis Wilson, sitting in on Murray Saul's Friday night "Get Down," suddenly broke down in tears after Murray's yelling reminded him of this own father, named Murry, with whom he had a troubled relationship. *(Janet Macoska)*

16. The WMMS broadcast studio, circa 1978, with Matt the Cat at the microphone.
(Anastasia Pantsios)

17. Members of Kiss were regular guests on WMMS throughout the seventies and early eighties. Gene Simmons was a natural on the air; he had a standing invitation from me to be a guest DJ whenever he was in town. *(Anastasia Pantsios)*

18. Tom O'Brien, Southside Johnny Lyons, Rhonda Kiefer, and Denny Sanders in the WMMS production room. Southside was listening to the playback of personalized IDs he cut for the airstaff. *(Anastasia Pantsios)*

19. Mick Fleetwood of Fleetwood Mac in my office at the Cleveland Plaza, working on a promotional idea. (That's Bruce Ravid of Capitol Records, partially obscured). WMMS was strongly identified with Fleetwood Mac's national breakout. *(R.J. Farrell)*

20. With Kid Leo in the WMMS on-air studio. Behind Leo are the commercials on "cart." Below them are bins containing the current albums we were playing. The cart racks on the studio table featured celebrity IDs and rare, unreleased material. The albums in the back of the room were a small portion of our total album library. *(author's collection)*

21. Plasmatics leader Wendy O. Williams being interviewed by Dia Stein. Wendy had been arrested the night before on an obscenity charge for simulating sex on stage and wearing only shaving cream at a WMMS Monday Night Out appearance at the Agora. She was later acquitted. (*Anastasia Pantsios*)

22. Actor Mr. T takes on Ed "Flash" Ferenc in the WMMS hallway in 1982. He appeared on Jeff and Flash's morning show to promote *Rocky III*. (*Janet Macoska*)

23. Kid Leo, me, and Don Novello as Father Guido Sarducci. I pitched the idea of Father Guido Sarducci doing "phone-in confessions" on Leo's show. The feature was a big success and was later imitated by other radio stations. We received one complaint, from the Cleveland Catholic Archdiocese. (*Anastasia Pantsios*)

24. Malrite Broadcasting President Carl Hirsch and Chairman Milton Maltz (at center). Carl Hirsch was a true broadcasting visionary and his backing and support of WMMS helped achieve our success. *(Janet Macoska)*

25. The final show at the Agora on East 24th Street with the Ricky Medlocke and Blackfoot. The club was destroyed by a fire just hours after his performance. *(Anastasia Pantsios)*

26. WMMS staff photo, 1983. Everyone is wearing a different Buzzard T-shirt. (I'm wearing a bootleg I bought from a street vendor.) *Top row, L to R:* Walt Tiburski, Bill Smith, Pam Barker, Jim Cszar, Ron Forrai, Len "Boom" Goldberg, me, Denny Sanders. *Third row:* Michelle Martoff, Beth Manuk, Rita Henderson, Cindy Tausch, Rhonda Kiefer, and Bill Salvo. *Second row:* Gaye Ramstrom, Irene Dardis, Sue Dixon, Tom O'Brien, Dia Stein, David Helton, Ed "Flash" Ferenc, Matt the Cat. *Bottom row:* Terry Lockett, Jim Marchyshyn, Judy Goldberg, Kid Leo (portrait), T.R. (Tom Rezny), Unidentified. *Not pictured:* Jeff Kinzbach *(Janet Macoska)*

27. Impromptu photo of Dia Stein, "Captain" Kenny Clean, me, Denny Sanders, and Matt the Cat in the WMMS broadcast studio, 1985. You would often find WMMS staffers working side-by-side on various programming projects. *(Anastasia Pantsios)*

28. Ohio Governor Dick Celeste guest hosted the morning show in 1986 and surprised us by knowing all the Buzzard Morning Zoo characters and features. *L to R:* Ed "Flash" Ferenc, me, Jeff Kinzbach, Dick Celeste, Ruby Cheeks. *(Anastasia Pantsios)*

29. WMMS print ads from the 1980s. Here's the Buzzard in a superhero costume, which we dubbed his "Buzzard Nuclear Army" uniform.

30. A custom ad for the national *Performance* magazine highlighting the unusually close relationships WMMS had with promoter Belkin Productions and the Blossom Music Center, Agora Ballroom, and Front Row venues—a level of cooperation rare in most other cities.

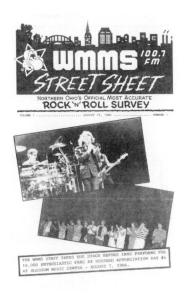

31. The "WMMS Street Sheet" was a throwback to the 1960s, when radio stations issued weekly surveys charting the position of albums and singles based on sales, airplay, and requests. *(Courtesy of Anastasia Pantsios)*

32. Not all of our publications were for outside consumption. This was one of a series of comics made for the staff, with plenty of inside jokes.

33. Staff photo, 1984, in the lobby of WMMS-WHK and Malrite Corporate offices. *Back row, L to R*: me, Bill "B.L.F. Bash" Freeman, Tom "T.R." Rezny, Ed "Flash" Ferenc, Jeff Kinzbach. *Front row*: Elisabeth Pick, Rhonda Kiefer, Matt the Cat, Denny Sanders, Betty Korvan, Len "The Boom" Goldberg, Kid Leo, Dia Stein, Tom O'Brien, Jim Marchyshyn. *(Janet Macoska)*

34. Malrite "Office of the President" chief Gil Rosenwald (left) and National Program Director Jim Wood (right). In less than a year, their interference in programming and marketing and encouragement of office politics tore apart WMMS. *(author's collection)*

35. Another WMMS "hype sheet," this one noting that WMMS had been the number one rated radio station in Cleveland for 20 consecutive ratings periods going back to October-November, 1975.

CHAPTER 15

THE BUZZARD AND THE BOSS

No recording artist was more closely associated with WMMS than Bruce Springsteen—especially after he played our tenth anniversary concert in 1978. And probably no one at the station was more identified with Springsteen than Kid Leo.

It wasn't a case of love at first listen. Leo's tastes were eclectic, but he did have quirks. When Culture Club's first album came out in 1982, for example, Leo didn't want to play it because he was concerned about Boy George's cross-dressing. He felt our audience would react negatively to his style—even though David Bowie, in his pre–Ziggy Stardust phase more than a decade earlier, looked like Lauren Bacall, and there were many other gender-bending artists in the seventies, including the New York Dolls. "Leo," I finally said, "this guy sounds like Smokey Robinson. How can we go wrong?" Though nearly all album rock stations were scared off by Boy George's image, it was good music for its time, and Leo agreed.

He had similar reservations when Madonna's "Borderline" single was released in 1983. It arrived as a twelve-inch disc, in a package that opened into a poster of Madonna. She was a bit blurred, like Dylan on the cover of *Blonde on Blonde*, and Leo was convinced she had an Adam's apple and was a transvestite. He was sure we'd be laughed at for playing the artist. When he was assured that Madonna was a woman, his opinion on her music changed.

It took Leo longer to pick up on Springsteen, whose first albums—*Greetings From Asbury Park, N.J.* and *The Wild, The Innocent & The E Street Shuffle*—sold poorly and received little play on WMMS after they were released in 1973. Denny Sanders, David Spero, and Matt the Cat were early boosters who liked and played a few tracks, but Leo was still heavily into hard rock and "glitter band" artists from Britain—Bowie, T.Rex, Sparks, and Mott the Hoople—as well as their American counterparts the New York Dolls and lesser-known hard rock acts like the Heavy Metal Kids and Hawkwind. Springsteen was being called "the new Dylan," and Leo thought he was working too hard to fit the part. And Leo didn't like Dylan.

Springsteen was, unquestionably, working hard. Though his record sales were weak enough to concern Columbia, his relentless touring was making him a darling of critics and starting to bring him an audience beyond the Northeast and the Jersey shore—especially in northeast Ohio. When he played his first show in the area, opening for Black Oak Arkansas at Kent State University in January 1974, he made such an impression that *Scene* gave him his first magazine cover anywhere—although they panned his Cleveland opening appearance for Wishbone Ash the next month.

Springsteen's next Cleveland date was a WMMS Night Out at the Agora, four months later on June 3, 1974. The club was a little over half full, with a smattering of college students from the Jersey Shore and Philadelphia. (That show, which has appeared on numerous bootleg CDs and sites, is often listed as taking place in February, because of a show that was canceled.) Despite an offer from Columbia Records to be their guest at the show, Kid Leo had no interest in attending. Springsteen played just short of two hours that night, and the concert was edited to fifty minutes for its Wednesday night broadcast on WMMS.

For Leo, and Springsteen, *Born to Run* made all the difference.

Rich Kudolla, the branch manager of Columbia Records in Cleveland, visited WMMS a few months after the Agora show to play an early version of the record for Leo, Denny, and me. It featured double-tracking of Springsteen's voice and was backed by full orchestration. We were impressed. Leo felt the song captured the essence of Phil Spector's "Wall of Sound," and didn't sound like that "fuckin' Bob Dylan." The only downside was a slight hiss on the recording. Kudolla let us keep the tape and gave us approval to play it. Springsteen was still a virtual unknown in Cleveland, so any exposure WMMS gave his music could only be positive.

Kudolla returned a week or two later with a cleaner copy of "Born to Run" without the hiss and minus the double-tracked vocal and massive orchestration. A better take, it became the version we used on the air, and the one Springsteen selected for the album, which was still months from release. The song took on a life of its own, so much that it became the official lead-in to Murray Saul's Friday Get Down. We revisited Springsteen's first two albums, with Leo now playing a cut from one of them daily, and their airplay on WMMS translated into sales. Both showed up on legitimate top twenty album lists in Cleveland, Akron, and Canton.

Springsteen's next Cleveland appearance, on February 18, 1975, was at the John Carroll University gym in University Heights. Co-sponsored by us, it was booked by Tim Russert—the host of NBC's *Meet the Press*, who graduated from John Carroll in 1972, and was president of its University Club while attending law school in Cleveland afterward. He had booked a number of concerts in college and agreed to help this time because he could use the money for law school. Russert suggested Springsteen, got him for $2,500, and worked with fellow fraternity members as a roadie—setting up the stage and the band's equipment, and working security.

I had to hand it to Columbia. If their plan was to establish Springsteen's first two albums only months before his third, it worked. Besides playing his previous albums, we started building a library of such unreleased tracks as "Thundercrack," a live performance recorded at a club in Philadelphia by WMMR, the first station in the country to play Springsteen. Like Michael Stanley in Cleveland, Springsteen had already achieved superstar status along the Jersey Shore and his influence and popularity continued to grow further south to Philadelphia. WMMS got a lot of credit later, because of our reputation for breaking new music, but most of our early unreleased Springsteen material came from influential WMMR announcer Ed Sciaky. He was Springsteen's original champion, even prior to his first Columbia release, and he became a source and friend to us.

Another unreleased track was "The Fever," which became a hit although it hadn't been officially released to the public. Charlie Kendall, our music director and morning man in 1975, was leaked a version notably different from Springsteen's. The artist was listed as "Southside Johnny," with no other information. Leo didn't like it, preferring the Springsteen version, but Kendall championed the tune—playing against Leo for listeners—and also fueled rumors that Johnny might be Springsteen in disguise. It was the kind of thing you do if you're a popular culture radio station, and even better when you are trying to build morning and afternoon drive ratings. Feuds can be good. Within days, we learned there really was a Southside Johnny Lyon, and that his Asbury Jukes were another popular band along the Jersey Shore. Springsteen occasionally joined them on stage at the Stone Poney, the Asbury Park club where he got his start, and the band's cofounder was Miami Steve Van Zandt, before he joined the E Street Band. Their first album was a masterpiece of blue-eyed soul, and a perfect fit for us. After Kendall left WMMS, Jeff Kinzbach assumed "ownership" of Southside Johnny along with the morning show. But Leo, knowing that Southside essentially had Springsteen's endorsement, also got behind him in a bigger way and because of his Springsteen connection, Leo became synonymous with Southside Johnny as much as with Springsteen.

All of it worked for Springsteen. By the time *Born to Run* was released, he was a superstar in Cleveland. The album quickly jumped to number three on the national chart, and it was the top seller in every record store locally. Most ran out of inventory, which was another plus for WMMS; we were the main station playing it, and listeners knew they wouldn't have to wait longer than an hour to hear a cut. In August 1975, Springsteen played triumphant shows at the Akron Civic Theater and Allen Theatre. In October, he appeared simultaneously on the covers of *Newsweek*, whose story quoted Denny Sanders, and *Time*, which proclaimed him "Rock's New Sensation." Over the next year and a half, he returned for four engagements in Northeast Ohio—of which two were at the Allen, and one, finally, at the Coliseum.

Clevelanders loved him, and Leo became the surrogate who expressed their passionate appreciation and spoke to the man directly. Springsteen returned the affection, giving Cleveland attention on a par with Philadelphia and New York. He visited WMMS only once—before his April 1976 shows at the Allen, for an interview with Leo in which it was hard to tell which of them was more nervous—but he obviously spent time listening. He knew the station, and he either fit right in or was a better actor than anybody dreamed. We couldn't have created a better artist to represent what WMMS stood for.

Even then, however, Springsteen's position was precarious when *Darkness on the Edge of Town* was released, in June 1978, because of a royalty dispute with his former manager. His success was built on his live shows, but record labels still considered annual album releases the norm. *Darkness* was Springsteen's first in almost five years. Columbia wanted to use it to reignite his career, or ignite it where he hadn't yet broken big. They suggested a series of free concerts, broadcast from key markets on ad hoc regional radio networks. Cleveland, where Springsteen was well established, was not among them. The label suggested doing the Midwest show in Detroit and wanted WMMS and other stations to simulcast it.

Steve Popovich and others at the label insisted that Springsteen do Cleveland and the Agora, which he believed was the best rock and roll club in America. Fortunately, it turned out to be an easy sell. Everyone in the Springsteen camp wanted the deal, too. The tie-in would be WMMS's tenth anniversary, the Agora would be the venue, and we would broadcast the show regionally.

The tenth anniversary tie-in was a natural, even though the anniversary itself was somewhat artificial. It marked the change of call letters from WHK-FM to WMMS, which came six weeks after the original progressive format was installed in August 1968, and it overlooked the fact that WMMS had other formats in its early years. To me, it was a useful marketing and promotional tool—a way of celebrating our past and presenting an image locked to a long future. It worked, locally and nationally, bringing a cover story in the *Plain Dealer*'s *Sunday Magazine*, a commemorative edition of *Scene* magazine, a special supplement in the national trade magazine *Record World*, and coverage in other trades including *Radio & Records* and *Billboard*. A week rarely went by without stories about WMMS in national trade magazines.

But nothing matched the Springsteen show. It was set for Wednesday, August 9, 1978, and we drew postcards from listeners to give away almost 1,200 tickets. Springsteen and the band, who'd been touring nonstop since May, added to the anticipation and festival atmosphere by arriving in town a day early to hang out with fans such as Jim Kluter, Joe Juhasz, Bill Spratt, and Johnny Kusznier—working-class West Siders who were so obsessed with Springsteen, before his stardom, that they'd driven to New Jersey to meet him and become known as his "Cleveland Boys." By showtime, the band was so relaxed that they cleaned out a pan of homemade lasagna Leo's mother sent backstage. Even Springsteen dug in, violating his rule of not eating before going onstage.

I was nervous, as I've always admitted. This was a major event for us, our listeners, and the other stations simulcasting the concert: WABX in Detroit, WDVE in Pittsburgh, WEBN in Cincinnati, WLVO in Columbus, WXRT in Chicago, KSHE in St. Louis, and KQRS in Minneapolis. A missed cue or a channel cutting out would have made us look bush-league. I wanted this to be the best radio concert of them all. I needn't have worried. To handle the broadcast, Columbia hired Sam Kopper, a former announcer at Boston's WBCN, who had purchased a school bus years earlier and equipped it with a remote recording studio for the specific purpose of broadcasting concerts. Production was supervised by Jimmy Iovine—a young engineer from New York who made his name by being part of John Lennon's comeback entourage and went on to become head of promotion for the Universal Music Group. One audio feed from the Agora went to the bus for radio; a second went upstairs to Agency Recording for a possible "live" album.

The air was literally electric—muggy and rainy outside, with summer lightning crackling, and fans jamming the Agora almost two hours before showtime. Some had even slept on the sidewalk the night before, because it was a general-admission show and they wanted to be up front. They whistled, clapped, and chanted in the background as Denny signed on the broadcast to welcome radio listeners. Leo did the onstage introduction: "I have the duty and the pleasure of welcoming, ladies and gentlemen, the main event. Round for round, pound for pound, there ain't no finer band around—Bruce Springsteen and the E Street Band!"

"He must have memorized that at home. I know you did!" Springsteen answered, obviously delighted. "Cleveland, how you doin'? Are you ready to shake them summertime blues?"

The band launched into Eddie Cochran's "Summertime Blues," and then "Badlands." The segue was like launching a rocket. Each song just kept building and building and building.

I know of only one thing that went wrong. Clarence Clemons never showed it in his performance—at one point, he even pulled the future wife of one of the Cleveland Boys onstage to dance—but he was upset because somebody had stolen his portable Nakamichi stereo from his room at Swingos. Springsteen turned the theft to advantage, however, by making a joke about it during a thirteen-minute version of "Growin' Up," in which he told his classic "Teenage Werewolf" story about going with Clemons to meet God. Springsteen also came close to knocking Leo off his feet during the story, by ad libbing that they met him along the way: "I go, 'Kid, what are you doing?' He says, 'Praying for more watts. I gotta blast this baby all the way to New Jersey!'"

The show went on for twenty-one songs, in two sets, and an encore ending with "Raise Your Hand." "I'd like to thank Cleveland for supporting us," Springsteen said. "When we first came here, we got some respect." The broadcast ended past midnight, after more than four hours. Leo read the credits but fully expected Springsteen would do one more encore. Springsteen, nearly spent, returned one more time for a surprise encore of "Twist and Shout" for the Agora crowd. It wasn't carried live, though we broadcast it later. Tape was still rolling, and it was flawless. The broadcast was also flawless, however, which might explain why Columbia never issued it as an album. The radio audience was estimated at three million, and the show was one of Springsteen's most-recorded and most-bootlegged.

Max Weinberg, drummer and currently bandleader for *Late Night with Conan O'Brien*, once called it the best show the E Street Band ever did. One of the greatest compliments I ever got came a few years later from Bob Seger. He said, "Man, I heard the concert you guys put on with Springsteen. That was the greatest rock 'n' roll show I ever heard." He told me he was one of the listeners who ran to his tape machine to record his own copy.

Cementing his ownership of Cleveland, Springsteen returned just three weeks later to play a three-hour concert at the Coliseum. After it ended, he and the E Street Band made an unannounced midnight run to the Agora—taking the stage to perform with Southside Johnny and the Asbury Jukes. A video of the show was shot for a *Live at the Agora* TV show, but Miami Steve would not allow Springsteen's portion to be broadcast. It turned up later on bootleg copies and, much later, on video-sharing sites on the Internet.

In the summer of 1978, Cleveland was sliding into default. Mayor Dennis Kucinich faced a recall election less than a week after our tenth anniversary show. He and the city council were snarling at each other like rabid dogs. Crime was high and the business climate was deteriorating. Under better circumstances, the Springsteen concert would have been an amazing high. In 1978, it seemed like all we had. The Buzzard was circling, and rock and roll was one of Cleveland's few salvations.

CHAPTER 16

COFFEE BREAK CONCERTS

When you don't have the money to promote and market, you have to be creative. For us, that included special programming that would generate talk. We had to make every minute count by creating an environment where our listeners knew that if they weren't listening to WMMS, they were missing something. It could be an interview, a live broadcast, or a concert announcement. Some were surprises, while others were fixed-positioned (at regularly scheduled times), like Murray's Get Down, Leo's Bookie Joint, Bash playing "Maggot Brain," or Flash's cutting-edge newscasts.

The *Coffee Break Concert* was one of the fixed positioners. It debuted in March 1972, well over a year before I got to WMMS. Billy Bass, who was program director and about to become general manager, came up with the idea when Elektra records offered him a live performance by singer-songwriter Carol Hall, who had just released her first album, *Beads and Feathers*. Bass accepted, and Hall performed in WMMS's small production studio.

Other *Coffee Break Concerts* from that era included Cleveland blues singer and guitarist Robert Lockwood, Jr., North Ridgeville native Martin Mull, an acoustic set by Cleveland's Glass Harp, and a young Michael Stanley. The *Coffee Break Concert* label was also used on a five-hour Sunday show for a live audience at Chester Commons, featuring Jesse Colin Young and local artists Alex Bevan, John Bassette, and Orville Normal. Another Sunday *Coffee Break Concert*, billed as "A Folk Special for a Sunday Afternoon," featured an acoustic performance by Peter Laughner and his Wolverines.

But the standard format was live, at 11 a.m. on a weekday, in the cramped production studio. Len Goldberg and later Matt the Cat hosted the show, and Denny Sanders took over bookings after Bass left. Booking was a thankless job. It meant holding auditions, and Denny had to work around the production department's schedule for them. There were many times I'd see him with the patience of Job, sitting through another young singer's cover of a Neil Young tune, though he was able to spotlight some true local talents.

One was black folk singer John Bassette, who wrote Jamie Brockett's "Remember the Wind and the Rain." He moved to Cleveland's Hessler Street neighborhood from Richmond, Virginia, and for many years was one of Cleveland's best known performers. Another semiregular was folk singer Jim Glover; he recorded a couple of albums for Verve with partner Jean Ray, under the name Jim & Jean, after playing in another duo, the Sundowners, with his Ohio State roommate, singer-songwriter Phil Ochs. Alex Bevan, whose mid-1970s "Skinny Little Boy" became one of Cleveland's most popular and requested songs, was also a semiregular.

Most of the *Coffee Break Concert* artists were young local singers and songwriters who relied heavily on cover material. Some performed originals, and some performed originals you'd wish they hadn't. Denny was always on the lookout for national talent, though any act we booked had to be able to play acoustic—and, if a group, work two to three on one mic. Despite the odds, Denny was able to book such well-known performers as Ramblin' Jack Elliot, who was one of the original sixties folk singers and a major influence on Bob Dylan; Tom Waits; Tim Buckley, Warren Zevon, and Harry Chapin.

A memorable incident happened in the mid-seventies, when singer-songwriter Buzzy Linhart, a Pittsburgh native who had some Cleveland roots, showed up at WMMS early one Wednesday morning demanding to be put on the air for a *Coffee Break Concert*. Pulling a "Don't you know who I am" routine, based on Bette Midler covering his song "Friends," he insisted that he replace the scheduled artist. He managed to convince receptionist Verdelle Warren that he was the scheduled performer, and managed the rare feat of sneaking into the station when she wasn't looking. When I told Lin-hart it wasn't going to happen, he replied, "I know the people over at M105. They'll put me on." I told him it was a great idea and that he should leave immediately. He was escorted out of the building. I scanned over to M105. They didn't put him on the air either.

We occasionally found a gem. Singer-songwriter Marc Cohn was one of them. He did a *Coffee Break Concert* on July 6, 1977, the day after his eighteenth birthday, and it was one of those performances in which you could measure the performer's musical depth. Cohn was signed by Atlantic in 1991 and released his first, self-titled album, featuring the hit "Walking in Memphis." His peers, among them David Crosby, Jimmy Webb, and Bonnie Raitt, consider him a brilliant songwriter. Another artist who impressed me was Barrow Davidian, a singer-songwriter and twelve-string guitarist who gave a brilliant performance. Denny, Matt the Cat, and I were certain he'd break nationally, but we never heard from him again.

When we heard an artist we felt had talent to go the distance, as we did with Cohn and Davidian, we sent tapes of their *Coffee Break* performances to A&R (Artist & Repertoire) directors we knew at major labels. From there, it was up to the label and the artist. Unfortunately, many brilliant performers were unable to take the next career step. There was interest in a number of acts, but Cleveland lacked good management to follow up and negotiate deals. In many cases, managers were also doing illegal double duty as booking agents—making guaranteed money by having their acts play around the region. Taking time to cut an album in a studio was not making money. Doing a national circuit, either on club dates or as an opening concert act, was a risk—and when a band went on the road, the manager would have to tour with them. Most decided against it. For example, when Mike Belkin was manager for the Michael Stanley Band, he would only go on the road to cities that had antique stores to his liking. It was this small-time thinking that prevented a number of excellent acts from breaking out of Cleveland. A couple of local managers were also known for snorting up their bands' profits.

Moving to the Cleveland Plaza gave us a much larger studio for

Coffee Break Concerts, but it was still not conducive to electric performances. Both its benefits and limitations were evident when Kenny Loggins and his band performed. "You know," he commented to guest host Shelley Stile, "this nonelectric, acoustic performance is pretty cool. Too bad we couldn't videotape it." Actually, there was video, but we never thought of taping the entire performance. WJW-TV was taping portions of songs, which they edited together with an interview with Loggins for *PM Magazine*.

Little did we realize that we would be an influence on MTV for its *Unplugged* series, which I was told was patterned after the *Coffee Break Concerts* and was suggested by an MTV staffer with Cleveland roots. At the time, it was more pertinent to us that Loggins, who had just split with Jim Messina, barely managed to get his band set up in this larger but still tiny studio. Matt, Denny, and I also believed we had run the course with the acoustic singer-songwriters. Though we'd occasionally land a gem or a national act, most of the artists— even those who auditioned well—were mediocre at best. We had to evolve the show and take it to the public stage.

Opportunity arrived in 1979 when Bobby McGee's, a nearby club in Playhouse Square, expressed interest in working with us. It gave us the chance to try an idea that was initially looked at as the dumbest one imaginable—a *Coffee Break Concert* with a live audience. The result was a short-lived and largely forgotten experiment. Since it would have cost a prohibitive $600 to set up fixed stereo lines between the club and the station, such as we already had with the Agora, we set up a dual-transmitter microwave system to broadcast what was essentially a club version of our in-studio show. The first one first featured an acoustic performance by Alex Bevan. The second one, almost an omen, featured Buzzy Linhart— and Denny had to play the drums at the pre-broadcast soundcheck because Linhart's drummer was late. The third show never came off: no one showed up to open the club.

That could have been the end of it. But Denny, the keeper of the *Coffee Break*, was both upset and tantalized, and he insisted on approaching Hank LoConti and the Agora. The only reason we hadn't gone to him first, despite our good relationship, was that Bobby

McGee's came to us first, and it seemed like a longshot that Hank would open his nighttime club for a daytime show. But he immediately said yes. We had already switched out *WMMS Nights Out at the Agora* to a live remote broadcast, making this a logical addition.

With that, everything changed. We moved the show from 11 a.m. to 1 p.m. in hopes of drawing a live audience, because it was easier for more people to delay lunch than take an early one. The extra two hours helped with musicians, too; they hated getting up that early in the morning. And Hank was all for it—club admission would be free, but the booze wasn't. Serving alcohol at one in the afternoon was found money.

We gained the ability to offer performers the option of going electric, performing acoustically, or using a full band. Those options would allow us to make the CBC acts even more diverse, adding national stars and pop culture favorites to up-and-comers and the local artists we felt had potential. Most performers chose to go electric. Among the exceptions was John Cougar Mellencamp, who consented to do a CBC after long deliberation and did not want the show rebroadcast. He preferred acoustic, and his show stood as one of the best performances in the Agora series. Felix Cavaliere, formerly of the Rascals, used the show's freedom in a different way, doing a solo performance with just keyboards—another amazing show.

Other acts included local and regional favorites: the Michael Stanley Band, American Noise, Wild Horses, The Godz, Lucky Pierre, Love Affair, I-Tal, and Breathless (formed by Jonah Koslen after he left the Michael Stanley Band), and the Jerry Busch Group, among others. National artists included U2, in one of their first performances in America, Chris Hillman, Boxcar Willie, Foghat, Bryan Adams, Cyndi Lauper, Quiet Riot, Fastway, Aldo Nova, Kix, Artful Dodger, UFO, the Fixx, and Alcatraz, a Swedish band featuring then-unknown guitarist Yngwie Malmsteen. Cox Cable videotaped a few of them for its local access channel, though its cost couldn't be justified by the cable company's bean counters; one can only imagine what video from those shows would be worth now.

Admission was free and first-come, first-served, except if we pulled off a coup like a Mellencamp. I wish we'd distributed tickets for Boxcar Willie, too, because he drew such a curiosity crowd off the high level of camp from his TV commercials. His stage show blended jugband, country band, and rock band, like a country Grateful Dead, and I'd never seen anything like it before or since. It turned out to be another of the best shows we ever did.

Booking the CBC was a pain. Local or regional acts not connected with labels were easiest, since Denny could deal directly with a band and its management. National acts were different, and securing name performers took massive coordination and cooperation. Usually, I would start by contacting labels, managers, or third-party record promoters like Bruce Moser from Buffalo to ask if they would let an act play the *Coffee Break*. I'd pitch the basic premise of the show and why they should do it—an hour of commercial-free air time on a station that had become a major force in breaking new product. Once they gave approval, Denny took over the complex part of dealing with the labels and management and coordinating dates with availability. Because almost all *Coffee Breaks* ran on Wednesday—Mellencamp was a rare exception—it was always a complicated proposition, and due to the show's "breakout" status for new music, labels encouraged managers of up-and-coming artists to book their tours so they could play the CBC on Wednesday.

Even with name performers, the CBC was not a costly proposition for WMMS. Acts were never paid for it; they played for exposure, or because the label or management wanted it. What was frustrating to Denny and me was that most of the labels didn't grasp the promotional and marketing tool the *Coffee Break Concert* provided by giving their artists a full hour, live, on the top-rated rated station in town. Most did it strictly to stroke WMMS and missed the bigger picture.

But there were some wise managers and labels. One of the best was Bruce Allen, who managed a number of well-known Canadian acts including singer-songwriter Bryan Adams. Allen was one of those rare managers, like Irv Azoff, who could always see the big picture years ahead. When he learned about the *Coffee Break*'s potential from Bruce Moser, whose Could Be Wild company did independent promotion for smaller labels and artist management, Allen had Adams' label, A&M, set up a major promotion for his appearance on the show, early in January 1982.

A&M did a promotion with forty-two major retail music outlets, including Camelot, Record Theater, Recordland, and Peaches—the major stores of that period—to create a store display for Adams's album *You Want It, You Got It,* prominently including our call letters and logo and mention of the CBC appearance. Allen took full advantage of the post-Christmas blahs by turning the appearance into an event, two days before Adams began his first U.S. tour with the Kinks. A week later, the album was number one in the majority of our store reports. A year later, on March 1, 1983—two months after the release of his breakthrough third album, *Cuts Like a Knife*—Adams did a second *Coffee Break Concert* for us. He was established nationally, but he had already reached star status in Cleveland, and our listeners considered it a very special event. A&M considered it so important that famed producer Bob Clearmountain was flown in to mix it.

Every show wasn't flawless. In 1983, against my better judgment, I let Bruce Moser talk me into booking a Scottish band, Big Country. They had a reputation for sloppy shows and for showing up late, often drunk. The band also had thick Scottish brogues, which would make it difficult for Matt to conduct an interview. Moser finally called in a favor—sort of like a trade for a high draft choice later. Because he had been straight with me, I discussed the matter with Denny, who was also assured by Moser there would be no problems.

There were.

A few moments into the performance, lead singer Stuart Adamson stopped the show, said "we can't do this," and marched off the stage, catching Matt the Cat completely off guard. It also caught the engineers back at WMMS off guard. They routinely did what we called "preventive maintenance" to the studio board and equipment during the CBC's. They had the board open and were cleaning the "pots," or potentiometer control knobs, when the show suddenly came to a halt, forcing quick completion of the maintenance to a return to the air. Because it was so unexpected, there were a few minutes of dead silence, which to me seemed like an eternity.

Big Country's management claimed Adamson suddenly lost his voice. In reality, and true to what I had heard about them, the problem was actually with bassist Tony Butler, who was suffering from a dagger-pain hangover. By that time, every song we added and every act we presented were being watched by the national radio and records industry. A nod from WMMS meant an opportunity for labels to get their acts on other stations. A bad move, like Big Country's, could kill a band, and it did.

I usually spent half my time at the station during a show, to hear how it sounded, and the other half at the Agora. Denny, however, would be at the Agora by 10 a.m. or 11 a.m. to supervise a 1 p.m. show, and he stayed until the end or, more often, long afterward—and this following a 6 p.m.–10 p.m. airshift the night before, with another looming in a few hours. It was a huge commitment. He might have been the highest-paid evening announcer in Cleveland radio, in a deal he negotiated himself, but it didn't acknowledge the added time, easily ten to fifteen hours each week, consumed by his work as a programming assistant and producer and director of the *Coffee Break Concert.*

The *Coffee Break Concert* series at the Agora came to an abrupt end in October 1984. Heavy damage from a fire following a *WMMS Night Out* with Blackfoot, a band fronted by Strongsville's Ricky Medlocke, forced the club to close. The show returned on February 15, 1985, relocated to Dewey Forward's Peabody's Down Under in the Flats, with the band Giufridda. We installed permanent lines in the club for the series, as we had at the Agora, but after a few months it appeared the show had lost its cachet, either because of the four-month hiatus or the location of the new venue. By that time, we were doing so many free concerts and WMMS Buzzard Appreciation Day shows that the *Coffee Break Concert* no longer served the purpose it once had.

Unfortunately, the *Coffee Break Concert* tapes—like everything else stored in the WMMS archives room—were lost, destroyed, or stolen when the station, still owned by Malrite, moved from the Statler to Tower City Center in 1992. The company was reducing its square footage and refused to sign off on additional space to store tapes, memorabilia, and history. *Coffee Break* performances by Warren Zevon and Tom Waits have been heavily bootlegged, but their source was an on-air broadcast, not the master tape. Others, like Bryan Adams, Foghat, and Harry Chapin, have shown up on BitTorrent sites with fair sound quality. Besides the memories, they're all that's left.

CHAPTER 17

BEATLES BLITZ

We kicked off 1979 with the biggest on-air undertaking in station history, our round-the-clock, commercial-free *Buzzard Beatles Blitz*. No station had tried anything quite so ambitious before, and I don't know of any others since then.

It wasn't simply a marathon of Beatles music, although the music—with live tracks, outtakes, solo work, and unreleased material—went far deeper than a standard retrospective. Weeks of work went into preparing it. We sifted through hundreds of hours of interviews with the Beatles—and people connected to them. For months leading up to the BBB, as we called it, we asked every celebrity who came to the station to cut actualities, or interviews, for it, and they ranged from Gene Simmons of Kiss to Charlie Daniels. For a local edge, we solicited calls from listeners, who talked about seeing the Beatles at Public Hall or Municipal Stadium or camped out in front of their hotel.

What made it unique, and different from such productions as Bill Drake's enormous *History of Rock & Roll*, is that the highly detailed and specialized programming was done live by our air talent. The jocks weren't taped, and their maneuvering through the tightly timed, scripted, and formatted hours, plus the usual demands of a winter weekend, was a major testament to their skills.

Interviews came from hundreds of sources. The Beatles interviews alone came from nearly a hundred, and included never-broadcast material. We found an interview with Tony Sheridan, whom the Beatles backed on an album in Germany, when Pete Best was their drummer. We had a John Lennon interview with London journalist David Wiggs, in which Lennon said he didn't want to be compared to someone like Gandhi as the voice of a "revolution," because Gandhi got shot by being one.

With the exception of Mick Jagger, who sent back audio after we submitted questions, we did all the other interviews live, in person, or on the phone, including *Saturday Night Live* producer Lorne Michaels, Ann and Nancy Wilson of Heart, Carl Perkins, Rick Derringer, and Doug Feiger of the Knack among many others. One of the highlights was singer Ronnie Spector admitting to a brief affair with John Lennon when the Ronettes opened for the Beatles on a European tour. She revealed that Lennon wrote "Norwegian Wood" about the affair. She also admitted the previously unknown fact that Phil Spector refused to send her on the Beatles' 1966 U.S. tour, when the Ronettes were on a bill with the Cyrcle, Barry and the Remains, and Bobby Hebb, and had a substitute singer in her place.

From the Beatles camp we had road manager Nat Weiss, Joy Hall, who handled radio promotion for Apple Records and gave us her autographed copy of *Abbey Road* to give away, and Ken Mansfield, a former president of Apple Records who was then married to actress Joan Collins. Mansfield revealed that the Beatles wanted to do a farewell concert in a U.S. desert, and that one suggested site was Black Rock City, Nevada, later home to the annual Burning Man festival. Logistics and the growing rift between Lennon and McCartney put an end to that plan.

Local interviews included Jane Scott of the *Plain Dealer*, who interviewed the Beatles and covered their shows; Brad Bell, who managed Melody Lane, a cutting edge record store in Lakewood; Bruno Bornino, who covered the Beatles for the *Cleveland Press*; Norman Wain, who brought the Beatles to town for WIXY in 1966; and Stu Mintz, son of Record Rendezvous founder Leo Mintz. From our own archives, we had what I feel was the best interview ever heard on WMMS, the one Denny Sanders did with Lennon in September 1974.

· · ·

Lennon was my favorite Beatle. I had spoken with him on the phone a few months earlier, albeit for about ten minutes, because of connections going back to late 1969, when I signed WNTN to Lennon's Peace Network—a group of progressive rock stations which would be involved with his "War Is Over" campaign and which never really got off the ground. This time he was pitching his forthcoming *Walls and Bridges* solo album.

Once the album was released, he made himself available to promote it to radio on a limited basis. But Capitol, his label, like most labels at the time, did not know how to work album rock stations, and they began to push the single "Whatever Gets You Through the Night" by setting up interviews with Top 40 stations. I managed to track down my Lennon connection, who put the wheels in motion to make an exception for WMMS. In the end, only five stations in the country got interviews. Since the others were in Boston, New York, Chicago, and San Francisco—all top radio markets—it was a coup for eighteenth-ranked Cleveland.

Denny was my only choice to talk to a former Beatle. I waited for the confirmation of the interview from Capitol. Nothing. After a few days, I finally got a call from a label rep at eleven o'clock on a Thursday morning: Lennon would be calling sometime after noon, and I should have somebody ready for the interview because he has a limited amount of time. That was as tight as they could pin it. I had expected at least a day or two of lead time. I called Denny at home, waking him up. He was exhausted. The previous day he had produced a morning *Coffee Break Concert*, worked in programming all afternoon, and handled an evening air shift. But he was excited.

"Two o'clock," he said. "What day?" He'd planned to prepare for the interview—which we weren't even sure would happen—over the weekend. Somehow, he was showered, shaved, dressed and at the station by noon. The WMMS production studio wasn't set up to take the call. It would have to be relayed to WHKs production room to be recorded. We wanted to have the interview in the can before we promoted it, and we didn't want to risk doing it live, considering the unreliability of our equipment and the near impossibility of putting any phone call on the air. But WHK's production director refused to vacate the studio; he had his own production to do, and he couldn't give a rat's ass about John Lennon. He was more of a Ray Conniff guy. Denny appealed to general manager Hal Fisher, needing an executive order for the production room. John Lennon was calling!

"You know," Hal said, "he's one of my favorite actors."

"No," Denny replied. "It's not Jack Lemmon, it's John Lennon."

"Who's John Lennon?"

"Hal—he's one of the Beatles!"

"Didn't they break up?"

WMMS was still "the FM." Find Me. WHK's production director refused to relinquish the studio, but he found a tape machine so old it had tubes. We figured it hadn't been used since before the Beatles were formed. With alligator clips, tape, and rubber bands, a makeshift line was fed into an old phone receiver, with wires running down the hallway to the FM studio to make the connection. Denny was still testing equipment when Lennon called. Receptionist Verdelle Warren paged him, but Denny couldn't hear it in the production room. I used to call Verdelle "Lieutenant Uhura," after the bridge communicator on *Star Trek*, because she remained calm in the most stressful of circumstances—but this was John Lennon. On hold. She tried paging me. Luckily, I heard the page in the hallway intercom, alerted Denny, and he fired up the tape machine.

There was occasional crackle and static during the interview, caused by people walking on the wires in the hallway. The old phone also had a mute button, which created static anytime Denny moved his hand. Once, fortunately during a pause in the interview, someone picked up on the line and asked, "Who are you holding for?"

Denny was able to make a tight edit, and his interview was a masterpiece. Transcribed, it ranked as one of the best interviews Lennon gave. It was more of a conversation than an interview, and Lennon enjoyed it. Capitol loved it, though we later learned that a rep from the label was holding up a piece of paper in Lennon's face, which said "Push the album!" whenever the interview turned away from *Walls and Bridges*. My Lennon connection loved it. The label gave us permission to transcribe the interview should anyone want it. We pitched it to *Rolling Stone*, whose editor turned it down because, "If we want an interview with John Lennon, we'll do it ourselves." They did, and it wasn't as good.

Denny's entire interview was repeated during the *Buzzard Beatles Blitz*, but not as one piece because of the special's fast movement. We cut it into individual questions matching the follow-up song. We tried to keep all interviews, excerpts, and celebrity contributions to a minute or two at most to keep the program flowing. Because it was commercial-free, we could maintain a tempo.

It was programmed for twenty-four continuous hours, starting at midnight Friday, a dumb move on my part. Though the motto back then was "Sleep is out of the question," Rhonda Kiefer and I stayed up all night finishing the treatment of the next few hours. I got home at 6 a.m., took a three-hour nap, and was back at the station by 10 a.m. to finish up the rest of the programming. We heard from listeners who followed similar schedules, which was one reason the BBB was memorable and a true event. Making it an experience was the reason it could be both commercial-free and profitable. Thanks to the power of WMMS, and the aggressiveness of our great sales team, we had each hour sponsored by a specific client, who paid a premium for three mentions per hour, delivered in a manner similar to National Public Radio's acknowledgments for program underwriters. Clients knew that when WMMS did a special, we would have listeners locked in for long periods of time. The sales staff sold it out more than a week in advance.

We taped the entire BBB, and we planned to syndicate it to other stations. The idea was to get everyone a few extra bucks, and to open the door for other WMMS syndication possibilities. Remarkably, the idea was shot down by Gil Rosenwald, who believed we'd just give other stations the "plans" on how to do it on their own. A number of listeners made their own tapes, and some ended up at other stations. Even when we started getting calls from stations asking if we would syndicate, Rosenwald said no. Like Murray's Get Downs, the *Buzzard Beatles Blitz* and its sequels ended up being bootlegged around the country, without Malrite, WMMS, or any of us receiving any royalties for them.

We did a second BBB in the spring of 1980, months before Lennon was killed in December, and made it an improved version, assembling more material and spreading it out over three days. I was able to clear the time for it to run commercial-free; the sales staff sold out sponsorship weeks ahead of time. I planned to run a third BBB, but eventually decided twice was enough.

Malrite ultimately erased and reused the master tapes, as they did with all of the creative masterpieces, ranging from station promos to "Buzzard Theater of the Air" and "Dr. Destructo" specials, produced by Steve Lushbaugh, Jeff Kinzbach, and Tom O'Brien. Anything that might have survived in the archives was lost when the station moved to Tower City Center. It's lost in space now, and that's a sin.

CHAPTER 18

CHIMPS, RATS, AND BUZZARD KILLERS

When the Mercury label released the first Boomtown Rats album, in September 1977, Mike Bone, who was doing the label's national promotion, had the crazy idea to promote it by sending dead rats to key radio stations. Not sewer rats, but white lab rats, packed in formaldehyde and sealed in thick, clear plastic medical bags you'd need to attack with an ice pick to open. Mercury vetoed the idea, but *Billboard* gave it some coverage. I called Bone to tell him it was a great idea. He appreciated the call, especially because he was worried about losing his job over it, and said he didn't know what he was going to do with the rats.

I said I'd take them off his hands. I wasn't sure what we'd do with them either, I just knew we wanted them. Denny Sanders once called in excitement during a vacation in Boston to say he'd found a pile of radiation protection suits in Building 19, a closeout and salvage store. I said he should buy every one; we'd find a use for them someday. We stuck them in the prize closet, forgot about them, and ended up giving them away in a contest five years later. Free rats? I wasn't planning to give them away on the air, but we'd think of something.

A package arrived a few days later with at least a dozen rats. Bash wanted one immediately. Somebody else put one in the WHK studio as a joke. Terry Stevens, WHK's program director, found it and reported it on his daily "discrepancy sheet": "Found dead rat in plastic bag. Concerned about hygiene."

Sending one to M105 seemed like a natural. It was too outrageous to do on my own, so I shared the idea with Walt Tiburski. The Arbitron ratings were coming out. Why not send a rat to Eric Stevens when the book arrived—like the message that Luca Brasi was sleeping with the fishes? Walt took it a step further. Since we were in a constant battle with M105 to get new music first, why not see what was scheduled to come out, and send a rat labeled as "exclusive" with a note attached not to tell WMMS. It was delivered by Walt's administrative assistant, Chris Hernandez, as if it came from a messenger service.

The prank became "the rat story"—a classic that inevitably grew in the telling to involve dozens of rats, all but plague infected. Like urban legends, stories about the competitive harassment we perpetrated became so exaggerated I hear them to this day. Some never happened, and others were wrongly attributed to us. When another station hired a program director who was fresh out of rehab, somebody sent him a case of booze and pictures of his ex-girlfriend, a jock at his previous station who'd gone on vacation and married somebody else. I had nothing to do with it, but suspicion fell on me and WMMS anyway.

It all reflected the intensity and frequent prankishness of the competition in the years before radio stations were owned in "clusters" by big companies that carved up markets like the Five Families. Head-on or indirectly, we battled at least a dozen stations for listeners and ad dollars at WMMS.

WNCR fell first, torpedoed by its own conservative ownership. Uncomfortable with a "progressive" format, they went to Top 40, easy listening, and finally country, under the call letters WKSW, or "Kiss FM," and ultimately as WGAR-FM. WIXY went next, a powerhouse victimized by a weak AM signal, a teeny-bopper image, and the fading of Top 40's ability to be all things to all listeners. It entered a series of sales and changes that made it soft-rock WMGC in 1976, and all-talk WBBG three years later. WCUE-FM in Cuyahoga Falls, which featured an album rock format, became WKDD and changed to "Mellow Rock" in 1977. (Unfortunately, the station attempted to create a "Mellow Rock" mascot, which most thought resembled a turd with a face.) Any competition from them might have seemed marginal, but Akron and Canton were important markets for WMMS.

We also fought an interesting battle with WGAR-AM, despite their oldies-oriented, adult contemporary format. We did it with a unique form of dayparting I called "environmental programming"—knowing where your audience is and what they're doing, and creating a soundtrack to fit that mental picture. Middays, for example, were softer and would mix Carly Simon and Fleetwood Mac and Eagles tracks with mainstream rock, old and new, to build our "at work" audience—picking up some WGAR listeners by taking advantage of FM's superior "in building" signal. We went light on hard rock until after 3 p.m., when schools let out and the at-work audience was pretty much wrapped for the day. (Neil Young was an example of the perfect artist for us. We could play his softer stuff during the day, and his harder-edged material later in the day and evenings.) It helped us when we shared music with WGAR. Though it's perceived as a liability in most radio circles, and many stations will remove songs from their playlists if stations in other formats adopt them, I wanted to flood WGAR with "WMMS music." I thought listeners who liked some of the music they were playing would be attracted to WMMS, which played even more of it. It worked.

From our standpoint, the best decision by WGAR's owner, Nationwide Broadcasting, was not moving its format to FM. WMMS was just a blip in morning drive, which was owned by WGAR's John Lanigan—or at least shared with Gary Dee on WHK. Had Lanigan and company moved to FM, WMMS would have had a much tougher battle to win the masses. It wasn't until Lanigan left town for a year in 1984—partly because WGAR was losing so much audience to FM—that we won mornings.

WMMS had another challenge for a short time after Detroit-based Booth Broadcasting changed the format of ethnic programmer WXEN to Top 40 in 1977. Renamed WZZP, or "ZIP 106," it mainly battled WGCL for the teen audience—but we had to keep our eye on them, since we had to court that audience for future victories. WZZP became a bigger concern when they hired Beau Raines, a

Top 40 programmer from Pittsburgh. Quickly grasping the market's WMMS influence, he began playing a few well-selected, hard rock album tracks he called "Buzzard Killers." Unlike most programmers, and like me, he was very concerned with environmental programming; he'd rearrange music rotations to suit the weather, and periodically increase the number of "Buzzard Killer" tracks. But hard rock was a hard road. WZZP found a softer and more successful one in 1984 as "Lite Rock" WLTF. We battled WLYT-turned-WRQC at the bottom of the dial, WDMT at the top, and everything in between. But no rivalry was longer and harder than the war with M105.

I always likened it to *The Enemy Below*, a 1957 movie about the Battle of the Atlantic in World War II and the cat-and-mouse maneuvers of a U.S. destroyer and a German U-boat. The commanders, played by Robert Mitchum and Curd Jürgens, were both experienced, determined to win, and had much in common. Each had to anticipate the other's moves, knowing that only one would survive.

Eric Stevens, my counterpart, was a worthy foe who made a fun target and knew how to fight back. We gave everyone nicknames in those days. He was the Chimp, and sometimes El Chimpo Wimpo— partly because of a "WIXY's gone bananas" promotion he had while at that station, but mostly because we liked it. M105, naturally, became the Monkey House. It fit especially well. Until 1978, when the station moved to the old WIXY studios at 3940 Euclid Avenue, their jocks worked on public display, behind a window under a stairway in Park Centre, the building a block from WMMS that later became Reserve Square. Our "war" was less visible. Everybody in the radio and music business knew about it, but we never mentioned M105 or the Chimp on the air. Listeners didn't know what was going on behind the scenes until the mid-1980s, when we battled WGCL, but the fight with M105 was bigger.

M105 was not as musically adventurous as we were, which made us their proving ground for new music. When we broke an act, M105 would jump on it like it was their own. They never reached our ratings numbers, but they had respectable enough ratings to live off our spillage in advertising. WMMS was always sold out; if a client needed a spot on the air, M105 always had room. And their operating costs were much lower, because they weren't a union shop and their air talent was paid barely over minimum wage.

When it came to promotion and marketing, we got the most bang for our buck. WMMS had one of the smallest promotion budgets of all the radio stations in Cleveland, but we managed it carefully. We bought television and print wisely, spending money for maximum impact, and traded time with TV stations whenever possible. We were similarly careful with billboards. Instead of the "scatter buys" of most stations, in which a number of billboards ended up in areas unimportant to reaching a specific audience, we pinpointed boards we wanted—and what others considered throwaway boards, we saw as ways of reaching our audience in transit.

We even made a profit on our greatest promotion and marketing campaign: merchandising. WMMS invented radio merchandising. We flooded the market with bumper stickers that we paid for, in advance, by selling the backs as coupons for clients. We did a minimum of two T-shirt designs a year, and sold them in stores throughout Cleveland, Akron, and Canton. The shirts always sold out. We also expanded from T-shirts to long-sleeve winter jerseys. We flooded the market with Buzzard buttons for special events, Frisbees, teeny halter tops, scarfs, and hats—the latter two items in conjunction with the Olympics Board, which chose us over a merchandising campaign from WGAR. Some of our earliest items were WMMS roach clips, which today net top dollar on eBay and other auction services. We even marketed Buzzard Bars, a candy bar, through Malley's Chocolates. Our merchandising even topped that of the Cleveland Indians, a neglected, losing team in those years. There were far more Buzzard stickers than Chief Wahoos.

We acted as if we had a bottomless pit of promotion and marketing dollars, just to make other stations overspend for less than what we got at no cost. Thanks to Dan Garfinkel, our promotion and marketing genius during the M105 war, and Carl Hirsch, who knew how to get the most for what we spent, we had the most enviable marketing of any radio station in America.

M105 learned how deeply WMMS worked into Cleveland popular culture when they "traded," or exchanged, on-air spots for services with the Roman Gardens restaurant in Little Italy for a year-end staff party in 1977. M105 had suffered a morale-busting fall season, and the party was intended to boost spirits. The night of the party, however, the M105 staff was greeted with banners reading "Welcome WMMS Buzzards!" Because M105's WWWM call letters were not widely known, someone misread them as WMMS and assumed it was our party. The party went on, but it wasn't a happy one, and the Chimp was convinced we had something to do with it—though we didn't, this time. We weren't even aware of it until someone from the restaurant called WMMS the next day.

Sometimes, M105 got caught in crossfire. After I refused a Belkin Productions request to have Kid Leo announce a 1978 Queen concert as "the most dynamic exciting concert Cleveland has ever seen," they awarded an upcoming Boston concert to M105. Though we had a very good relationship with Jules Belkin and sponsored most of the concerts coming through Cleveland, it was one of their occasional attempts to "teach us a lesson," and an intentional slap. WMMS broke and played Boston even before stations in Boston did. We'd even been the only station allowed to carry a Boston concert, when the band played a *WMMS Monday Night Out at the Agora* after the release of their first album. I called my friend Paul Ahern, Boston's manager, whom I knew while living in Boston. Ahern was as upset as I was about the co-sponsorship, but promised he'd do one better. He gave us a huge block of tickets to give away, commenting that we should do something special.

We learned that tuxedo companies often discard their apparel after a certain number of uses. We contacted one of them and purchased dozens of white tuxedo jackets, which we silk-screened with the Buzzard in a flying saucer, Boston's logo, and "WMMS Welcomes Boston to Cleveland." We told ticket winners they had to wear the jackets to the show. They did, and you couldn't miss them. They were at concession stands, in hallways, and—since all our tickets were together—formed a wall of white in the seats, becoming a huge billboard. Even better, after Ahern tipped off the band, singer Brad Delp thanked WMMS for being the first station in the country to play them. To the Chimp and M105, it was curses, foiled again. To Belkin, it proved that we would not go quietly.

A similar situation occurred when Belkin awarded M105 a Cheap Trick concert at the Allen Theatre. Just before the doors opened, the WMMS Buzzard van showed up to pass out a few hundred "WMMS Welcomes Cheap Trick to Cleveland" T-shirts. A spy reported that Eric Stevens and Ellen Roberts, his music director whom we nick-named Piggly Wiggly, stood in the lobby beaming over their victory—until they spotted the WMMS shirts everywhere.

In both cases, Columbia Records ended up picking up the tab, because we went over the head of the local promotion guy for money to cover the cost of clothing and silk screening. Columbia was notorious for playing both sides against the middle. We made it work to our advantage.

We had to be cautious not to get baited into a rival station's trap. On several occasions, the labels or Belkin tried to manipulate us to benefit them, claiming they'd take an act to M105 or WGCL if we didn't add the artist first. Most of the time we called the label's bluff, and we had good reason. We were not going sit on a song or an artist that we felt could go the distance for us—emphasis on "for us"—or make an add against our judgment.

Columbia wanted us to add the first Steve Forbert album. Not a bad album, not a great album. Chances are we would've tried it out, if not for the label's demand that if we didn't add it immediately, they would take it to M105 and do a concert with them. If we didn't add the record, the artist wouldn't be booked for the *WMMS Night Out at the Agora*, meaning Columbia would have to find another venue if they carried out their threat. They pitched the Agora, as it turned out, even offering to pay "rent" to book the show them-selves. Buddy Maver, who was booking acts for the Agora, turned them down. It wasn't worth the skirmish.

Figuring they'd encroach on what they believed was WMMS territory, Columbia pitched the student union at John Carroll University. That was the site of a WMMS-sponsored Bruce Springsteen concert, and it was a Catholic Jesuit school—which carried less weight than they thought it would with me, but some weight nonetheless. It was billed as a low-dough show, $1.05 per ticket. One-oh-five! Columbia would pick up all costs. JCU would make its money at the door. The show was announced on M105, and Columbia pushed for major mentions in *Scene*, *Cleveland Press*, and the *Plain Dealer*. Advance tickets went on sale. Not a single one sold. M105 upped its promotional mentions. Still nothing. Columbia took out print ads. Zilch. Despite M105 running promo announcements every hour and playing a Steve Forbert track every three hours, tickets weren't selling. Desperate, Columbia tried to buy commercials on WMMS. Though labels always paid top of the card rates to advertise on radio, and this was a hefty buy, Walt Tiburski backed me and refused the advertising, claiming we were sold out.

Tickets had to be given away free at colleges and high schools. Tickets were even handed out on Coventry during the Saturday shopping rush. A few record stores also gave away tickets, and Columbia tossed in a near-total discount on Forbert's album at Record Revolution on Coventry. If you took a free ticket, they'd sell you the album for $1.05. One-oh-five! The show went clean. Every seat was filled. Never underestimate the value of the word "free." But the promotion cost Columbia dearly. A week later, we opened the trades to find a photo of Eric Stevens and Rich Kudolla, the Columbia branch managers, holding a "sold out" sign at the Forbert show—with no mention that every ticket was given away.

Despite the promotional push from Columbia and M105, sales never materialized for Forbert. The album didn't do well anywhere, and he'd end up best known for his cameo in a Cyndi Lauper video. When we did our weekly survey of record stores, only a couple listed Forbert—and in the number one position. Knowing how Columbia operated and how suspect those reports were, we knew they had bought that listing, probably for a box of clean Cheap Trick albums from which the band would never see royalties.

Were we being unreasonable to the artist? No. Blame the label. Had Columbia not played the M105 card, we probably would have added the record when we had room on our playlist, and Forbert would have done a *WMMS Night Out at the Agora*—giving him a full hour's live exposure. If listeners liked what they heard, they'd call with requests and comments. It worked for every other artist. That's how acts broke out of Cleveland.

No matter what move M105 made, WMMS always got there first. For a brief time, they duplicated every song we played every hour, an idea supposedly raised by David Spero while he was doing morning drive there. When WMMS launched their annual rock and roll survey with the *Plain Dealer*, Spero went on the air with an imitation—even using the same title.

Spero started at M105 in early 1977, replacing "Mud," nee J. Mudcliffe, nee Wyn Rosenberg. He sold himself to M105 partly on the promise of "inside information" about WMMS and partly on music industry connections. He liked to brag about having Ringo Starr on speed-dial, and being on a first-name basis with Neil Young, but he learned the world had changed. When he couldn't deliver celebrities for his new morning show, Spero ran edited versions of interviews he had done on WMMS, and even WNCR, between 1972 and 1974. Listeners heard through the ruse and called WMMS to complain. We never mentioned our competition on-air and didn't want to call attention to a lower-rated rival, but we did begin to run tape on the interviews to forward them to appropriate managers. M105's image was damaged. Management of many acts that caught M105 running dated and doctored interviews even refused to allow their other artists to be interviewed on the station.

Stevens soured on Spero, who lasted barely a year. When his contract was not renewed, it was another victory for Jeff and Flash, who were closing in on being the longest-running morning show hosts on a contemporary music station in Cleveland. In a story that's never been told, the victory could have been their swan song. It's not clear who made first contact, but M105 made Jeff and Flash an offer to jump ship. The groundwork had been laid when they hired attorney Avery Friedman to represent them. Friedman, widely known for his civil rights work, represented some local radio and TV talent. By the summer of 1979, Jeff and Flash were rising stars, and Friedman enjoyed having them in his stable. We enjoyed having them, too. We'd made a substantial investment in them as morning hosts, even promoting them in station merchandising that included a popular T-shirt, "I wake up with Jeff and Flash" (whose back side read, "I go to bed with Betty Korvan").

Snatching them would have been a coup for Stevens and Tom Embrescia. The offer was a well-kept secret, though I had heard about it through an anonymous source, which led me to believe that Friedman leaked it so it would get back to us. When I learned of it, I told Carl Hirsch, who had heard the same story and was about to tell me. He wasn't surprised. After Kinzbach returned from his brief stint at WABX in Detroit, Carl cautioned me that Kinzbach "wasn't a lifer," and that he'd likely jump from WMMS if he felt he could get a better deal.

We decided to let this one play out, knowing that Jeff and Flash, in spite of their creativity, would have a tough time battling the WMMS infrastructure and the campaigns we'd launch to protect our turf. We believed they knew it, too, and that they recognized their deal with WMMS wouldn't be matched or beaten elsewhere in town. Besides, we learned that the Research Group, a firm M105 hired for a market study, argued that Jeff and Flash were too closely identified with us; if they jumped ship, Arbitron diary holders would still credit them as being on WMMS. In the end—after negotiations so theatrical that Stevens and Embrescia supposedly showed up at one meeting with a suitcase full of money—they couldn't reach an accord. Carl and I never let on that we knew about it. And I never told anyone else, not even Denny, about the aborted defection. It would have produced a rift between Jeff and Flash and the rest of the fiercely loyal staff that would have been challenging to mend.

M105 eventually replaced Spero with Joe Benson, from Malrite-owned WZUU in Milwaukee. Like Mud and Spero before him, he made little impact against Jeff and Flash. When Stevens himself left M105, the station had a party for him and local record guys at a restaurant in the Chesterfield on East 12th Street, just down the street from our Statler Office Tower home. We heard about it, but had no idea it was his farewell. Somebody—it wasn't me, and I was glad under the circumstances I didn't put anyone up to it—called the restaurant and asked them to please page Mr. Chimp.

CHAPTER 19

INTO THE '80S

WMMS hit 1980 as Cleveland's leading contemporary radio station, increasingly dominant among listeners ages eighteen to thirty-four and rising steadily in the twenty-five- to forty-nine-year old demographic. Overall, we usually ranked in third place, behind the easy-listening music of WQAL-FM and WERE-AM's news-talk format.

Our music covered a wide range. We played the obvious Van Halen, Humble Pie, and Nazareth rock anthems, included the theatrical rock of bands like Kiss, Triumph, and Angel, and got strong reaction for Marianne Faithfull's *Broken English*, John Cale's *Ready for War*, and Warren Zevon.

It went against the advice of most radio consultants, who recommended playlists be "modal," a trendy word for sound-alike music. The consultants increasingly based music programming decisions on "call-out research," in which random respondents were asked to rate the appeal and familiarity of a dozen to twenty-five songs based on short snippets called "song hooks." That was programming for a passive audience, and I took the opposite approach. Rock was an active format, and I didn't believe most rock listeners preferred one particular style over a variety.

Spring was shaping up to be a four-way war for us, against M105, WGCL, and WLYT. I noticed some carefully crafted changes at WGCL, a CHR ("Contemporary Hits Radio") station that was playing an unusually large amount of rock product because of the

WMMS influence. Any song from a rock artist was referred to as an "album track."

That was no accident. Our spies there reported that on the first day of the important spring ratings period, WGCL threw a "Kill the Buzzard" pep rally in their building, even bringing in some high school cheerleaders to perform. WGCL began doing "commercial-free" hours against us, and then doing triple-plays of album rock artists like Led Zeppelin, the Rolling Stones, and the Eagles. And the station landed a tenth anniversary supplement in *Scene*, whose relationship with WMMS was never all that cordial to begin with. We also knew that Gary Bird, an independent record promoter, was spending considerable time with WGCL program director Bob Travis. It figured. A sizeable amount of the music WGCL reported to the music industry trades that it was playing did not match actual airplay. The reports included "paper adds," which were useful for record promotion but received no airplay, but did not include album tracks and rock tunes the station was playing.

M105 had briefly experimented with new wave but was now turning in a mainstream direction. They were making desperation moves, like running tracks from our tenth anniversary concert with Springsteen (which I never understood because they reeked of WMMS), and we were tipped off that they might move the station to classic rock, an unknown format at the time. They were getting bolder and more active promotionally, even renting a plane towing an M105 banner over our World Series of Rock in July. They landed a good morning host in Joe Benson, the best M105 ever had, but he was victimized when the station's music veered off the mainstream highway of hits. He was moved to overnights and eventually moved to L.A., where he enjoyed success on album rock radio for years. When M105 returned to the mainstream, the station I was counting on to be the spoiler, WLYT, abandoned its short-lived hard rock format and moved back to CHR.

Ratings aren't black and white. A station doesn't necessarily gain audience directly from another, and increased competition in a format can be a good because it increases overall time spent listening. I viewed music programming as a tune-for-tune war in which we had to be highly conscious of what our competition was doing while not losing our individual flavor and flair for breaking new music. It wasn't uncommon for me to monitor WMMS, M105, WGCL, and WLYT simultaneously. I started jotting down results for the airstaff to see what we were up against. The notes were a snapshot of rock radio in 1980.

Some examples: When WMMS was playing "Hurricane" by Neil Young, M105 was playing "Last Child" by Aerosmith, WGCL was playing a live version of "Lovin' Touchin' Squeezin'" by Journey, and WLYT was playing "Don't Fear the Reaper" by Blue Oyster Cult. When WMMS was playing "Heartbreaker" by Pat Benatar, M105 was playing the live version of "Freebird" by Lynyrd Skynyrd, WGCL was on "Another Brick in the Wall" by Pink Floyd, and WLYT had "Love Stinks" by the J. Geils Band. When WMMS played "Precious" by the Pretenders, M105 played a live version of "Baba O'Reilly" by the Who, WGCL had Springsteen's "Born to Run," and WLYT played "Jane" by the Starship.

Our edge was our incredible airstaff and support staff, but music did most of the talking. I made sure we always broke for commercials before the competition, allowing us to get back into music first—giving us an advantage to hold button-pushing listeners longest. We made liberal use of our huge library of live tracks, giving listeners something they couldn't hear elsewhere. And to add to our element of surprise, Rhonda Kiefer created the WMMS Rock & Roll Dice. Against M105's commercial-free "Home of Continuous Music Hours" campaign and WGCL's "Free Rides," we became the Music Marathon Station, using the dice to roll out how many tunes we'd play without commercial interruption.

We regularly played a fair number of former Top 40 hits, from Motown and Stax/Volt to the Beach Boys' greatest hits, but I felt we needed a regular show to feature all oldies. We had done a few "Solid Gold Sundays," which were well received. I thought we needed something weekly. Sunday morning was the logical daypart, and Boom was the perfect choice to host. He was already doing Sunday mornings, and he had direct connection to the sixties, when he owned a teen rock club in Denver and later put Teen

Fairs on tour. He sold time on WIXY in its last days as an influential Top 40 station. Most importantly, Sunday morning was WGCL's highest-rated weekend daypart, when they carried Casey Kasem's *American Top 40* countdown.

Boom, Denny, and I worked out the logistics of the show, which we called *Solid Gold Sunday Morning*. The music covered all genres and generations, added a "spotlight" act that had three or four hits in a row, included a weekly bubblegum tune, and featured something we called a "Solid Gold Sickie," usually an offbeat novelty tune. We called the oldies "Solid Goldbergers," and added some awful WMMS jingles from the brief moment the station was Top 40 a decade earlier. John Chaffee enthusiastically approved it, and it was an immediate success. Boom was flooded with calls and letters, and it actually brought in new listeners who had assumed WMMS was all hard rock.

Within a month, both WGAR and M105 started their own oldies shows. WGAR put theirs opposite ours on Sunday morning, where it died a quick death. M105 carried theirs on Saturday afternoon, which made little sense to me—that was the weekend daypart when a station should sound most like itself, to take advantage of the huge early afternoon in-car audience. But I wasn't going to tell them that.

We gained more first-time listeners, especially from WGAR, when Jeff and Flash kicked off their *Class of* series for spring, highlighting a different year every day in music and news stories, from the mid-1960s to 1977. Listeners from those years' graduating classes called in with their own stories. Jane Snow, whom I discovered in the WHK news department, joined Jeff and Flash to assist with news and do traffic reports. To raise her profile, I also scheduled her for afternoon newscasts and occasional weekend air shifts. Jane's real last name was Disko, and in retrospect I should have let her use it. Harriet Peters announced her arrival in the *Cleveland Press* by noting that her last name was a slang word for cocaine.

Dia Stein, who at the time preferred using only her first name, joined us as a full-time part-timer. A Syracuse University graduate, she started as a production assistant and was also given the highest-profile weekend shift, from Saturday noon to 6 p.m., to give Matt the Cat a well-deserved five-day week, and the same time on Sunday, providing a break for Denny. Dia's first weekend was Buzzard boot camp—on Saturday she interviewed Ronnie James Dio, who at the time was the new lead singer for Black Sabbath, and on Sunday members of Blue Oyster Cult. Both were in town for a double-bill concert at the Coliseum.

Thom Darden was in his eighth year as defensive back for the Cleveland Browns and knew he had only a couple more good seasons in him. WHK carried the Browns, and, planning for the future, he approached Gil Rosenwald about learning more about the radio business, specifically sales and management. I'd already given him a Friday afternoon feature with Kid Leo, where they talked about the coming Sunday game—sports and rock make good partners. Because jazz was his favorite music, I gave him a one-hour weekly show, *All Pro Jazz*, which he did year-round on Sunday nights.

The only problem was that he didn't always show up. I'd be the one to get the call from a frustrated board operator asking how to fill the hour. I finally decided to stop promoting the show and scheduled other programming in its place. On the rare occasion that Darden did show up, we'd simply preempt whatever was scheduled in place of Darden for Darden. He picked up the name "No Pro." I tried having him come in during the week to cut his show in advance. It meant taking one of our production rooms off-line, which was no easy task at our station, where both rooms were usually going full-time to record commercials and special programming. That idea was scratched after Darden did two shows without turning on his mic. When I finally canceled the show after more than a year, in late November 1981, he failed to show up for the last two. I called in Murray Saul, who knew enough about jazz to cover them.

Off the air, we had a new chief engineer in Frank Foti. He had worked at a few stations around town but was a solid rock and roll and WMMS fan, and he knew exactly what we wanted and needed with audio processing. Listeners might not have known his name, but his engineering miracles made WMMS the envy of the business.

Adding to our full-time part-timers, who were paid regular salaries for off-air duties, we had part-time part-timers. One was Jeff Koski, a Parma kid who liked rock and roll, had broad musical tastes, and had gone to high school with Pat Benatar's husband, Neil Giraldo. He didn't have much radio experience beyond broadcasting school. I didn't want another Jeff, since we already had Kinzbach, so I renamed Koski Al. He picked up the nickname "Bear" and the "The Bear in the chair" on the air. He was into black music and jazz, and turned Ronnie Laws's "Always There" into a respectable Cleveland hit.

A few months after he started, however, he was in a serious car accident that required surgery and an extended hospital stay. Jeff Kinzbach and Kid Leo, together, filled in to do his Saturday night show on the first weekend of the spring ratings book in April. The troubles began after Koski returned to work. He didn't always arrive on time, a cardinal sin at WMMS, and didn't always get his work done. I learned why. A weekender on WHK, who worked roughly the same hours as Koski, was a drug dealer. Koski fell prey. I gave him several chances to redeem himself, maybe one chance too many, and had no alternative but to let him go. It was unfortunate for both WMMS and Koski, since he had the stuff to be a great personality and on-air communicator. He later resurfaced for a short time at M105 using his real first name, Jeff.

Another part-timer I counted on was Neil Lasher, a native New Yorker who'd been at CJOM in Windsor and program director at WIOT in Toledo. He left radio for the record business, which paid better, and moved to Cleveland to do regional promotion for EMI. Having Lasher in town gave me another voice to use when I was short-handed. His identity had to remain deep in the shadows of the Buzzard's wing so as not to upset his relationships at other stations, so I named him Manhattan Max.

He emerged from the shadows in an unfortunate way in September 1981. I was at home watching the local TV news and saw a piece on a major drug bust—with Lasher among the people shown being led out of the home. I knew Neil to occasionally have a line or two, but in no way would he be trafficking in drugs, especially cocaine. It wasn't his style. As it turned out, he was in the wrong place at the wrong time. Larry Elkins, whose house was raided, was Neil's connection for an occasional gram purchase. Neil was dropping off a few promo copies of EMI product, maybe in exchange for a few lines of boola-boola, when the bust went down. He and five others were charged with trafficking in narcotics. I did what I could to get word to the right people that Lasher was a victim of bad judgment and not part of a drug ring. He was brought up on a lesser charge and, fortunately, served no time in the crowbar motel. We also rallied his bosses at EMI not to fire him for being in the wrong place at the wrong time.

There has always been a misconception that those of us at WMMS were tight with people like Bruce Springsteen, Bob Seger, Fleetwood Mac, the Eagles, Kiss, and the other superstars of that era. We weren't, really. Bands liked it that we played their music and gave them exposure. You may become professional friends in those circumstances, but you don't become buddies. The artists live in a different world. As much as people liked to think stars dropped in to have dinner at Leo's house, it wasn't like that. When we had lunch or dinner with an act, it was all business.

Still, musicians were always welcome at WMMS. After a few years, we had acts returning for second, third, fourth, and even tenth interviews. Though I considered our air talent to be skilled interviewers, there does come a point when fresh material is needed. We evolved our interviews by turning many into guest disc jockey segments, which allowed visiting artists to choose and play some of their favorite music. Word traveled fast, and Ted Nugent, Meat Loaf, Southside Johnny, and Peter Wolf all jumped at the chance.

But other performers and celebrities also came to play. Two were Rick Moranis and Dave Thomas, then of *SCTV*, for Second

City Television, the long-running syndicated TV show produced in Canada. Because the country's Radio and Television Commission insisted it had to include a "Canadian content" segment in every show, Moranis and Thomas created "The Great White North"—a routine in which they played a pair of beer-swilling brothers, Bob and Doug McKenzie, who wore heavy winter clothing, called each other "hosers," and often used the interjection, "Eh?" When the skits unexpectedly became one of *SCTV*'s most popular features, Moranis and Thomas followed up with a single, "Take Off," featuring guest vocals from Geddy Lee of Rush.

In the U.S., the song broke out of Cleveland. Moranis and Thomas visited Leo's show in January 1980, playing their favorite music—Canadian—and taking calls from listeners as Doug and Bob. WKYC-TV gave the appearance a lengthy feature on newscasts, and Moranis and Thomas repaid the favor by occasionally mentioning WMMS and Cleveland on *SCTV*. The relationship was so good that when CBS approached *SCTV* to do a pilot for a network show, they called it "From Cleveland" and taped it in Cleveland. One of the skits was about a Cleveland gang named the Buzzards. David Helton did their logo, and the skit included a cameo by Kid Leo. CBS didn't get the show's humor, however, and it wasn't picked up as a regular series.

We found another link to *SCTV* by chance, and soon afterward, when the Pretenders were in town for a show, that was a homecoming of sorts for Akron native Chrissie Hynde. Their debut album was an out-of-the-box bestseller, their Agora appearance sold out well in advance, and Cleveland was the band's breakout market. Their label, Warner Brothers, brought their heavyweights to town, and Leo and I had lunch with the brass.

As label people do, they pitched a forthcoming album from Don Novello, formerly of Lorain, who was a writer and producer for *SCTV* but known best for the Father Guido Sarducci character he developed on *Saturday Night Live*. I was intrigued by the idea of Father Guido Sarducci doing on-air confessions. The Warner people initially felt it couldn't be done. But it was, and Novello sat in with Kid Leo, hearing phoned-in confessions. Despite a few complaints, including one from the Catholic diocese, it was one of the funniest features we ever did. Our only regret was that we couldn't do it on a regular basis.

We became friends with Novello. When one of the 1980 presidential debates between Jimmy Carter and Ronald Reagan was staged at Cleveland Public Hall, he planned to cover it for a *Saturday Night Live* sketch. When the bit didn't make the show, we invited Novello to do his review on WMMS. We were becoming a "must visit" stop for celebrities and even newsmakers. Just before the debate, Jimmy Carter's mother, Miss Lillian, stopped by WMMS for an interview, which was good for an item in the *Washington Post's* gossip column.

Then there was Paul Simon. Paul Simon was an ass. At least to me. He was in Cleveland to film a movie he wrote and acted in called *One Trick Pony*—having picked Cleveland as the setting for the movie because "you couldn't get any lower than playing some club in Cleveland." Excuse me?

I enjoyed his intelligent music and considered him a great songwriter, musician, and producer who could match world music with pop sensibilities. In my few meetings with him, I found him to be a self-centered, egotistical, thoughtless little man. When he solicited an opinion or asked a question, he'd already have the answer and dismiss you with a wave. When I mentioned to him that I had the original acoustic *Wednesday Morning 3 AM* album and his first solo album, which had only been released in England, he responded by saying he didn't have to be reminded of his own music.

I had my own agenda. I wanted WMMS to figure into the movie, which it did with the brief showing of a Buzzard bumper sticker on an amp case and a phony aircheck. I say phony because we initially provided Simon with airchecks from both Leo and Denny, which is what he wanted. Afterward, he decided he wanted Leo to cut a special aircheck for the movie, with Leo as our overnight DJ and Flash doing news.

I wanted to do a Cleveland premiere, pulling out all the stops, but the movie opened without any fanfare. *One Trick Pony* was as bad as Simon made Cleveland look. The movie, starring Simon as a has-been singer-songwriter named Jonah Levi, had a dull script and wooden acting. It should be best known for reuniting the original four Lovin' Spoonful members for one last time, for a cameo appearance by the B52s, for the reuniting of Sam and Dave (Sam Moore and Dave Pratter), and for an appearance by saxophonist David Sanborn, both of whom made the best of a bad situation. Harry Shearer was in the movie, too, though I don't think he wanted anyone to know.

We broke news of a new Led Zeppelin tour, supporting their *In Through the Out Door* album, and secured prime-spot tickets for giveaways for the two scheduled nights in Cleveland, October 26 and 27. That changed with the news on September 25 that drummer John Bonham had died of asphyxiation caused by choking on his own vomit after a night of heavy drinking.

A few days later, we received an announcement from the band's manager that the tour was off, and on December 2 we were first to announce that Led Zeppelin had disbanded. But the show must go on. No shame there. We did two nights of Led Zeppelin music on the air on the nights the band was scheduled to play Cleveland— staging the concert that would never be, by using the set list Rhonda Kiefer compiled when she attended their concert at the Knebworth Festival in London a few months earlier. We rounded out the tribute to six hours, playing a good portion of the Led Zeppelin library and tossing in a few rare and unreleased tracks.

I was home watching *Monday Night Football* on December 8, 1980, when the news broke that John Lennon was shot. A few minutes later, a second report said he was dead. Howard Cosell, who knew Lennon and had interviewed him on *Monday Night Football* in 1974, said, "This, we have to say it, is just a football game, no matter who wins or loses. An unspeakable tragedy, confirmed to us by ABC News in New York City. John Lennon, outside of his apartment building on the West Side of New York City, the most famous perhaps of all of the Beatles, shot twice in the back, rushed to Roosevelt Hospital, dead on arrival."

Like everyone who had grown up with the Beatles, I was stunned—and knew that we'd be the prime source for news updates and further information. I called Betty Korvan and told her to check the newsroom, turn on the TV, and watch the wire. Denny, who'd been about to leave, took over operations. We called every contact we knew in New York, including Lennon's management and record label. We picked up feeds from NBC Source. We played continuous sets of John Lennon's music, solo and with the Beatles. Denny went to the archives for his interview and others with Lennon.

By morning, everyone on our staff was contributing. With music, interviews, commentaries, and phone-ins, we dedicated the entire following Sunday to John Lennon's memory. It was heartfelt, something we were uniquely positioned to do, and—like our Zeppelin coverage and our coverage of the presidential election a month earlier—more proof that WMMS was moving toward being the full-service station Denny and I envisioned almost a decade earlier.

CHAPTER 20

PRIDE OF CLEVELAND

Chrissie Hynde wasn't the only Akronite breaking out in 1980. Rachel Sweet's album was winning critical acclaim. The sixteen-year old already had received international exposure when a track of hers was included on the English-based Stiff Records release, *Akron Compilation*. Stiff signed her to a contract that led to her album *Fool Around*, recorded with the English power pop band the Records. The album didn't sell well nationally but was a major hit in our listening area. Rachel's cover of the Carla Thomas hit "B-A-B-Y" received heavy airplay on WMMS.

Rachel's lack of album success, despite critical praise, was more proof that an act had to move from Cleveland or Akron if they hoped to achieve national success. Northeast Ohio had no lack of talent, but it had no infrastructure to take artists beyond the region. Rachel's album was produced by Liam Sternberg, who also wrote four of its eleven tracks and produced Stiff's *Akron Compilation*. He was a major player in the Akron alternative rock scene that spawned Devo, the Waitresses, the Rubber City Rebels, Tin Huey, and Chi Pig. When he left for Los Angeles, he gained national attention as a songwriter, composer, and producer, working with acts as diverse as the Bangles and Ratt and composing the theme to the TV show *21 Jump Street*. The Rubber City Rebels, who were also featured on the *Akron Compilation* album, moved to Los Angeles when their local management couldn't secure them dates outside the region; after making the move, they toured internationally. They scored airplay and requests on WMMS with "Bluer than Blue," from their

Capitol album produced by the Knack's Doug Feiger, which should have been a national hit.

By 1980, Cleveland had developed some fine talent in search of a deal to take them beyond the city limits.

American Noise, made up of brothers Craig and Bruce Balzer, Tommy Rich, George Sipl, Greg Holt, and Jerry Moran, got signed to Planet, a boutique label distributed by Elektra. Love Affair, led by Rich Spina, was signed by Radio Records, which was distributed by Atlantic. Local reggae rock band I-Tal put out a single, "Rockers," whose popularity in Cleveland rivaled any track by Bob Marley.

Wild Horses broke with "Funky Poodle," the song of the summer. The Jerry Busch Group, from the fringe of the WMMS signal in Madison, followed their well-received album *Demo Tapes* with a second including the tracks "City Boy" and "Nobody Does Me Better." Another band, the Wild Giraffes, hit with a cover of Elvis Presley's "Burning Love."

"Go, Joe Charboneau," a novelty song dedicated to the Indians outfielder, did well for a group put together by singer-songwriter Don Kriss; they recorded under the name Section 35, where they had their Indians season tickets at Cleveland Stadium. Proof that we'd give any local act a chance, we even added the Baloney Heads' "I'm a Drunk," which was actually a pretty good song, probably better than the band thought it was.

We even stole Walt Masky's *Ohio Homegrown* show away from M105, probably just because we could. M105 used it primarily to claim they were playing local music, too—except they did only once a week at 11 p.m. Sunday, when radio listening was at its lowest. I always felt that if a station wants to make a commitment to playing local bands, they should do so in regular rotation, which is what we did.

We called our local talent a *Pride of Cleveland*. At one point, nearly 20 percent of the music we were playing came from local and regional artists—and it helped, not hurt, our ratings. The response was so positive, Denny and I planned a *Pride of Cleveland* album as part of a campaign to promote local talent. Conceived in August 1980 and targeted for release during the October–November Arbitron ratings period, it represented the variety of music being created in Greater Cleveland, from rock to reggae to pop to folk to country-rock.

The album, which was quarterbacked by Denny, featured an unreleased track from American Noise, "Out in the Streets," which I picked from their demo tapes; the Jerry Busch Group's "Nobody Does Me Better"; I-Tal's "Rockers"; Don Kriss's "Where's the Fire"; Alex Bevan's "Love Stays Beside Me"; a live version of Wild Horses' "Funky Poodle," from a WMMS *Coffee Break Concert*; the Generators' "I'm A Generator"; Rapscallion's "Anytime"; Love Affair's "Mama Sez," from their debut album, and Flatbush's "Snug as a Bug in a Rug."

It was a compilation even *Scene* couldn't do a bad review of, and its release garnered a favorable editorial in the *Plain Dealer*. It became a rare case of Cleveland getting the "rising tide lifts all ships" concept. In-fighting between managers and artists vanished, and artists started promoting one another, with all of them increasing their fan base.

Although we promoted it through the Christmas season, production delays kept it from stores until December 15, which put us in direct competition with Fleetwood Mac and Blues Brothers albums—and Talking Heads, Cheap Trick, and REO Speedwagon. But we did get plenty of stock to stores, and the album sold briskly enough to rank among the five top-selling albums well into the new year. All the profits went to a music scholarship fund at Cleveland State University. (An unofficial CD version, minus the American Noise track, was available for a brief time in 2005.)

Two of Cleveland's biggest local groups, the Michael Stanley Band and Jonah Koslen's Breathless, planned to be part of the compilation but were left off when their manager, Mike Belkin, told us we'd have to pay $600 to $700 for a track to be mixed and mastered, and that we'd have to wait until Jonah Koslen returned from out of town before he decided whether or not Breathless should be on the compilation at all. We reluctantly decided to release the album without them. Time was short, and the deal would not have been fair to the other acts, which had paid for their own mixing. Their absence didn't hurt sales nor did it affect our relationship with the bands. Mike Belkin later let Breathless do a *Coffee Break Concert* under the provisions that someone of his choosing would mix the show, with us picking up the tab; that tickets had to be distributed in advance; and that we would support it with heavy promotion and print ads. But all the posturing went for nothing—the group broke up before their scheduled appearance. I doubt that Michael Stanley or Jonah Koslen even knew of the tactics Belkin used to play hardball with their careers.

We actively promoted local bands to national labels. I put out a memo to the staff:

> Don't let up on your push of local talent. Talk up Pride of Cleveland support for Love Affair, American Noise, I-Tal, Rapscallion, Michael Stanley Band, Breathless, Flatbush, Dawn Bewley, Alex Bevan, Eric Carmen, etc., etc., etc. Also play those Cleveland-oriented tunes, "Cleveland Rocks," "Hello Cleveland" (Dawn Bewley), "Cleveland Boys" (Love Affair), "No Surf" (Euclid Beach Band), etc. As Matt the Cat said (and everyone who heard it is quoting him), "This could be the summer that Cleveland's rock and roll scene explodes." It's up to us.

Of special note was Dawn Bewley, a young woman from the West Side who looked much younger than her twenty-one years. Typifying the passion we wanted to recognize, she worked as a cashier at a Gold Circle store to save up money to record her single.

Doing our best to put local bands in front of the masses, we did three days of Pride of Cleveland concerts with I-Tal, the Generators, and Flatbush—improbably tied to the "50th birthday" of the Terminal Tower.

A few major labels were interested in Cleveland talent, but the lack of good management killed every deal. No one in Cleveland knew how to manage an act outside of Cleveland. In Michael Stanley's case, the result was being a big fish in a small pond, though I have no doubt he would have been a big fish in a big pond. Other bands had problems because myopic managers were more concerned about making a few bucks playing a local club than taking the chance to broaden an act's base.

Not that management elsewhere was all-knowing about new music. After former New York Doll Sylvain Sylvain released a solo album with an excellent cover of Clarence "Frogman" Henry's "Ain't Got No Home," we brought him to Cleveland for a *Coffee Break Concert*; his album didn't get airplay elsewhere due to lack of promotion, and the label never even stocked Cleveland stores with copies. We also liked a band called the Tourists, who did a respectable *WMMS Night Out at the Agora*; but their label, Epic, did not know how to promote them to other stations and unceremoniously dropped them. A few years and a name change and new label later, they returned to Cleveland as the Eurythmics and headlined a free WMMS Appreciation Day at Public Hall.

We closed out 1980 on a sour note when an on-again, off-again New Year's Eve concert starring the Michael Stanley Band was canceled in another last-minute decision by Mike Belkin. The show was to be broadcast live from the Coliseum, and MSB's label, EMI, agreed to pick up the costs. Belkin nixed the deal when he learned that the charges would be deducted from the band's and his royalties, as was standard operating procedure, instead demanding that WMMS pick up all costs but not have exclusive rights to the broadcast—meaning it could be carried by other stations in the market without our permission. We didn't learn about the cancellation of the concert until the morning of December 31. The decision had nothing to do with Michael Stanley and his band, who wanted to have the show carried live.

We stayed solidly behind breaking MSB. Michael was a friend of everyone at the station. We took to calling the band "Cleveland's favorite sons." But the relationship with Mike Belkin remained stressed. We saw the consequences again the following summer.

EMI Records, whose executives believed they could go the distance nationally with the band, used their Blossom Music Center dates at the end of August 1981—a Sunday, a Monday, and an added sold-out show on Wednesday—to fly in national rock critics, out-of-town radio decision-makers, and other influential people who could spread the word. We did a live remote with the full twenty-three-song set—eighteen songs, plus five encores.

The logistics were a nightmare, but our always determined Frank Foti checked the terrain and figured we could do a direct wireless link from Blossom to our transmitter in Seven Hills. It worked, and everything went smoothly—almost. The group had just begun using wireless microphones, which were still relatively new technology, and had them tuned to the same frequency as the highway patrol's. In the middle of one song, a police call went out over both the Blossom sound system and our live remote.

We pitched the radio network NBC Source to record our show, which would give the band airplay in markets where they hadn't been heard before. It was edited down to fifty minutes for syndication, and NBC Source told affiliates it would be available in mid-September. We called friends at other stations, urging them to carry it. Only a small number did, however, because Mike Belkin provided the rival *King Biscuit Flower Hour* with a recording of the same show. Since most album rock stations carried the weekly *King Biscuit* show, they opted out of the NBC Source special, scheduled for a week earlier—unfortunately, since *King Biscuit* used barely twenty minutes of MSB's concert. We ran both shows at the end of September, *King Biscuit* on a Sunday and NBC Source the following Wednesday, and explained why on the air—meanwhile putting on Michael and bandmate Kevin Raleigh as guest DJs to keep interest alive.

CHAPTER 21

VIDEO STARS, RADIO STARS

When MTV made its debut on August 1, 1981, its first video was the Buggles' *Video Killed the Radio Star*—a song virtually unknown except in Cleveland, where it was heavily requested on WMMS. But we hadn't yet seen the video, and we didn't see it then. Cleveland still wasn't cabled, and neither were most of its suburbs.

We were fully aware of this new entity, Music Television, which was being described as FM rock radio for television. For more information, however, we had to depend on trade magazines and the few people we knew in the industry who had a relationship with the channel. Former Clevelander Nina Blackwood, who'd been one of the winners of our *Playboy*-sponsored "Girls of Cleveland" spread, was announced as one of what they called "video jocks," or VJ's. But it mostly was a great unknown, which was frustrating. Would it be friend or foe? Was it a medium we could link to, or were they out to compete directly against rock radio?

Its early playlists included an abundance of British music from the "New Romantics" movement that launched Duran Duran, ABC, and Spandau Ballet, and gave heavy exposure to such cutting-edge bands as Blondie and the Talking Heads, which were considered somewhat left of mainstream. They also played a few mainstream acts of the time like the Pretenders, Pat Benatar, Hall and Oates, and Billy Squier, augmented by videos from the Rolling Stones and some acts getting airplay on Top 40 radio (and WMMS), including Kim Carnes ("Bette Davis Eyes") and Rick Springfield ("Jesse's Girl").

Duran Duran was an act we knew about. "Planet Earth," their first single, did marginally well on WMMS. Exposing new trends and artists was part of our popular culture format. Unlike most album rock stations of the time, we refused to pigeon-hole ourselves in what was becoming a "greatest hits" format featuring artists that labels felt would reach "stadium" appeal—acts like Kiss, AC-DC, Journey, and Boston, which could deliver power ballads and driving, hard-rock pop.

But we didn't expect what we started to see on request sheets and store reports. Every week, we called virtually every retail outlet to check on what was selling, and where, for the chart we counted down on Thursday evenings. We also compiled requests to factor in "turntable hits," since sales were not the only measure of a song's popularity. One week it just happened. Rhonda Kiefer, who supervised and made most of the retail calls, noticed a couple of record stores in Akron showing strong sales for "new wave" acts, while other stores continued the status quo. We first wondered if the labels had got the stores to dish out phony information for free goods, but they weren't those kinds of stores. Their reporting had always been honest. Some of the reported albums were from acts that we either weren't playing or playing only occasinally. Akron was quick to pick up on new music before it went mainstream, but these unusual reports came from specific and scattered locations. Rhonda called the stores for their read on what was influencing sales.

It was MTV. Cleveland didn't have cable, but portions of Akron did, and they had MTV. It explained why some store reports in Akron paralleled our airplay while others didn't.

We faced something new and relatively unpredictable. This was a time when communities were just making deals to be wired for cable, which meant the MTV influence could and would be springing up in various neighborhoods with no set pattern. I was also concerned if some of the new music breaking out of Akron through MTV would sound good exclusively in audio; videos were adding new twists. When it came to songs like "She Blinded Me with Science," by Thomas Dolby, we realized we were stretching our musical limits. We wondered if the mainstream rock listener of WMMS who tolerated our wide variety would tune out for some of the MTV-influenced, cutting-edge music.

Music videos were nothing new. The Beatles used them instead of touring. Former Monkee Michael Nesmith released one of the first video albums, *Elephant Parts*. In the early 1930s, Max Fleisher introduced what might have been the first music videos, *Screen Songs*, which featured popular tunes you could sing along with by "following the bouncing ball." Cable's USA network, which was more widely carried than MTV, debuted a late-night video program, *Night Flight*, a month before MTV launched. But MTV's influence was larger and undeniable. In tandem with it came a new format, started at KROQ in Los Angeles, called Rock of the '80s—a Top 40 hybrid that played nothing but new music from new artists in tight rotation.

At WMMS, we had to fit more of this on our playlist without sacrificing our existing audience. The youngest end of the baby boomers, and the "Gen-Xers" born later, wanted their own music and style. If we ignored them, the results would come back to haunt us as they aged into what was then the money demo, adults ages eighteen to twenty-four. Were we better off joining MTV than trying to fight it? My mind was made up at my first chance to see MTV, when it was really music television. Ann and Nancy Wilson of Heart were being interviewed by a VJ, and Ann said, "We'll have to send you some of our videos, I didn't realize you were playing them." Straightforward and unrehearsed, it sounded like a WMMS interview—except they had video, too. This was not a medium we could fight. It was only a matter of time before our entire listening area would be wired for cable, and most of it would get MTV. It wasn't direct competition per se, but it was an opportunity for someone to watch music on TV instead of listening to WMMS. We had to make the two compatible.

We identified other markets with MTV. Most of the album rock stations we talked to either ignored MTV or tried to launch campaigns against it. We decided to contact MTV and establish a relationship. We backed their "I Want my MTV" promotion when they were trying to land cable franchises. We did copromotions. We invited Nina Blackwood back to Cleveland, where she was interviewed by Jeff Kinzbach. For MTV image reasons, we promised not to mention the fact that she'd been a finalist in our "Girls of Cleveland" promotion. Whenever and wherever possible, we bought time on MTV through the cable companies equipped in those early days to run local commercials. Cable was relatively inexpensive to buy, and only a couple hundred dollars could buy us more than a hundred spots.

It didn't take long for some to assume MTV and WMMS were connected in some way, maybe common ownership, and we didn't bother to correct them. Early MTV was primarily a rock station, with only a minimum of pop music, and paralleled most of the music we were playing. The perceived MTV connection gave us the street cred needed to play acts like Culture Club, Talking Heads, and the Eurythmics, which were being ignored by most rock stations (which wondered why their ratings were declining).

In some ways, MTV's videoplay of Michael Jackson, Prince, Sheila E., and the Time made it easier for us to add them to our playlist; artists like Cyndi Lauper and Madonna, already exposed on WMMS, had careers jump-started by heavy video rotation. We also married our audio to video by simulcasting a weekly Live at the Agora concert, and we went after other opportunities, such as simulcasting a Rolling Stones concert on Premiere, the short-lived, encrypted-signal pay service carried on Channel 61 in the mid-1980s before Cleveland was cabled.

Cable brought another opportunity when Warner Cable used Columbus as a test market for QUBE, an interactive cable service. For an extra $2 a month, a subscriber could run a cable to a radio receiver and receive WMMS. We didn't know it until we started getting calls and mail from Columbus. Seeing potential—though more bragging rights than revenue—we took out an ad in the *Columbus Planet*, an alternative weekly, which we later learned did not sit well with WLVQ, the Columbus album rock station, which ran a comparatively tight playlist.

We acknowledged QUBE listeners on the air, welcoming Columbus to the growing list of cities able to hear WMMS—since we learned around the same time that a cable service in London, Ontario, was carrying WMMS as the audio on a text channel. When we gave our phone numbers, we'd add, "area 216 if you're listening in Columbus on the QUBE or in Canada." QUBE's coverage was limited and hardly full-market penetration. But we were quite satisfied to count our out-of-town listeners one by one.

Boom's oldies show was pulling such strong numbers that on long weekends we brought back Super Solid Gold Sunday, as we called them—a full Sunday of oldies music. I decided to do one on Memorial Day weekend to cap a very positive month. We received the winter Arbitron results, which we topped overall and dominated by a wide margin among both men and women aged eighteen to thirty-four; scored exclusives from Tom Petty, Van Halen, Peter Frampton, and the Moody Blues; and even got Cleveland Orchestra music director Lorin Maazel and Don Pardo, the voice of *Saturday Night Live,* to cut IDs. We started the holiday with eight straight hours of music on Friday night from our archive of remotes and *Coffee Break Concerts.* On Saturday night, we did a Styx and Stones concert, featuring Styx in a first-run concert recorded in 1977 and the Stones in a previously unaired concert from 1978. Mondays, we played sets of our most-requested artists and rolled the "rock and roll dice" for even more artist in-a-row tunes. The phones lit up all weekend.

On the Tuesday after Memorial Day, with morale high, I got a call from Milt Maltz's secretary. He needed to see me right away. I was barely in the door when Milt growled, "What was that I heard on Sunday?" I told him about our Super Solid Gold Sunday. "How dare you take my station and change format?" I gave him the reasons. "Don't ev-v-ver-r-r do that again! I'm a broadcaster, and I know programming, and you don't DARE alter your format at a whim." Later in the day, John Chaffee called to say he had convinced Milt that what we did was good for the station. Milt, who never said a word to me about our successful ratings, never apologized. When I ran into Carl Hirsch later in the day, he apologized for Milt. Carl, now the president of Malrite, was doing a lot of that.

Total secrecy covered a promotion we launched at the end of August 1981 for two sold-out Journey concerts at the Coliseum. As cars pulled into the lot to pay the then-outrageous $5 parking fee, parking attendants outfitted in WMMS T-shirts told them that WMMS was picking up the cost—and handed out a "souvenir" flyer saying we did it to "thank you for making WMMS the #1 rock and roll station in America." It became one of our most talked-about promotions, even more successful than we'd imagined. Journey's management was also pleased, because it meant that concert-goers had an extra $5 to spend on Journey merchandise.

Opening Labor Day weekend, we hosted night-before festivities for the three-day Cleveland Air Show. Wild Horses performed, and between their sets we staged the "World's Largest Yeah"—a mass shout to show support for the Cleveland Browns that was entered into the *Guinness Book of Records*.

We did have occasional botched promotions. I've always found it best to get out of a bad deal as quickly as possible, and one of the worst we ever did was the Buzzard Card. Though it encouraged listeners to be "card carrying" listeners of WMMS, its purpose was to tie in with local retailers for discounts. It never caught on, because retailers questioned what was in it for them if they discounted merchandise for our listeners. A second problem was discounts being offered to Buzzard Card holders by retailers who didn't advertise on WMMS. We phased it out, but it must have had some attraction. By Christmas, some street vendors and kiosks in shopping malls in Akron were selling bootleg Buzzard Cards.

Toward the end of 1981, at Gil Rosenwald's insistence, we debuted a new Sunday night hosted by Leo, the *Grand Jury of Rock and Roll*. Gil Rosenwald, who nixed syndication deals for other projects, figured we could sell this to a national syndicator. No one bit. It didn't do much except inspire a local group, the Balls, to record a tribute song titled "Kid Leo"—which they hoped would become its theme song.

Our biggest misstep came in advertising. Denny and I believed that everything we did at WMMS—programming, promotion, and marketing—had to be home-grown. Our print advertising was original and drawn by David Helton, not off some ad agency's assembly line. Our TV spots were animated by David Helton and his hand-picked assistants. We didn't want rubber-stamped, agency-produced spots in which only the call letters changed from market to market. We didn't want a campaign the same as anyone else's.

That changed when an excited John Chaffee approached me about a TV spot he'd seen for WEBN in Cincinnati, featuring a model in a thin tank-top dancing to some corporate rock song. At the end of it, she ripped her top off, forward toward the camera, and said, "Now, you try it." I thought it wasn't bad for a typical dirtbag rock station, but it wasn't for WMMS. Denny and Leo agreed. But Chaffee insisted it was for us. I'd have fingers left over if I counted the number of times he overruled me on a decision, but he was the boss and this was one of those times.

A week later, Chaffee, Helton, and I were on a plane to Cincinnati to cut the WMMS version of the spot. Frank Wood, a brilliant radio strategist who owned WEBN, was at the taping. I asked what other stations picked up the campaign; fortunately, none within our television market did. The last thing I wanted was some Youngstown, Toledo, or Columbus station using the identical spot.

The model, who had the personality of stale bread, went through her motions and nailed it in three or four takes. Chaffee couldn't wait to get dubs to local TV when our master copy arrived a few days later. I believed that most guys watching, except for the lugs, would expect more from WMMS—and that women would consider it third-rate. And that's exactly what happened. TV stations said they expected better from us. We heard complaints from listeners, and from our own staff. The only favorable comment about the spot came from a listener who added a closing complaint: "You fuckin' guys sold out, man. You shoulda had her show her tits."

The spot was pulled after a brief run, never to be seen again. It was so generic that, fortunately, some people I knew were not even aware it pitched WMMS. Chaffee never approached us with another exciting ad campaign.

The wildest listener parties I've ever been to were hosted by Jeff and Flash at Surfside Six (or "Surfside Sex," as it was often called), a club in Lorain, three summer weekends a year. Whether there was something in the drinking water in Lorain or, more likely, an abundance of controlled substances the partygoers were holding, the parties were uninhibited orgies of sex, drugs, and rock and roll. The club owners were adamant about keeping drugs off the premises and sex off the dance floor, which meant most would go to their cars, trucks, and vans to toke up, toot up, or get a quickie, then return to the club with illicit smiles. My guess is the club moved more alcohol on those Jeff and Flash Sundays than they did on St. Patrick's Day. Jeff and Flash also hosted sold-out WMMS Friday night parties for years at the Mining Company, at State and Brookpark roads, near the Peaches record store. But nothing came close to the debauchery of the Surfside Six events.

The popularity of Jeff and Flash did not go unnoticed by Gary Bauer and Geoff George, two entrepreneurs who, separately and together, owned a number of clubs around Greater Cleveland. Bauer approached Jeff and Flash about fronting their own club in Lorain. They were given a piece of the club and royalties on the use of their names and likenesses. Bauer and George, understanding we would not share in any liabilities but that he needed WMMS to make the club work, chose an artist other than David Helton to do the logo and caricatures of Jeff and Flash—a subtle indication that the club was not linked to the station. The club was called Jeff and Flash's Monopolies, and it was far enough under the radar not to be noticed by Milton Bradley, the Monopoly game company. Except for opening week, the Jeff and Flash appearance commitment was limited to weekends. The club had a few good months but closed a year later, in part due to a changing neighborhood, though it did well enough that Bauer later reunited with Jeff and Flash to launch Noisemakers, in the Flats, and Cadillac Beach, in North Ridgeville.

When the Rolling Stones came to town, it was an event. They had incredible marketing savvy, and we did, too. We landed the rights to call ourselves the "Official Rolling Stone Station"—and had to cease-and-desist M105 for using that slogan, which they changed to "Your Real Rolling Stones Station." For their two nights in Cleveland in November 1982, we played nonstop Rolling Stones each day from 2 p.m. to 6 a.m., including rare and unreleased live and studio performances. We had Rolling Stones giveaways every hour, including their current album, *Tattoo You*, plus tour shirts and other paraphernalia.

We landed an exclusive interview with Bill Wyman, which Kid Leo did on the afternoon before the first show. Wyman was promoting his own self-titled album and its single "(Si Si) Je Suis, Un Rock Star." Bob Travis, program director at WGCL, fumed but there was little he could do. It wasn't a pay-for-play single, so he never played it. We were the only station in town that did, and that gave us the exclusive arrangement. Gary Bird, the independent record promoter close to WGCL, pleaded with me to allow their Bob Travis to get an interview. I refused. Exclusive meant exclusive, and Bob Travis was the last person in town I was going help. Bird also tried to get Wyman to cut an ID for WGCL. He wouldn't. Our interview went so well, and Wyman revealed enough news about the Stones, that excerpts and the special Stones programming on WMMS made the Associated Press internationally, picked up by newspapers in the U.K., South Africa, and France.

Every so often our renegade image needed a boost, and the Stones gave us one. We launched an event called the WMMS Rolling Stones Orgy, playing nonstop Stones on the evening and day of their WMMS World Series of Rock concert at Cleveland Stadium. Some listeners actually believed we were breaking FCC rules by doing so. We didn't bother to correct them. Local TV covered the

Stones Orgy on their newscasts, though one station refused to use the word "orgy" and substituted "party."

We made sure the entire Stones organization was outfitted in Buzzard gear, and we provided Mick Jagger a Browns jersey to wear on stage—promoting in advance so everyone would know where it came from. After each concert, to lock in the audience driving home, we played the tunes back in the same order the Stones performed them in concert. It didn't stop there. Rhonda Kiefer worked with the Akron Civic Theater, arguably one of the best theaters in the country, to do a weekend of Rolling Stones films, featuring *Gimme Shelter*, the concert film *Ladies and Gentlemen, the Rolling Stones*, and Jean-Luc Godard's *Sympathy for the Devil*. At the end of November, we simulcast a full Rolling Stones concert, live, in conjunction with the Preview pay-TV service on Channel 61.

When you said Rolling Stones in Cleveland, you said WMMS.

CHAPTER 22

"BRING THE NEXT ONE ON"

"We are about to have our most serious radio war in the history of this station," I said in a confidential memo to the airstaff at the end of February. Larry Robinson, the community activist and owner of the area's best-known jewelry chain, was buying M105 and its AM sister, WBBG.

Some of our department heads felt that Robinson knew nothing about radio and was getting involved in an industry that would confuse and confound him. I felt differently and argued for Robinson's expertise as a marketer. His Robinson Jewelers corporate office was in the Statler Office Tower, and I'd occasionally run into him in the lobby or on the elevator. We had a few lengthy discussions about advertising and marketing, and I considered him a positive and gifted businessman who always asked the right questions—the first rule in research, one too often ignored. I believed he was spending a good deal of time researching the Cleveland radio market, on his own terms.

And Robinson was a ruthless winner. I recalled when Richard's Jewelers mounted a serious image campaign against Robinson in the 1970s. Robinson conducted a brilliant media counterattack, promoting his store as the classy joint everyone could afford. In his commercials, Robinson said he would not be undersold. He insisted that you visit his competition first, and promised he would beat any deal another jeweler offered—and he did it.

He already knew what radio could deliver. By buying bulk advertising on radio, with a limited budget, he'd made Robinson

Jewelers one of the most visible retail outlets in Greater Cleveland. And every Robinson customer was asked to fill out a card with the prominent question, "What radio station do you listen to?" There was a much-told story that Norman Wain and his partners put WIXY up for the sale when its ratings started to drop in Robinson's store survey. I believed that WMMS was undoubtedly the leader in Robinson's survey, on a scale that even outstripped WIXY's golden years because of its limited AM signal. If I were Robinson, I'd see opportunity, especially when the number two rock station had less than half the audience of number one. Tom Embrescia's M105 was already living off the advertising spillage of WMMS, and there was plenty of room to grow.

Carl Hirsch agreed there should be no underestimating Robinson. But we disagreed on strategy. He asked me about consultants, who provide stations everything from advice to formats, playlists, and promotions. There were three in album rock radio: Lee Abrams, Jeff Pollack, and newcomer John Sebastian, who was pounding competitors with a hybrid rock and Top 40 format that I felt was closest to what we had, minus our adventurous and local music. Most of the top fifty markets had at least one rock consultant serving a station, and I always assumed one of them would reach Cleveland. I was frankly surprised that M105 hadn't signed earlier, and I expected Robinson to hire one or more.

Carl stunned me. He wanted to buy up all three consultants—pay them off—and I wouldn't have to use them for anything unless I elected to. It would keep a costly battle from erupting. Carl's thinking was that the consultants were going to record labels for promotions for the station groups they were building. In some markets, the consultants had total control of music selection and rotation, which made them important to the labels—which are only as loyal as the last time you added one of their songs.

I could attest to the success of consultants. After John Sebastian, a former Top 40 programmer, put together a seamless rock format for WCOZ in Boston, using a playlist that relied heavily on weekly call-out phone research, it blew past WBCN, one of the first album rockers in the country. When I drove along beach roads in Boston that summer, nearly every portable radio was blasting WCOZ. But I liked the fact that we were pure and not influenced by a mass-market playlist, even though I carefully studied every playlist and read any research I could get, from any market. I didn't want to just buy out a consultant. On one hand, we'd be buying insurance; on the other, we'd never have the chance to take on one or all as competitors. I consulted Denny and Leo. Like me, both preferred going the distance. WMMS owed its success to its accept-any-challenge attitude.

Carl decided to buy out the consultants before they signed with Robinson. Carl assured me it had nothing to do with any lack of faith in my programming and competitive ability. It would send a message that our turf was not for sale and we'd guard our borders with any means necessary. Robinson tried to hire Sebastian, but Carl got to the table first to sign him and Abrams within a week. Robinson got to Pollack first. We had two out of three, which gave us the opportunity to pick and choose what we could use from their services, including staff and research about music and lifestyles. We weren't about to change our way of adding and rotating music, but we had another element to use. As it turned out, one of the two consultants did not charge us for their services. Alignment with WMMS was enough. The relationships did not change us in any way, but the access to research was a distinct plus.

Jeff Pollack was already throwing his weight around, using his twelve to fourteen consulted stations as leverage with labels and artist management. Pollack's format made its debut on M105 on March 15, featuring roughly 400 library titles and 25 to 30 current album tracks. Within twenty-four hours, I made a connection to procure a copy of Pollack's master music list and detailed information on special features. M105 also cut commercials to six minutes per hour, with generic slogans like "More rock, less talk" and "Cleveland's real rock radio station." It would've made a mark in other markets. In Cleveland, you couldn't do generic with the improvisational Buzzard around.

We learned that M105 was preparing a three-hour *Beatles at the Beeb*, featuring thirty-seven previously unreleased performances from the BBC. Knowing that most of that material was available on bootlegs, and that we had dozens of additional unreleased Beatles tracks, we went a week earlier with our own Beatles weekend featuring six tunes every hour. We also tied in with Beatlefaire, an event organized by fans Janet Macoska and John Awarski at the Agora the same weekend, and gave away copies of *Reel Music*, a new Beatles soundtrack collection. M105's show ended up sounding like a pale copy of ours.

It was a hard sell, but I got approval for commercial-free hours, something that Sebastian-consulted stations programmed. Because we were sold out, however, I was limited to 6 p.m.–midnight, Monday through Saturday, and all day Sunday.

We also decided to start a twin-spin contest, awarding $1,000 to the first caller noticing if we played two tunes by the same artist in any given hour. It wasn't my favorite kind of contest, but it was a simple promotion any station could do, and we wanted to do it first. Besides, I knew it could increase time spent listening, which would translate to higher ratings. We did it daily, a grand a day, and called it the Buzzard $25,000 Double-Play Contest, because that was the total amount I had to play with. M105 countered with a $5,000 five-in-a row promotion, planning to award one listener with $5,000 for catching a set of five tunes. It ended up costing M105 $10,000 when a miscalculating T.R. (Tom Rezny, who would later work at WMMS) accidentally played an unscheduled five in a row one evening.

In early June, I took a week off to go back to Boston to visit family and friends. While I was away, the *Cleveland Press* announced it was folding. That was national news I was sorry to hear, since it meant we would lose a media outlet, and having two papers made each one better.

But the real news was that Larry Robinson pulled the plug on M105. He was being wooed by Mike McVay, an out-of-town programmer who pitched for a job by showing Robinson the station should adopt a soft-rock format appealing heavily to women that was growing in popularity in other cities of similar size.

It brought to a close one of the great radio wars of all time. Winning was reason to celebrate, but we also knew we'd miss the competition that turned us into a war machine. Our new slogan inside the station was "Bring the next one on." To insure that another station wouldn't jump to album rock, and to prove a point, Carl Hirsch signed Jeff Pollack, M105's former consultant. We felt a minor backlash from the usual gadfly types, who accused us of being a "monopoly" in rock and roll radio. Tough. Without M105 to play against us, every record weasel in town was now trying to become my new best friend, promising endless exclusives—to which I said, "Every song we play now is an exclusive." M105 became WMJI, and its staff was on the street. I felt that T.R., Tom Rezny, could be molded into a Buzzard air talent, so I hired him to do weekends and fill-ins.

Now that M105 was history, we'd have a little more breathing room for creativity. But we weren't about to let down our guard, and we continued to program and market as if we had a hundred competitors. I thought we were one step closer to my dream of making WMMS a massive, mass-appeal station, and my new goal was to get back into double-digits in the overall ratings and to increase our lead in all demographics under thirty-five.

Len Goldberg had hit the milestone of ten years with WMMS in May—not counting the number of times he quit and returned in the seventies—after giving us a huge scare. In early March, Boom suffered a heart attack that sidelined him for more than a month. Fortunately it was mild and served as a wake-up call about his diet and lifestyle. Listeners sent hundreds of get-well cards, and his return to the air on April 24 got so much press that one record weasel moaned, "I wouldn't be surprised if Gorman somehow talked Boom into having that heart attack to capitalize on the ratings."

He was kidding. I think.

Hitting summer, Denny and I stole an idea from the station wars we remembered from our youth in Boston, the WMEX Beachcomber. This character roamed local beaches to give $15.10—matching the AM/1510 frequency—to anybody whose radio was tuned to WMEX.

It was a nice payoff for a teen audience and effective against stations with far bigger budgets. But we always wondered if there was a real Beachcomber, since we never heard anything about winners. We wanted a real WMMS Buzzard Beachcomber, giving away prize packages, and we wanted to mention winners on the air with Jeff and Flash on Monday morning. And since we had only three real beaches—Edgewater, Huntington, and Mentor Headlands—we added the Buzzard Rock Ranger, who cruised the Metroparks to reach a larger number of WMMS listeners.

While other stations went on automatic pilot over the July 4th weekend, I kept our regular airstaff lineup on the air and had John Webster—the WHK news director who occasionally filled in for Flash as Buffalo John—cover the Cleveland 500 at Burke Lakefront Airport. We listed fireworks displays throughout the area in a way that gave the illusion we were presenting them all. And many believed we did.

I was hot on adding more forward-motion, high gloss sounders and features. One was the "WMMS weekend weather eye scanning the sky," which was a fancy intro, with a sound-effect bed, for the forecast. We also added a marine forecast, using a bell from a buoy and the sound of waves crashing as its bed.

Our top-of-the-hour IDs adopted a summer style, too, with, "The station that reaches the beaches, shakes the lakes, and rocks the rivers" for sunny days—and the "Thundering Buzzard" for stormy ones.

We knew it was only a matter of time before another station switched format to challenge us. I just didn't want it to be a surprise. We hadn't had much advance notice of the format change at M105, and our intelligence needed improving. Getting information from other stations wasn't difficult. When jocks from rival stations came to WMMS to apply for potential spots, I tried to greet them personally and give a tour. I was amazed at how readily they'd give information when they felt there was a possible job for them at WMMS—though anyone who would tell tales out of school would never work for me. Some actually stayed in touch, giving me updates without realizing it. Just saying, "Your station sounds really good" would get me all the behind-the-scenes information I needed to know.

One such meeting with a jock at WLYT tipped me to a format change they were planning. He called to tell me that the station was going to change its call letters to some form of "Rock" and had signed a deal with the ABC Rock Radio Network.

Within twenty-four hours, I confirmed that WLYT had applied for the call letters WRQC, a fact few knew at that station. We also learned they'd be called "92 Rock" and would pattern themselves after WLLZ in Detroit, a "hit rock" station. M105 ran a tight playlist against us (fewer tunes in frequent rotation), but WRQC would be even tighter. And we learned their new program director was Tim Spencer, formerly of KISS, an album rock station in Dallas that had success with a homogenized format—one that worked for the many newcomers in a fast-growing market.

Within forty-eight hours, I had a memo smuggled from the station's general manager Zemirah Jones: "Cleveland is a two AOR radio station town. We may seem like David going up against Goliath. WMMS is an excellent radio station. WMMS, however, never had a strong promotional campaign against them. We plan to out-promote and out-program WMMS. Many feel WMMS to be somewhat complacent. Our research shows the need for a second AOR station in the market."

Finally, we learned that they were readying a press release to go public in mid-August. Our first line of attack was to notify everyone, from local papers to record labels, of the coming change. That way, when someone from a label or newspaper called to confirm, they'd mention WMMS as the source of the information. Most of what I learned came from sources outside the station, and even included the tip that the format would change on Labor day weekend; word would travel fast around schools that there was a new rock station in town. We found that the station would spend around $150,000 for thirty-second custom TV spots produced by John Dykstra, the special effects director for the first *Star Wars* and *Star Trek* movies and creator of the series *Battlestar Galactica*. Their TV buying included MTV. They were serious.

In a staff meeting, Zemirah Jones positioned WRQC between WMMS and WGCL. Jerry Hroblak, president of the station owner, United Broadcasting, told the *Plain Dealer* WMMS had "broadened beyond album-oriented rock" and was "trying to do something for everybody." He was right. What he didn't understand about WMMS was that it was never a true AOR; we were called that only because we were closest to that format and had to be labeled something. But we were growing ourselves as a full-service pop-culture station that programmed far more than just music. But that didn't stop Ross Salupo, whose ad agency was hired to buy WRQC's TV time, from putting out a release saying, "Within a few months, 92 Rock will be the most talked-about radio station in America—or I'll eat a buzzard whole." (I'd eventually send him a Buzzard chocolate bar with the message, "Choke." I never got a response.)

When WRQC made its debut, I thought they were pretty good, but somewhat generic. With few commercials, they immediately jumped into "92 commercial-free minutes" of music, and initially kept Sunday and Monday commercial-free all day. It sounded highly polished. I was impressed and, believe me, I didn't want to be.

Everyone on the air was fired up. We started the battle by immediately stealing the name "Rocktober" for October, using it in every mention of the month by mid-September. Something like owning the name "Rocktober" might seem silly or overblown, but it wasn't. You didn't win a war by winning a battle—you won by winning most of the battles and never losing sight of your goals. We had to be right the first time, every time.

Changing our "101 FM" monicker to 100.7 was another example. We were entering a digital world. Years earlier, I had insisted that time be giving digitally—five-twenty, instead of twenty past five. When I spotted a digital clock radio selling in a drug store for less than $10, and subsequently learned about 50 percent of new radios had digital readouts, I realized "101 FM" was obsolete. Someone looking for it might bypass 100.7. Changing it meant major retooling of advertising, promotions, and paraphernalia. We started in the fall—saying "one-oh-one, digital one-hundred-point-seven" on the air—and eliminated 101 completely in early 1983.

We kicked off fall with two successive weekends of Friday Night Live, where we played continuous live music—most of it from the WMMS archives of Instant Radio Spectaculars, *Coffee Break Concerts*, Monday Nights Out at the Agora, and other live remotes. Besides giving us energy other stations couldn't match, it racked up serious audience time, because many listeners taped what they couldn't buy in stores.

We jumped on news that a new Fleetwood Mac tour was scheduled but would bypass Cleveland in its first leg. I called Irv Azoff, the band's manager, and Wright Airlines, which flew to Detroit, and set up a promotion where twenty listeners would get to see the Mac there—via "Trans-Buzzard Airways," with the Warner label picking up the tab.

With football season starting, I wanted a Browns player on WMMS once a week before each game, in Thom Darden's former role, and I wanted Tom Cousineau. He was a natural fit as somebody who grew up in Cleveland as a fan of WMMS, played at St. Edward High School in Lakewood, and was a two-time All-American at Ohio State before being picked first overall in the 1979 NFL draft. Our game plan was to have him on with Jeff and Flash every Friday, but it worked out better to have Kid Leo do the segment on Friday afternoon. When a players' strike cut the NFL season to nine games, we turned that to advantage, too; on Sunday, radio's lightest listening day, we super-served the young male audience normally locked on football. Sports talk as a full-time format didn't yet exist.

Weekends were already the time when we did our best "world premiere exclusives," since I was able to make myself unavailable for cease-and-desist demands from labels. My personal favorite was an album Atlantic Records denied existed—a rumored Led Zeppelin album with some unreleased material that was being rushed out for the Christmas buying season. Atlantic denied it.

We even taped an interview with an Atlantic representative who was adamant there was no such album—and then announced our latest world premiere exclusive, Led Zeppelin's *Coda*. We played tracks from it all weekend.

One of our biggest events was buying out the Who's two Coliseum concerts in December 1982. The tour was billed as the band's farewell—as every subsequent Who reunion tour has been—and we got exclusive local ownership by putting up the guarantee and all costs in advance. The shows sold out in record time, and surveys at a number of sale locations showed that more than 99 percent of ticket buyers heard the concert announcement on WMMS. The official tour name, which had to be used in all advertising—even announcements on other radio stations—was "WMMS 100.7 FM presents the Who." We allowed other stations to buy tickets for giveaways, but they all had WMMS imprinted on them, and any alteration, such as running a marker streak over our call letters, made them null and void. Best of all, anyone using a check to buy tickets to the Who had to make it out to WMMS.

Three nights after the second show, WGCL picked up the "farewell" broadcast of a Who concert from Toronto that we passed on, because it would've cost us $2,000 that I couldn't justify. Instead, we did another Friday Night Live instead, including a previously unreleased concert Led Zeppelin did for the BBC. It blew away WGCL's Who concert broadcast, which was riddled with engineering problems.

CHAPTER 23

YOUR MODERN MUSIC STATION

I defended it then and I defend it even more strongly now: we made the right decision to play Michael Jackson and Prince. All the urban legends about that decision came from people who weren't in that music meeting of March 1983.

We'd often spend a week or two, or even more, discussing the merits of certain songs and artists and whether we should add them or not. We went back and forth about playing Sheena Easton's "Strut," since prior to being a Prince protégé and adopting a new and slightly slutty rock and soul image, she had recorded some pretty crappy adult contemporary songs, especially "Morning Train (Nine to Five)." We discussed "Smalltown Boy," by the gay British trio the Bronski Beat, about a boy who was shunned by his family and friends when they learned his sexual orientation; hardly another album rock station in America would play it, and even the label asked if we were sure. Yet—without incident or complaint—we added it. We actually spent more time debating whether we should play Madonna, whom Leo originally thought was a transvestite.

But Denny, Leo, and I didn't debate whether we should play the Jacksons for weeks or months, just as we never pondered about playing the Isley Brothers, Gloria Gaynor, Labelle, and George and Gwen McRae. We never anguished over playing Johnny Guitar Watson, Gil Scott-Heron, or B. B. King, or classic rhythm and blues and soul tunes from the sixties and seventies, from the Temptations to Aretha. They were the roots of rock and roll music. The hottest rock band in the world in the seventies, Led Zeppelin, freely borrowed music and even lyrics from rhythm and blues tunes.

We didn't have meetings with Milt Maltz, Carl Hirsch, Gil Rosenwald, JC, or anyone else before we added Michael Jackson. And we didn't do it to get a greater teen audience, as some suggested. It came down to one thing. Jackson was the hottest act in show business, his music was mass appeal, he was all over MTV, and as a popular culture station we'd be crazy not to play him. In fact, we were late for that party. WGCL had been on Jackson's *Thriller* album from the time it was released, and I supposed it threw a few ratings points in their direction.

A couple of days after we started playing "Beat It," which was a rock song, we added "Billie Jean," a masterpiece that already was an MTV staple. Within days they were the two most requested songs on WMMS and sounded as pop as anything else we were playing.

To us, Prince was a rock and roll artist and had been since his *1999* album. We knew we were backtracking there, too. Prince also had a roster of other acts like Sheila E., Apollonia 6, and the Time that quickly developed into WMMS staples.

I believed, as did Denny and Leo, that Michael Jackson would not alienate most of our audience. No one boycotted the station. We didn't get petitioned to stop playing him. Maybe ten people called or wrote to complain. We received far more complaints for not playing enough Allman Brothers or Jeff Beck. If Jeff Kinzbach didn't like the decision, as was widely reported, I never heard it from him. And actually we weren't the only album rock station to play Michael Jackson, though others tried and apologized for it. I heard one album rock station play "Beat It" and identify it as Eddie Van Halen (who played guitar on the track). Lord forbid you mention a black artist's name.

Within weeks, anything related to Michael Jackson was a hit for us. Any lingering concerns about Michael Jackson and Prince were put to rest by Arbitron ratings for the previous months. We were still in first place, but WGCL was only a hair away. We'd killed 92-Rock, which was the game plan, but paid the penalty for being late to Jackson and Prince.

The same week we started playing Michael Jackson, we also added Eddy Grant's infamous "Electric Avenue," Billy Idol's "White

Wedding," Rocker's Revenge's updated version of "The Harder They Come," which had been a huge song for us in the seventies by Jimmy Cliff, and a new track from the band Sparks. We were covering all the bases.

It was an exciting and stimulating time for new music. Seventies superstars like the Eagles had reinvented themselves as solo artists. The Clash provided a raw but mainstream edge with their brand of commercial punk. The English Beat took Jamaican ska and reworked it into pop music. Adam Ant was, for the times, a perfect left-of-center rock and pop artist, whose music and style complemented both radio and video. You also had second-generation rock acts. Led Zeppelin, for example, was heavily influenced by American blues, but newcomers Def Leppard used Led Zeppelin as their prime influence. Duran Duran was influenced by Roxy Music, Led Zeppelin, and seventies glitter bands. It was only after Capitol Records tried to reinvent Duran Duran as teen idols that they lost ground on album radio. Mainstream rock stations often stopped playing artists once they achieved Top 40 success—it was viewed as "selling out." I preferred to call it "buying in."

Leo, Denny, and I saw the "new wave" artists as perfect balance for the beginning-to-sound-tired corporate rock artists. The music could be quirky and off center, but that what's rock and roll was all about. There are no rules for popular music. The only constant is change. New music was our lifeblood. Our music reports made little sense to the trades. How could a station play Pink Floyd, the Stray Cats, Pat Benatar, and Haysi Fantayzee? We paid close attention to what was being played on college radio, which we used as a proving ground. We listened to everything, well beyond what we were hyped by the record weasels. It was how we were able to discover and play so many local acts—most of which were pressing their own records and lacked the resources to promote and market to radio.

One afternoon, while going through some music I hadn't had a chance to hear yet, I put on an album from some obscure Los Angeles label that caught my attention as nearly perfect for us. It was Berlin's *Pleasure Victim*. I had no doubt that "Sex ("I'm A . . .)," as the song was called, would be huge if given exposure. I played it for Leo and Denny. They loved it. I called Berlin's "Sex" a secret weapon. Since the album was on a tiny, unknown label, our competition would know nothing about it. They didn't dig deep into new releases. When we added it, listener requests exploded. Record stores immediately got calls, and other stations wanted to know where we got it. We did, too, actually. Eventually, we tracked down their small indie label and management to let them know how well their song was doing. I also turned them on to Bruce Moser's Could Be Wild company, which could promote and market them to other stations. Moser targeted key adventurous radio stations, and he often worked for artist managers rather than record labels.

Major labels took note of our airplay of Berlin, and other stations started to play it based on our "Sex"-cess. Geffen made an offer to the band and rereleased *Pleasure Victim* nationally. It sold 500,000 copies in just a few months, good for gold, and established vocalist Terri Nunn as a new voice and new name to rock and roll.

Attention to new music helped renew WMMS. Many of the artists we backed when they were "baby acts" were starting to cross into the mainstream, most notably U2, a band that bridged the gap between old and new music, appealing to everyone from classic rockers to cutting edgers.

U2's *War* tour came to Music Hall in May, and I was awed by how much the band had developed from its *Coffee Break Concert* a few years earlier. They weren't yet superstars, but I bet anyone willing to wager that U2 would be the next big thing. Bono and the Edge came to WMMS for a lengthy interview and to cut a station ID, and I spent a good part of the afternoon with them. They were thoughtful and intelligent and not your typical rock and rollers. Kevin Rowland of Dexy's Midnight Runners called while I was talking to Bono, and I put all of them on the speakerphone. My only regret was not being able to record the conversation. After their concert that night, I spent a few hours discussing religion with Bono. This was not your typical backstage after-show party. U2 became my favorite new group, and my gut told me they'd be the biggest act for WMMS since Bruce Springsteen—and would give us the solid eighties identity we needed to separate ourselves from other stations in town.

Not that we forgot the other side of our music. When Journey came back to play the Coliseum a week later, the WMMS staff was awarded platinum albums onstage for breaking and supporting the band. We had our pre- and postconcert programming down to a science. Before any major Coliseum show, we'd play an hour of the artist's greatest hits to lock in listeners en route to the show. After the show, we'd do another hour to lock in listeners heading back home. For a really major act, and Journey was among them, we'd play the songs in the same order they'd been performed in concert—and if we had live versions, we played those.

There was a slight divide between rock and "new wave." New wavers tended to be twelve- to twenty-four-year olds, and equally split between men and women, where the mainstream rock appealed to eighteen- to thirty-four-year olds. The only overlap was eighteen to twenty-four, which cautioned me to keep our musical balance under control. My demographic research showed that most research companies and radio stations viewed the center of the baby boom as the "1950 kid"—but that it was actually those born between 1954 and 1964 who had the greatest numbers and clout. True baby boomers, the group I should concentrate on most, were between the ages of nineteen and twenty-nine. They made up roughly 30 percent of the adult population in 1983. I began concentrating on the music most likely to appeal to that audience and realigned our music away from the "1950 kid." To avoid alienating our older, classic rock–leaning audience as we increased our "modern music," we used a sweep that Boom cut, saying, "More weird-ass music from WMMS." We said it before they said it, and it helped make new music acceptable to the older demos. If they thought it was weird, we did too.

I monitored our competition constantly and noticed a change in 92 Rock's music. They had been using the tag line "Vintage Music" but dropped it abruptly. Playing a hunch, I planted rumors through the record weasels that I was considering moving quickly in a "modern music" direction. I believed this might lead their program director, Tim Spencer, to jump the gun and own a new music position for himself, to be "cooler than WMMS." He did, falling into the same trap Phil DeMarne fell into at M105. Even better, he started having their jocks play unfamiliar music saying, "The other station isn't playing this one"—which made it sound even more unfamiliar and unfocused.

Over the years, we used WMMS as an acronym for such tags as "Where Music Means Something," "Weed Makes Me Smile," and "We're your Music Marathon Station." Rhonda Kiefer came up with, "We're your Modern Music Station." Boom cut a new ID, and David Helton was called to retool an ad for the *Plain Dealer* using that slogan, which ran in the *Plain Dealer* that week.

By the time 92 Rock put out a press release saying they had switched to "modern music," the response was, "Like some of that music WMMS has been playing?" Once again, we had moved our competition into uncharted territory and a corner they'd be unable to escape from. We gave 92 Rock six months before they abandoned the format, and were right on the money with our prediction.

What surprised me most was that WGCL ignored "modern music" entirely, even though many of the genre's songs were crossing over to the CHR format. They were still hell-bent on trying to out corporate rock us with Journey, Foreigner, and Boston album tracks. Had WGCL embraced modern music, it could have created problems for us with our younger demos. By the time they realized they were late for the party, we had the lock on the new music image. But we did have growing concern about WGCL. They were becoming the station our listeners would tune first if they didn't like something we were doing. In a way, we were helping build their audience.

Whenever we did a "WMMS World Premiere Exclusive" on an album we weren't supposed to have, the labels would send us cease-and-desist telegrams and faxes. By 1983, I had moved to a larger office and one of the walls, from floor to ceiling, was papered with cease and desist telegrams. I'd collected close to 150 over the years, for artists ranging from Paul McCartney to Pink Floyd to Led Zeppelin. They'd usually begin, "We are the exclusive licensees of the recordings entitled . . . " and continue, "the recordings have yet to be released. It has come to our attention that you have in your possession unauthorized copies of that album and that you have no authority to broadcast that album. We hereby demand that you cease and desist from any further use of said album. Your intentional and unauthorized use of this album constitutes a deliberate copyright infringement for which you will be held strictly accountable."

One of the best exclusives of that time was when we got a well-in-advance copy of David Bowie's *Let's Dance*, which turned out to be the biggest album of his career. The label and Bowie's management were so incensed they threatened to sue WMMS, and they hired a private investigator to track down the source of the leak, which they never found. We covered our tracks well.

An international incident erupted when we were leaked a copy of Robert Plant's album, *The Principle of Moments*. It was so far ahead of its release date that we knew neither the name of the album nor the song titles. We premiered it over the long Memorial Day weekend. On Tuesday morning, there was no cease and desist waiting. We later learned that the album, which was not scheduled for release for another month, was the subject of a lawsuit over who owned the master. Plant wanted out of both his management and Atlantic recording contract, so there was no one to "officially" serve us with a cease and desist. Due to the suit, the regional Atlantic records promo guy had no idea there was a Robert Plant album scheduled on their label until he heard it premiered on WMMS. By Wednesday, someone with the proper authorization sent us a cease and desist. We read it on the air, telling of the behind-the-scenes skullduggery, which amplified our rebel credibility with our listeners. We later learned that Plant was pleased the album leaked because it helped him renegotiate the remainder of his deal with Atlantic at a better royalty rate.

CHAPTER 24

BUZZARDLAND

I don't know who came up with phrase North Coast, but I loved it, and I knew Cleveland would, too. North Coast signified a new Greater Cleveland with a "coastal" identity. It caught on quickly. Within a year of its introduction we'd have North Coast Heating, North Coast Plumbing, North Coast Printing, and North Coast everything else. I wanted WMMS to have the lock on North Coast for radio—and we did. Boom cut a number of North Coast-oriented top of the hour IDs and sweeps, which we introduced in 1981 and turned up in '82, alternating between "Serving the Universe from the Rock and Roll Capital of the World" with "Serving the Universe from the North Coast of America." We worked North Coast into promos and general raps. When we added marine forecasts, we played up the lake as we would the ocean if we were on either coast.

The timing was right. The *Wall Street Journal* opened 1983 with a story including a quote from Matt the Cat on what they called the "new depression music," which was a sizable portion of what we were playing—such songs as Gary U.S. Bonds' "Out of Work," the Pretenders' "My City Was Gone," and Billy Joel's "Allentown." Matt said, "I don't want to be the harbinger of doom, but hard times are out there." Cleveland's manufacturing industry had been hit hard in the economic downturn. The subject was often discussed on the air, and Jeff and Flash were getting an increasing number of calls from listeners who'd been thrown out of work. The North Coast label gave Cleveland a better image to look to and to present the world.

WMMS, through its listeners, continued to do its part in 1983, winning the annual *Rolling Stone* Readers' Poll for the fourth straight year—although it was also a rude awakening as to how few votes were cast, since this was the first year that *Rolling Stone* provided exact figures for us. WMMS won with 476 votes. KLOL in Houston came in second with 345. WNEW-FM in New York was third with 286. KROQ in L.A., which had adopted a "new wave/ modern music" format was fourth, with 199, and WMMR in Philadelphia came in fifth with 182 votes. I expected more votes for all the finalists. The upside was that the other stations were top ten markets, including New York and Los Angeles, the number one and two markets. Cleveland, at the time, was in eighteenth place and shrinking.

Later, we learned that KLOL had mistakenly gone on the air to announce they had "beaten the Buzzard." They played it as the Sun Belt against the Rust Belt and featured daily negative news stories from Cleveland. KLOL was so hell-bent on winning, station reps called *Rolling Stone* daily for updates. Locally, WRQC and WGCL had even tried to "buy" entries after *Rolling Stone* ran the first ballot in November. "92 Rock" offered $92 to anyone bringing a filled-out ballot to the station, and "G98" quickly followed, offering $98. Both stations retreated from the promotions after a few days.

On the air, we had our first full-time staff change since 1978 when Betty Korvan, burned out from her 10 p.m. to 2 a.m. shift, gave it up but kept her Saturday night, 6 p.m. to midnight slot. To continue building a team around Jeff and Flash, but stay within budgetary constraints, I hired veteran WJW-TV sportscaster and all-around nice guy Dan Coughlin to do daily sports—and found a sponsor to underwrite the cost. He'd been a popular writer in the *Cleveland Press*, the *Plain Dealer*, and other area publications, and had appeal that crossed demographics. I knew if we were to grow mornings, I'd have to reach out beyond our core audience.

We also locked up rights to *Rockline*, a late-night talk and music show that ran Monday nights, and picked up the FM simulcast of

Rock 'n' Roll Tonight, a ninety-minute syndicated series that aired at 12:30 a.m. on WJW-TV, its last half-hour opposite *Saturday Night Live.* Though that was an unrated time period for us, I considered the late-night weekend audience important—and wide awake. The show was good, and strictly music, but I probably wouldn't do again. It did screw up Bash's regular Sunday morning *Maggot Brain,* which ran an hour later at 2:30, and its long spot breaks between music sets didn't help hold listeners. Its ratings barely dented *Saturday Night Live.*

In 1982, Walt Tiburski became the first of the core WMMS people to leave. He put together a group of investors, including Steve Blaushield of the Blaushield automobile family, Tim LaRose of the House of LaRose Budweiser distributorship, and Cleveland Browns defensive back Thom Darden, to form WIN Communications and negotiated a deal to purchase WQAL. Tony Ocepek replaced the investors as Walt's partner shortly after the sale was completed.

Following Walt's resignation, Gil called me into his office and said he was going to reorganize management. Walt's position would not be filled. Instead, he was creating a new position, station manager, which Bill Smith, formerly the sales manager, would hold—and I would retain my operations manager position for both stations.

Both would be equal positions. Bill and I would work together: he would concentrate on sales and I would continue overseeing programming, promotion and marketing, and engineering.

However, when Gil met with Smith, he told Smith that he would be a station manager—but his real title would be "acting general manager"—and that I would answer to him. It put Bill and me in an unusual position initially, because we had two different definitions of our positions from Gil.

And neither of us knew the other was told a different story.

Our promotion department was returning to its former glory with Jim Marchyshyn at the helm. The Duck had flown in 1981 when Dan Garfinkel, burned out from years in the thankless and stressful job of promotion and marketing director, left to form his own management company. Walt Tiburski's former administrative assistant, Chris Hernandez, replaced him with passion and dedication but lacked a marketing background. Marchyshyn had one, after seven years as director of advertising and promotion for Belkin Productions, when he took over in September 1982. He reorganized the department, cleared up unfulfilled prize awards and giveaways, and hired former intern Elisabeth Pick as his assistant to clear up accumulated paperwork. He also hired Hank LoConti's niece, Gina Iorillo, who started out as an intern. There was a renewed energy. Promotion and marketing was a thankless job, but at WMMS it was supposed to be fun.

I loved working with Jim. He and I came up with some pretty wild and original ideas, which turned into reality. One unintentionally competitive incident happened after he secured the highly visible sponsorship of the scoreboard clock at Cleveland Stadium. The Indians were drawing little more than flies, but the Browns still packed the stadium on Sundays. The fans were the point, but there was an extra dividend when we heard about a number of record label weasels taking WGCL music director Tom Jeffries to an Indians game, just to get him away from the radio war for a few hours. He met them at the ballpark, spotted the huge WMMS scoreboard, shook his head, then got up and left.

We joked about being our own country, Buzzardland, and decided to show it before a Crosby, Stills, and Nash concert at the stadium—on a tour where David Crosby was so strung out on freebasing cocaine that he'd come close to setting his tour bus on fire on a half-dozen occasions. Jim put together a "rally" that had dozens of cheerleaders carrying WMMS Buzzard flags marching around the stadium grounds. It resembled Soviet Bloc May Day festivities so much that the only element missing was a parade of tanks and long-range missiles around the stadium.

Jim ordered our first inflatable Buzzard, a monster-sized icon of the Buzzard logo, which we brought to station-sponsored events.

We didn't get mad, we got even, when WGCL won exclusive rights to signage at the Cleveland 500 on the July 4th weekend because its AM side, WERE, had broadcast rights. They overpaid for exclusivity, but according to the contract we could not display banners or other visible presence, even in our hospitality suite. It was a risk, but Jim bought up tickets to an entire bleacher section—a highly visible one that most people attending would have to pass by. We resold them as "Buzzard Bleacher" seats and threw in a free Buzzard/Cleveland 500 T-shirt with every ticket—encouraging our listeners to wear them, which almost all of them did. As a result, everywhere you looked, there was a sea of Buzzard/Cleveland 500 T-shirts. WERE and WGCL, which had spent so much for exclusive signage, filed a complaint with the Cleveland 500 producers the following week. It was immediately dismissed because we had done nothing wrong. The shirt giveaways fell under "corporate sales." In fact, the Cleveland 500 producers chided WERE and WGCL for not doing promotions of similar high visibility.

The Buzzard's influence even extended to New York, thanks to Malrite president Carl Hirsch, one of the most brilliant broadcasters in the business. He followed a doctrine of gut decisions, without expensive and paralyzing market studies and research, and he had a sixth sense for deal-making. He identified an obscure FM station in Newark, New Jersey, that broadcast "beautiful music" by day and soft jazz by night on a signal that weakly reached New York City.

He learned its transmitter could be moved to the Empire State Building, making the station a player in the number one radio market in the world. And he saw opportunity because the city had been without a Top 40 formatted station since WABC went all-talk in May 1982. For what the station was, Carl overpaid. For what it could be, he stole it for pennies on the dollar. He pushed Malrite to close the deal, and in 1983 changed the call letters of WVNJ to WHTZ, leaving no doubt what the format would be—Hits.

Dean Thacker, WMMS's national sales manager, was named general manager and relocated to New York. Dozens of CHR programmers applied for the position of program director, and Scott Shannon, a brilliant, likable guy who was mainly known as an air personality leading the *Morning Zoo* on a station in Tampa, was hired "I just wanna be number one," he told Carl Hirsch.

Initially, Shannon wanted to call the station "Pirate Radio," envisioning a "theater of the mind" image of an illegal station in a secret location on the Hudson River. But Carl wanted WHTZ to be a New York City radio station, not one pretending to be. Shannon suggested calling the station Z-100, since its frequency was 100.3. Z-100 signed on the air August 3 from the Empire State Building, and in seventy-four days it was New York's number one station. Borrowing a slogan from the Tampa Bay Bucaneers, Z-100 became known as the station that "went from worst to first."

I knew WMMS's aggressive Len Goldberg–voiced IDs and sweepers (brief identifying drop-ins between songs) could easily translate to Z-100, including paraphrasing our, "Serving the universe from the Rock and Roll Capital of the World." It was retooled for New York as "Serving the universe from the Empire State Building"—though that had to be changed to the "Gorilla Building" after the building's owners wanted some form of compensation for mentioning it over the air. More importantly, I saw Z-100 as finally giving us a link to another influential station in the same family.

The relationship was ideal. It allowed me to spice up Jeff and Flash's morning show with additional content and rename it the *Buzzard Morning Zoo*. We were able to share Z-100 content contributors like David Kolin, a dentist turned comedy writer who did a perfect Michael Jackson impression; John Rio, with his Mr. Leonard character; and J.R. Nelson, a former Cleveland air personality and production director, who produced uncanny song parodies. We were able to customize Z-100 content for WMMS use. Our artist, David Helton, took on the same duties for Z-100 and relocated to New York, though he continued to do some work for us. Staff artist Brian Chalmers at *Scene* started laying out our weekly ads and became Helton's backup artist.

WMMS and Z-100 snagged a New York exclusive when I called Scott Shannon on another matter and mentioned that we just scored a coup with three tracks from the next Stones album, *Undercover*. He asked if I could get it there. I caught a plane to LaGuardia, where Shannon had a limo waiting to take me to the studios in Secaucus. On the way, I heard their afternoon drive jock say, "John

Gorman's on his way with the new Stones"—and hoped I didn't get a cease-and-desist delivered to me as I walked into Z-100. It didn't happen. That night, I was in one of the apartments Z-100 had rented next to the office building that housed the station. While a Stones exclusive played on Z-100, I looked out over the Manhattan skyline, and the lyrics to another Stones song, "Get Off of My Cloud," came to mind: "I live in an apartment on the ninety-ninth floor of my block/And I sit at home looking out the window/Imagining the world has stopped." I knew Mick Jagger was in town preparing his publicity for the album's legitimate release, and I wondered if he was aware of the exclusive.

CHAPTER 25

TAKING THE FIGHT TO THE AIRWAVES

With M105, all of our warfare was off-air—mostly propaganda stuff. With WGCL, it was different. They were a little dirty, and they were gaining ground on us.

WGCL was a true CHR, or Contemporary Hits Radio station, and by 1983 they had become the alternate first choice for the majority of our listeners. The more successful we were, the more successful they were. They were shadowing most of our current music, which made it imperative to triple-check our music and look for elements they couldn't duplicate. The Arbitron from winter 1983 showed us in first place among listeners twelve and older, but with our lowest figure in years and with WGCL only a hair behind. The spring ratings reinforced those results.

They were good, no doubt about it. They were building their own, albeit teen-heavy personalities with afternoon driver Dancin' Danny Wright and night guy Jo Bohannon, and their names occasionally showed up in our research. WGCL was doing the right format for Cleveland at the time—a teen-leaning rock hits format that neither M105 nor 92 Rock ever quite mastered because neither took into consideration the importance of personality in radio.

My concern was that WGCL could beat us in cume. "Cume" means the number of times one listens to a station sometime during a week, and it can mean listening time as short as a minute. Teens are the biggest button pushers. For many, WGCL was the first choice. WMMS might have been second, but there were also other choices, too—plus older listeners for whom WGCL was second choice. It meant that as the war heated up, WGCL could beat us in cume, which would give them the right to call themselves "Ohio's most listened-to station." The math worked against us.

In one respect, our hands were tied. We couldn't afford to build our teen audience. The reason was beer advertising. We had the largest share of beer business of any station in the market. We had all the right numbers, specifically for men aged eighteen to thirty-four, where no one else came close. But the beer companies had a rule that they would spend less money on teen-dominated stations because they did not want to encourage teen beer drinking—though it was utter bullshit in reality. The beer companies wanted to influence older teens, and their advertising proved it.

We didn't want to beat WGCL's teen numbers. But WGCL's twelve to seventeens of today would be the eighteen to twenty-fours of tomorrow—and we'd need them. I couldn't afford to have them get too comfy with WGCL. I had to be very careful to court teens without winning too many to our side. To do that, we let WGCL have some exclusive artists to themselves, most of them least likely to fit our format. It was a tricky maneuver.

Another problem was that WGCL was a typical pay-for-play station. What they said they played and what they really played were two different lists. In those days, before the start of independent monitoring services, reporting airplay to the trades was on the honor system. WGCL's true on-air playlist included the best current hits on WMMS, but these they didn't report, because there was no money attached to them. Their reported playlist was essentially owned by an independent record promoter.

Independent promoters are part of the system. Most that I've known have been reputable and above-board. Their promotion routes date from the 1950s, when there were a number of small labels that couldn't match the promotion and marketing savvy and strokes of the majors like Columbia, Capitol, and RCA, which could afford to wine and dine key programmers, a practice that was not overtly illegal. The small labels hired "indies" to work radio and sometimes retail. The local label reps went through the motions and pitched new music, but it was just a front for the independent promoter, who was paid a retainer; by the 1980s the going rate was anywhere from $5,000 to $10,000 per add per station. Because a record weasel's job is to "get the add," no one protested about their pay-for-play routine. The station didn't even have to play the record—just report it to the trades, of which *Radio & Records* was the most important. Those records were known as "paper adds." The practice was widespread.

Though everyone looked the other way, it was beyond obvious WGCL was a payola station. We used that knowledge to fight back. Knowing that promoter Gary Bird was close to WGCL program director Bob Travis and music director Tom Jeffries, I routinely fed him false information about WMMS and played up our vulnerability. I'd play dumb and pretend to confide, to plant information to throw them off. We'd tell Bird, "Keep it secret, but . . . " and rattle off a list of tunes that weren't doing well, even though they were, or deride our hottest tracks as pure dogs. Worked like a charm. If I felt a particular air talent posed a threat in one of our dayparts, I'd say just the opposite—telling him how relieved I was they'd scheduled so-and-so opposite Matt, Leo, or Denny. A week later, I'd hear WGCL make a change. It was almost too easy.

It was like luring WGCL into our jungle and ambushing them. We'd done the same thing with M105, using label reps as the conduits. Some label reps are decent human beings, some are weasels, and many are gossip peddlers, like salespeople in any industry. The trick was knowing which ones would pass along "inside information" supposedly told them in confidence.

We had the ratings, but WGCL was what was called a Parallel One reporter for *Radio & Records*, then the most important of the trade publications, which gave them clout we couldn't match in the alternate universe of record labels. Because they falsely reported the music they were playing, they were getting promotions they didn't deserve. Making it worse, I had problems locking up promotions when WGCL started claiming they wouldn't add music from a label if it was doing a major promotion with WMMS. That didn't always work, but WGCL did successfully block a Culture Club concert we had spent months setting up.

Labels would not stock much of what WMMS was playing because it couldn't get reported. If it wasn't an AOR artist, the industry looked at it like we weren't playing it. At one point there were sixteen songs on our playlist from major labels that were not stocked in any store in Cleveland, Akron, or Canton. We were the first station in Cleveland to play Culture Club, Madonna, the Stray Cats, the Eurhythmics, and Missing Persons—but their music wasn't stocked in the stores until WGCL played them. That gave WGCL power they didn't deserve.

I was tired of playing this game with the labels. It had cost us one concert, and I knew there'd be others—and WGCL was getting more aggressive about locking up promotions. We had never before acknowledged our competitors on the air, but we decided to openly attack WGCL on the air only if they ever reached cume dominance and played up a "most listened to" line.

It happened early in 1984. WGCL beat us in cume, and, as expected, started boasting they were "Ohio's most listened-to radio station." It was time to launch an attack. Where M105 had been the monkey house, WGCL became the Temple of Baboons, playing off the movie *Indiana Jones and the Temple of Doom*, which was released that May. But where the Chimp and the monkey house had been inside, music industry jokes about an opponent worthy of respect, we decided to take this one public. We planned a regular on-air feature called "The Temple of Baboons," and we remade the song "99 Red Balloons" as "98 Dead Baboons."

The campaign kicked into high gear almost before it started, when we learned that Slade would be playing WGCL's Party in the Park opening Memorial Day weekend. We resented that for two reasons. First, the Party in the Park was sponsored by a different station every week in conjunction with the Greater Cleveland Growth Association. WGCL general manager Kim Colebrook sat on its board, and the station got the prime dates kicking off Memorial Day, Fourth of July, and Labor Day weekends two years in a row. WMMS was "awarded" the worst weeks. Second, Slade was a

British band we'd played as far back as 1974. We had just broken their first single in a decade, "My Oh My," and their new album was selling well in Cleveland based solely on our airplay. But they were suddenly working a single that WGCL added, so that station got the promotional concert for playing ball. We were furious.

About forty-eight hours before the show, we learned from a spy inside Epic Records that Slade was not performing live. They were going to lip-synch and pretend to play their instruments. Everything was on tape. Battle stations! The day of the show, Jeff and Flash started firing on the air: *This is a live music city, how dare they lip-synch? This is the rock and roll capital of the world, they're insulting us. Can you imagine if the national press picked up on this? What does this make us look like?*They gave out the local number for Slade's label, Epic, which jammed up their lines all day.

Listeners started calling in to the station, and they were angry. Not just kids, either—older adults called: *It's taken a long time for this city to turn around, we finally can say we're proud to live in Cleveland again, and now somebody does this to make us a laughingstock.* The show became four hours of that. It culminated with a call to our studio from the Epic promo guy, Joe Carroll (who was close friends with Kid Leo), screaming, "Flash? Fuck you personally! Fuck Gorman, fuck your whole fucking station! Put it on the air, I don't give a fuck!" A few minutes before nine o'clock, I got a call from Kinzbach saying, "You gotta hear this." He played the call over the phone. I asked if Tom O'Brien, our production guy, was there. He was. I told Jeff to give him the tape, bleep out the obscenities, and play it. By the time O'Brien finished the considerable editing, they were only able to play it once, close to ten o'clock. Kinzbach did his wrap-up, said no one called in favor of lip-synching, asked again how WGCL could do such a thing to listeners and the city (thereby tarnishing the image of the Rock and Roll Capital), and said he had one more call. He played the heavily bleeped tape, said, "OK, Joe," and explained who it was—adding he was surprised Carroll was able to make a call, considering the number of people flooding his phone lines. "Oh, and by the way, that number for Epic Records is . . . "

The attack didn't end with the morning show. Slade's "My Oh My" was one of the era's chest-pounding anthems. We played it all day, inserting Carroll's bleeped "eff you" throughout the song. Matt the Cat and Leo continued to slam the lip-synching baboons, and Flash even found a way to turn it into a story during our noon newscast. David Helton, meanwhile, drew a baboon under the circle-slash international "no" symbol—working off the logo for *Ghostbusters*, which was opening that week. It wasn't in our budget, and it was expensive, but Jim Marchyshyn rush-ordered 1,500 T-shirts printed with his design.

They were ready just in time for the show. We gave them away in increments of 500 to people going to the free concert, on Lakeside Avenue next to City Hall, making sure we got the early arrivals who'd be closest to the stage. We didn't know it, but WGCL had hired a crew to tape the show as a TV spot. That plan fell apart in a sea of Baboonbuster T-shirts. We watched from across the street, knowing we'd scored, and kept up the attack all weekend. *Wonder what those baboons are doing? Probably hanging their heads in shame. We're not going to let anyone damage our reputation.* Then we'd cue up Queen's "Another One Bites the Dust." Denny had a hat made that read "Fuck you, personally," which he wore in front of those who would get the joke. Anyone who saw it knew the meaning behind it.

WGCL's response was to tell listeners that "another radio station tried to ruin our concert," and to "thank all our fans" for attending their wonderful show. But the funnier response came when they sponsored the Party in the Park opening the Fourth of July weekend, featuring Weird Al Yankovic. After a sudden thunderstorm blew in, delaying the start of the performance, the emcee proclaimed that the show would go on—"And he's not going to lip-synch! He's going to be live!"

By then, we were a month into our "summer war." We made it our goal to drive out WGCL's program director by Labor Day, and we were relentless. I was constantly on the phone with J.R. Nelson at Z-100 in New York, who was producing and recording WGCL parody songs based on current and recent hits. Nelson could duplicate the style of the original vocalist so closely you couldn't tell the difference. Dan Hartman's "I Can Dream About You" became "I Can Lip Sync for You." David Bowie and Pat Metheney's "This is not America" became "This is not Baboonland," and maybe best of all, Ray Parker, Jr.'s "Ghostbusters," one of the summer's biggest hits, became "Baboonbusters." The lyrics played up lip-synching and payola. Nelson's version was so good it sounded better than the original and drew requests from club DJs for dubs. We put all the songs in heavy rotation, in all dayparts.

WGCL threatened not to report any product they were playing from Arista, Parker's label, to the trade papers if we weren't cease-and-desisted. More importantly, they pressured Donnie Ienner, who was running national promotion for Arista and had become one of Leo's closest friends. He appealed to Leo's friendship, but I refused to budge. I told him he'd have to cease-and-desist us to get us to stop playing it—and if he did, we'd read it on the air, explain the reasons why, and give out Arista's phone number. Instead of sending the cease-and-desist, Ienner contacted Columbia Pictures (no relation to Columbia Records) and had the order come from them. We read it on the air, and accused WGCL of hiding from the truth by censoring us.

We began producing "The Temple of Baboons," a series of "soap operas" for an eighties version of the "Buzzard Theater of the Air," which played off things actually happening at WGCL. There is no better source of information than disgruntled employees, and WGCL had plenty. They kept me updated daily. I was even provided the daily routine of everyone at the station. Whenever one of the baboons monitored WMMS, we'd mention it and the person doing the monitoring, on the air.

The "Temple of Baboons" episodes ran from a couple of minutes to five, depending on how much material we acquired. They usually involved a conversation between the program director, played by Spaceman Scott, and the music director, played by Denny. We never had to mention the station by name—just as "the baboons"—but identified it by having on-air personality Kenny Clean play someone who'd knock on the door, asking, "Hey man, is this the bus station?" And getting the reply, "No. It's across the street."

We didn't schedule the episodes. Whenever we had enough updated information, we produced a new one and rushed it on the air. When we learned that one of their jocks was arrested for assaulting his girl friend, we worked that into a "Temple" episode, followed by a public service announcement on where battered women could seek help. When we learned another had stolen from the station's prize closet, we used the news and identified the perp. In every episode we mocked an executive trading commercial time for personal lawn maintenance and ran a continuous loop of "Payola Blues" in the background. The local record weasels, most of whom did not like playing second fiddle to pay-for-play schemes, would check in to find out when the next episode would run. I knew they'd tip off Travis, which was good. We wanted him to hear them and quiver. The label guys also started feeding us information. We had more than we could use.

The attacks became too hot for the management of WGCL. The allusions to payola and other improprieties hit too close to home. The constant barrage and questioning of the way the station was operated began to affect sales. The labels needed WGCL for the *Radio & Records* charts, but the station's clout was diminishing, and the labels wanted no part of the war. Even K. Michael Benz, head of the Greater Cleveland Growth Association, was being asked about the group's relationship with WGCL. I'm sure he didn't appreciate the "Temple" episode in which general manager Kim Colebrook, renamed Dim Dolecrook, tried to secure key promotional dates from the Greater Cleveland Tumor Association. Carl received complaints from Colebrook and others to stop the series, but he ignored their requests. Episodes were churned out at a rapid clip and played on *The Buzzard Morning Zoo.*

On the Friday morning before Labor Day, Colebrook fired Travis. We had achieved our goal of getting him out by the holiday weekend. A few labels were upset to lose a station they could use to manipulate record charts, but their local and regional weasels on the front lines were ecstatic, hoping this would put an end to WGCL's Parallel One reporter politics.

We presented our final "Temple of Baboons" segment, the firing of Bob Travis, on the Wednesday after Labor Day. In it, we sent Travis to hell, where he was forced to listen to a tape loop of WGCL playing Slade's "My Oh My," the song that started it all, for eternity. We had calls and letters from listeners all week, thanking us for ridding Cleveland of the WGCL lip-synching baboons.

The new WGCL debuted almost immediately. Colebrook hired consultant Randy Michaels (later best known for his associations with Jacor and Clear Channel), and C.C. Matthews, his close friend, as program director. The playlist was slashed to a handful of currents in high rotation. From that point on, WGCL's music practices were under close scrutiny. Michaels, an unimaginative programmer but a pretty good bully when he had enough bodies to hide behind, wanted to do a campaign where WGCL would put the "Buzzard in a blender." It was immediately nixed. The last thing Colebrook wanted was another attack from WMMS.

We had beaten our rivals. It was our best summer, and we were having a record-breaking year.

CHAPTER 26

CHOOSING SIDES

We became the near-perfect AM-FM combination in April 1984, when WHK dropped its flagging country music format for oldies and adopted the new monicker 14-K. WHK played the roots of rock while WMMS played the best new music. We were covering rock and roll from the womb to the tomb. WHK's program director stayed on, and I was promoted to Cleveland operations manager to oversee the programming, promotion and marketing, and engineering of both WMMS and WHK.

It was a lot of fun being involved with a format of the music I grew up with. We made it clear to our potential audience that 14-K would be a gritty rock and rhythm and blues outlet with a large playlist; we wouldn't air the wimpy stuff like the Carpenters, Bobby Sherman, or Barry Manilow. That was WMJI and WLTF music: safe, nonthreatening oldies in bland formats. Music for people who didn't really like music. I was adamant about finding the original monaural versions and mixes of all the hits we played. The album version of a hit song often was not the version released as a single. Listen to "Time Is on My Side" by the Rolling Stones from their *High Tides and Green Grass* greatest hits album, and then listen to the same song on the original single release—a noticeable difference. I wanted to duplicate as closely as possible the original Top 40 listening experience. We even added a touch of reverb to sound authentic. I contacted area record collectors to locate the hit singles of local acts like the Poni Tails, Outsiders, and Grasshoppers and tracked down songs like "442 Glenwood Avenue" by the

Pixies Three, which didn't chart well nationally but were top ten in Cleveland. 14-K was to be as uniquely Cleveland as WMMS.

There's nothing more fired up, in a positive and motivating way, than a fired-up Carl Hirsch, and he was fired up about 14-K. He got Johnny Holliday, the former WHK afternoon drive announcer who had gone into network sports commentary, to help launch the station—and later brought him back as emcee of his high school reunion, which gave us a chance to make Johnny a guest DJ. We referred to 14-K as our "transistor sister," and borrowed Phil Spector's "Back to mono" slogan. David Helton gave it a logo that was different from WMMS's but obviously related. Keeping everything in the family, we used Boom's voice for the station sweepers. I let his *Solid Gold Sunday Morning* show, once the sole spot for fifties and sixties oldies on Cleveland radio, run until the end of July, using it to cross-promote 14-K in the interim. We had what I'd been waiting for—especially for our older demographic born in the late forties through the mid-fifties. They were fans of WMMS today, but grew up with the oldies. If they weren't listening to WMMS—I'd prefer they'd be sampling 14-K.

For years we discussed having a traffic service for WMMS, but it always got relegated to the bottom of the list. There were always items more pressing. Then WJW radio, a news-talk station, played a trick that forced our hand. Someone at WJW learned we were monitoring them for traffic reports. One morning they delivered a bogus report, which we copied. They immediately ran a corrected version of theirs, but our news department didn't catch the correction. We got flack from listeners upset that they were taking alternate routes for nothing, or that they were driving past the scene of the purported accident and saw nothing. This was in the days before cell phones, so the complaints didn't come in until after 9 a.m., past the commuting rush. Accuracy is a cornerstone of a morning show: we needed our own traffic service.

We signed with Baron Aviation, a small company run by the husband-and-wife team of Dave and Pat Baron. He was already doing traffic reports for WGCL as "The Red Baron," and I didn't want to use the same service as WGCL. Kathy Kodish at Baron arranged for us to get Pat. We had to come up with another surname for her, to avoid confusion with Dave. I thought of Pat Brady, which was the name of a character on the old Roy Rogers TV show. The new service cost us a few commercial spots, which we could easily add without much notice, and Baron could sell them for a greater price because they were on WMMS. I always felt we got the better end of the deal because Pat's traffic reports were more thorough than her husband's on WGCL, and her upbeat but authoritative personality was a natural for our morning show.

To keep our listeners updated on the latest music news, we set up a special recorded phone service, updated at least twice a day. It was an outgrowth of the WMMS concert information line, which updated listeners on the latest information for area concerts. We co-sponsored them with beer advertisers—Bud got the concert line, Miller got news. Rhonda also set up a system to update air talent continually with entertainment news. If a band like Deep Purple was getting back together, you'd hear it first on WMMS. We wanted listeners to consider WMMS the first choice for any entertainment news, with every show giving at least one "breaking" story daily. Everyone likes to be first with news, and the person relating it is often asked, "Where did you hear that?" I wanted the answer always to be "WMMS."

We landed national exposure in July on a USA Network special, *Radio 1999*, where they spotlighted the top albums we were playing and featured one of our animated Buzzard TV spots. I thought we might have an album of our own on the same month, when we secured John Cougar Mellencamp for a free *Coffee Break Concert* almost a year in the making. He performed acoustic and solo, as he hadn't before, in an intimate hour that was one of our most acclaimed shows. Contractually, we didn't have the rights to re-run it, which led to the hope his label might release it. Despite its excellence, they never did.

·   ·   ·

Internal politics were a factor we weren't used to at WMMS—Carl Hirsch didn't allow it. He wanted conflicts at the station to be external, not internal. That began to change with a new name I had started hearing in 1983. After Gil Rosenwald returned from a trip to the Bay-area Malrite stations, all he could talk about was Jim Wood, who worked for KSAN and KNEW, Malrite's stations in Oakland. He considered himself a computer specialist, and he jumped at the chance to offer his help to WMMS.

We had built our research department into a major force, and used it for polling purposes as well as for programming and marketing. It was overseen by Mary Ann Gambata, who started as an intern (with Nancy Alden, later the "Lady in Red" of WDOK) and who filled any research need we had, from election polls to pop culture. But Gil suggested I fly to Oakland for a few days to see Wood's operation. I did, and I wasn't impressed with the operation or Wood—a short, pudgy, sickly looking man who wore smoked aviator glasses too large for his face and chain-smoked cigarillos. After I told Gil I preferred the status quo, he went from suggesting to insisting that we switch to Wood's system, with computers and software Wood wanted us to buy from his connection in Oakland.

It took only a few weeks to realize Wood's motives. He wanted to learn everything he could about WMMS, and to take credit for success he had no part of. He contacted Rhonda Kiefer, my programming assistant, telling her I'd approved her providing him specific details on how we compiled our music—everything from calling stores for sales to whom we were researching and why. He was especially interested in knowing about the difference between musical tastes of the east and west sides of Cleveland. I learned of this when Rhonda copied me the cover letter she sent Wood with the information. Wood claimed it was a misunderstanding when I called to ask why he'd misled Rhonda and violated protocol by going directly to her. A few minutes after that call, I got one summoning me to Gil's office. He agreed Wood should have handled things better, but then he dropped a bombshell—he was creating a new Malrite "research" position, and Wood would be moving to Cleveland.

I hid my disbelief. When I met with Leo and Denny to fill them in, their response was the same as mine. We had built a first-class radio station, fulfilling and even surpassing all expectations. Why this? And I talked to the program director at one of our Oakland stations. It turned out he already knew Wood was headed to Cleveland and added, "He's your problem now, not mine. Watch your back. The guy's a real sicko and lives to create problems. I give him a few weeks before he claims to have invented the Buzzard."

Though we had become dominant and somewhat respectable, we were still a lightning rod for controversy, and we were giving heavy airplay to Prince and his associated acts, who were responsible for numerous sexually charged titles. Prince's "Erotic City" contained the line, sung to Prince by Sheila E.: "we can fuck all through the night." Vanity had a song about ejaculation, "Pretty Mess," and Apollonia 6 had "Sex Shooter." Prince was also attacked for "Darling Nicki," a track from his *Purple Rain* soundtrack, about female masturbation.

Cleveland Councilman Lonnie Burten claimed to have heard the unedited version of "Erotic City" on the radio, and "on the radio" quickly morphed into "on WMMS." He proposed a nonbinding "emergency resolution" urging radio stations "to refrain from broadcasting or playing recordings containing sexually explicit language." Passed without hearings by City Council on October 1, it was signed the next day by Mayor George Voinovich and took effect on October 4.

"Erotic City" was, for a few weeks, our single most played and requested track—but we had edited out the offending word with a drumbeat. It later turned out that both urban stations, WDMT and WZAK, had played the unedited version, as did Top 40 WRQC. After the resolution, however, they cleaned their playlists of all the suggested sexually explicit songs. We didn't. I took the other approach and compiled a list of every purportedly explicit song from the 1940s through the 1970s, and transcribed "Sixty Minute Man," a popular rhythm and blues tune by the Dominoes in the early fifties, to prove my point. That made it a dead issue, and I got Vanity to be a guest on Jeff and Flash's show to celebrate. Touché.

That same year members of the Cleveland chapter of the National Organization for Women (NOW) asked for a meeting to discuss our programming. Matt the Cat was slightly embarrassed because his sister was one of the three women in the NOW delegation at the meeting. I figured there would be little concern about our operations. We had women on the air doing their own programs, and not playing the common role of morning show laugh track. Programming assistant Rhonda Kiefer worked in management with independent duties. We played a wide variety of female artists. We had a "no chick" policy about names that could be considered derogatory.

NOW had only one major complaint. It was our occasional airplay of a song by the Sensational Alex Harvey Band titled "Gang Bang," with the chorus, "Ain't nothin' like a gang bang/to chase away the blues." All eyes in the room locked on me. The comment caught me by surprise. Trying to think of an appropriate answer, I began rambling about lyrics in general and how easy it is to misinterpret them. The stalling didn't work. A NOW rep asked, "Why are you playing that song which is not only highly derogatory toward women, but also promotes rape and violence?"

I said there was no way WMMS would condone or promote any crime against women, and doing my best to think quickly, explained that there is a difference between a gang rape and a gang bang. I said, "A gang bang, as the lyrics suggest in this song, means the woman's enjoying it . . . ," and they never even heard me say "and it is consensual." They took turns berating me for insensitive remarks. The end result? They got their own half-hour weekly public affairs program on WMMS, *A Woman's Place Is NOW*, for which we provided NOW our production facilities and promotion and marketing.

We might have been late with Michael Jackson's *Thriller*, but we made the party with *Victory*, the 1984 album for which he reunited with his brothers for the first time since 1980's *Triumph*. Actually, *Victory* was more like the Beatles' *White Album* or Fleetwood Mac's *Tusk*, a collection of solo projects on which the brothers, as a group, did not appear on every track. Its first single, "State of Shock," featured Michael in a duet with Mick Jagger, and the group used a stand-in for Michael on the video for its other hit single, "Torture." But he was still a red-hot superstar, and his participation in the album marked his first new recordings since 1982.

Coinciding with its release, a *Victory* World Tour was announced. It reunited all the Jackson brothers, including Jermaine, who had not performed with them since they quit Motown Records in 1975, but not Jackie, who was on the album but didn't tour due to a knee injury. Like most events involving Michael Jackson, the tour was unconventionally supported and financed. Charles Sullivan, the son of New England Patriots owner William "Billy" Sullivan, would no longer risk any stadium shows without up-front guarantees. Sullivan had invested millions in the tour and was coming up short when a number of the dates he fronted failed to sell out. The initial announcement had the group playing fifty concerts in the U.S. and Canada.

Cleveland was not among them. Carl Hirsch threw out a suggestion to me about bringing the Jacksons to town ourselves.

Knowing our musical direction, a direct relationship with Michael Jackson and the Jacksons would expose us to a wider audience. Despite our unique format, some non-WMMS listeners still assumed we were a hard rock station. Carl and I agreed that being a popular culture station made far more sense than being pigeon-holed as an album rock or a CHR or whatever. Carl knew I wanted to have the best radio station in America, and he was always there to back the attack. He asked a lot of questions before he'd back you, and he asked all the right questions. It was Carl, not Milt Maltz or Gil Rosenwald or Jim Wood, the naysayers, who built Malrite into one of the most respected radio chains in the country. It was Carl who provided autonomy when I and others needed it. Carl never threw away money. Every dollar he invested, he got back ten.

I agreed that the tour was worth the gamble. Carl did the numbers and made the deal. It guaranteed the Jacksons $2.7 million up front for two nights at Cleveland Stadium. For that, we would get "WMMS Presents" on all the tickets and be the exclusive distributor. Belkin would produce the shows. We faced problems from the start. One was simply that October was, for all practical purposes, too late in the year and unpredictable for an outdoor stadium. Financial reasons, and the stadium's large capacity, gave us no choice but to take the risk. We had to sell out those two nights at Cleveland Stadium, or come close, to cover costs, and that raised another problem: we were right under the gun. The tour was set up six to nine months past Jackson's peak popularity. A few weeks later would've been too late.

Prince had replaced Michael Jackson as our most requested artist, and we were giving Prince and his associated acts heavy airplay. We upped the rotation on a number of Jackson songs after we announced the concerts, even adding a few tracks from *Off the Wall* we hadn't played before, and did our best to butt them as close to Prince as possible. In other circumstances, we would have played Prince even more and Jackson less. Of more concern to me was early news of ticket sales for the Prince tour that followed the runaway summer success of his movie, *Purple Rain*. It was scheduled to open at Joe Louis Arena in Detroit on November 4 and 5, and demand was so great that two nights were added—followed by two more, which sold out immediately, and a fifth. Ultimately, Prince sold 104,600 tickets in seven sold-out shows, breaking the record of former champ Neil Diamond. We also got word that Prince immediately sold out three dates at the Capitol Center in Landover, Maryland—where the promoter was seeking additional dates and claiming that the Jackson concert at RFK Stadium a week earlier did not set any records.

Prince's tour included two dates at the Richfield Coliseum for Cleveland in December. Because of the Jackson shows, Carl Hirsch and Jules Belkin agreed to slightly delay their announcement and ticket sales. It wasn't Belkin's problem, it was ours, and we knew it.

Then Cleveland Councilman and self-promoter Jeffrey Johnson accused us of shortchanging the minority community, claiming we had only recently begun to play Jackson. He fired us off a long letter which he copied to what appeared to be half of Cleveland, saying, "The deal disgusts me and should be changed." I told Carl we had been playing black artists as long as I'd been at WMMS, probably longer, and we had the files to prove it. He answered Johnson, saying, "Black artists have been played on WMMS for years. WMMS is not a white station, nor a black station, but a Cleveland station. I know of no other station or company willing to put up a guarantee of $2.7 million. Furthermore, our business arrangements are such that not one cent of the proceeds go to WMMS." Johnson shut up.

Leading up to the shows, the *Buzzard Morning Zoo* did a week of live remotes from Cleveland Stadium. The idea was to illustrate the stage being set up and to interview nearly anyone connected with the tour. It wasn't my favorite kind of radio, but there was that $2.7 million investment—and a growing chasm between Carl and Milt, who attacked the project as too risky from the start.

We lucked out on the Cleveland dates, October 19 and 20, with unseasonably warm evenings. The ticket tally for the first night, a Friday, was at 34,210 and 47,186 for Saturday. It came out to exactly 8,604 unsold tickets, of a total 102,000 tickets for both shows. I went the first night, reasoning that I'd catch the song list, check the demographics of the crowd, and spot anything we could improve to promote night two. I got backstage but didn't get to meet Michael. In fact, I was told to look away immediately if I did see him—no one was to have eye contact. I'd been to more backstages than I care to remember, and none had a weirder vibe than the Jacksons'. I couldn't think of anything to compare it to, and it was an environment I wouldn't want to revisit. I'd never want to see a Jackson family reunion.

It turned out to be the worst night for me to watch the show. I went up to the Malrite loge to get away from the crowd and decompress, but instead was waved over by Maltz, who was in one of the outside seats. He had a sour look on his face. Without even a hello, he launched into a tirade about Carl, which put me in an uncomfortable spot. I agreed with Carl about the investment in the show and could see the end result. All Milt could see was the here and now. To him, that was money sprouting wings and flying out of the stadium. I listened without comment. "What do you think of Carl Hirsch now?" he snarled, then spent ten minutes telling me how Carl "violated" the company rules by not presenting the concert to the board of directors before making a decision as president and chief operating officer.

Just before the concert began, Milt tapped me on the shoulder and barked, "Look over there," pointing to the west side of the stadium. "How many empty seats do you see?" I did a quick scan and said, "Seven, eight, nine . . . " He stopped me. "I see . . . one, two, three, four, five, six, seven, eight, nine, ten, eleven, twelve, thirte-e-e-n." With each empty seat, he cocked his finger as if he were shooting. I lost count. He stopped at fifty. Throughout the concert and during every song, he would interrupt me to say, "This wasn't worth it" and "CAR-r-rl wasted the company's money."

The concert was only slightly memorable. Michael had the stage presence; his brothers didn't. We pulled off a major coup when Kid Leo was approved to introduce them, thanks to our connection with Michael's manager, Frank DeLeo, who used to be a regional record promoter for Bell Records, with WMMS part of his territory.

The concerts cost us $258,120. Based on the $30-ticket, we would have broken even with a sell-out. The real winners, of course, were the Jacksons. They were guaranteed $2 million for two shows, and they got it up front, long before Milt was counting heads. But it was a success all the way around. Overnight, we enlarged our audience and enhanced our image. To me, and to everyone except Milt, Gil, Jim Wood, and Malrite's chief financial officer, the money was well worth it as promotional and marketing expense. My job was to translate that newfound audience into listeners who would spend significant time with WMMS. Having the best on-air team, a great support staff, and Carl's backing, I had no doubt. We had a respectable 10.9 percent share of audience in the fall ratings book, despite John Chaffee's calculation that no station would ever again see double-digit numbers on Cleveland radio, and a year later we would increase our share to 14.5.

That didn't silence Maltz, who looked for any opportunity to slam Carl in public. He acted as if he were disowning Carl and disparaged him daily, calling him "Reckless" Hirsch. They stopped speaking. Rosenwald and Wood took the opportunity to side with Milt like a couple of teacher's pets, getting his ear and criticizing Carl for promoting the Jackson concert.

But there was nothing reckless about the decision. It would have been reckless not to have taken the chance to do it. If anyone was reckless, it was Maltz with his public execution of Carl. It fueled politics that spread from corporate through the glass into WMMS and WHK. For the first time, everyone had to pick a side.

CHAPTER 27

"WMMS CAN CALL ITSELF ANYTHING IT WANTS"

WMMS couldn't be categorized. We weren't like every other album oriented rock station. We transcended formats. Nationally, I sparked controversy by challenging the complacency of AOR radio. In an interview in *Billboard* magazine, I said,

> AOR is going to have to get back to the original reason it happened in the first place. AOR used to be a broad-based, no-holds-barred format where you could play a wide variety of music and make it all work. But AOR got a little too structured and researched in the seventies and Top 40 took the ball and started playing the wide variety of music AOR once did. Last year was very healthy. There was activity in a lot of different forms of music. Unfortunately, in most markets it took a Top 40 station to show all of those different forms were compatible. AOR should have been there first . . . but the format had become too complacent and boxed itself in the corner.

My views put me at odds with radio consultants who were still preaching the "modal" gospel that most AOR music should sound the same—like what discontented listeners were calling "corporate rock." Having successful ratings while playing Cyndi Lauper, the Eurythmics, Culture Club, Duran Duran, and many other new music acts went against their grain. They didn't know how to do it, so they told their clients it couldn't be done. At WMMS, we were breaking music we weren't getting credit for because we were classified as an AOR station. Being lumped in with the others prevented us from doing promotions with non-AOR artists. Over half the music we played didn't fall into the AOR category, but it meant nothing to the record weasels.

Finally, in 1985, we formally declared ourselves a contemporary hits radio station. It was considered a bold move. In reality, we weren't much closer to traditional CHR than AOR. We didn't play jingles. Our announcers didn't scream. We reached an older audience that appreciated new music. But the announcement caused major rumblings in both the radio and record industries. The highest rated and most respected AOR station in North America was "abandoning" the format. Some called it a defection that would hurt the format. We stressed that the opposite was true and argued that it was unfair to listeners that we were denied the right to do promotions with acts we were playing because the record companies labeled them something other than what our format was. We were also weary of the bias many clients had against the format, which generally was driven by men aged eighteen to thirty-four. We led the market in women listeners.

Every trade paper covered it as a front page story. I told *Radio & Records*, "It's not that we have abandoned AOR, it's that the format abandoned us." We did it for no other reason than to take credit for, and do promotions with, acts we were playing—and to be taken seriously by the labels as a station that broke new music. Steve Feinstein, the AOR editor of *Radio & Records*, wrote: "WMMS can rightfully call itself anything it wants. It's a format unto itself. The station's never been restricted by the do's and don'ts of any format's unwritten code. WMMS defies format labels; calling it CHR instead of AOR is swapping one inexact format for another."

Could Be Wild's Bruce Moser told trade paper *Friday Morning Quarterback*, "I remember John Gorman speaking about the direction he was going to take the station three years ago at the *Billboard* magazine convention and people laughed and thought he was out of his mind. Meanwhile, the ones who were laughing are now out of business and WMMS is still highly successful."

My plans for WMMS countered what album rock consultants were pushing. They were saying narrow; I was saying broad. They were saying modal; I was saying variety. They said to shut up the jocks; I pushed for personality. When I said the format would have to be innovative and do new things, they said that's not what their research told them. I had talked to the heads of promotion for major labels about being given dual status, because of the current music we were breaking, but we were considered radicals against the grain. WGCL and other rival stations distributed every article on WMMS to clients and radio and TV editors, hoping some would question our move. None did.

We were not the first station to make the switch—just the one that got the most attention because of our wide playlist. We were the same station, regardless of format distinction, but there was one major difference. When we became designated a CHR, we became the most influential music radio station in the country. Stores stocked what we played, and others took notice. We were breaking more acts than ever before, because what we were doing was now being noticed by other stations that played new music.

We had built an extraordinary brand with a deep and wide heritage. We were constantly evolving with our listeners, and we had become the soundtrack of a young Cleveland. We knew how the system worked, and we knew we'd be more successful doing everything our way. If we noticed a song or an artist getting attention in other markets, regardless of format, we'd check it out for ourselves. We watched other stations live and often die by research, and we didn't want to follow. I called it paralysis by analysis. Our mistakes would be our own; the successes would also be. We knew what our listeners in Cleveland wanted and expected; they preferred us being a new music leader and not a follower. We played the hits, the hits to be, and even the misses, but let our audience decide which were which. We supported local artists, scheduling their music in regular rotation and not relegating it to late Sunday night.

We couldn't be all things to all people, which would have failed, but wanted to be the most things to the most people. We had to be a positive energy force in an often negative city. The Rock and Roll Capital of the World, words from an old Get Down that Murray Saul did, became our identity. It's an adage of radio that "as the morning goes, so goes the station." Most stations programmed accordingly. We considered ourselves to be in drive-time twenty-four hours a day.

A few days after Thanksgiving 1984, at a Christmas party in Hudson, I overheard that Fred Anthony, who managed a couple of Akron radio stations—news-talk WAKR and beautiful music WAEZ—was flipping WAEZ to classic-leaning album rock on New Year's Day 1985, with the new call letters WONE-FM.

Their company also had a classic-leaning rock station in Denver. I called the program director at the Malrite station in Denver, asked him to run a few hours of tape on it, and alerted Denny and Leo we were about to get some new competition from the south. Denny took a drive to check their signal strength in our metro survey area. He found they reached much of our turf but had a huge hole in Parma because of a ridge to the south and interference from nearby FM antennas there. I spent a couple of days with the cassettes from Denver, studying their music, rotations, and general sound. I believed WONE would adopt the same format. I was impressed and also annoyed. It went deep on tracks by familiar artists and played some forgotten songs: "Callin' Me Home" by the Steve Miller Band, "Low Spark of High Heeled Boys" by Traffic, "Sea of Joy," by Blind Faith, and "In Memory of Elizabeth Reed," by the Allman Brothers.

It could be a difficult challenger. We were heading in a different, new music direction. WONE would be playing our past. A certain percentage of listeners would try a new brand just because it was there. The station wouldn't make much of a dent in Cleveland, but it could hurt us in Akron, and its classic rock lean could hurt us with older males. Unlike our powerful, in-your-face format, theirs recalled the earlier low-tech days of album rock radio. Fred Anthony had it right. We had strong numbers in Akron and Canton and took considerable money out of his market. He studied it and determined that his FM station should adopt the format running in Denver.

I proposed a "Classic Rock Weekend" on WMMS before WONE-FM signed on the air. We'd have to make it work in tandem with our current format, and we had to act fast—the coming weekend—to be far enough ahead of WONE-FM so it wouldn't appear we were heading them off at the pass, though we clearly were. Denny and I assembled a special card-file system and enough tracks to keep any repeats to a minimum. And we'd need to secure greatest-hits albums from classic rock artists for giveaways. We billed it as a unique venture into the past "as only the Buzzard could do it." Jeff Kinzbach and Tom O'Brien produced cinematic promos, which we ran nearly once an hour starting on the previous Wednesday. We pulled out a few classic rock chestnuts during the week as a sneak preview. Knowing we had acquired an audience with little of our album rock past, and that the weekend had to be palatable to them, too, we called it something that never had been done before—thereby making it a first-time experience. We billed it, in other words, as one of those cool things that only WMMS could do. You had to listen.

It was a smash. Everyone on the air stressed that "once in a great while it's OK to visit the past, as long as you don't live there," and that we were playing music reserved for "this special occasion." We knew that we'd be back to our usual format on Monday, and we didn't want listeners saying, "Why can't you sound like that all the time?" Response was so strong, we went on with a new promo saying we were breaking all the rules and announced a second Classic Rock Weekend the following week. Two in a row. We made it sound like what were doing bordered on illegal, and once again stressed we were visiting, not living in, the past. The second week, we used our "often imitated but never duplicated" line. We made subtle mentions that anything this good was bound to be copied, but imitation is never close to the original.

We might have overdone it, but listeners never knew. When WONE signed on, its format was something that WMMS had already done—twice. The debut was anti-climactic, and we lost no ground in Akron and Canton. Had we not presented our weekends as we did, they easily could have backfired and provided an entry for WONE. Subtleties made the difference. We also had MTV on our side. Akron had lived with it since it started, and we rode the wave of its new music influence. Still, the Classic Rock Weekends proved to me that we had to respect the listeners who brought us to the dance. Though we had changed and they had changed, I felt we needed a more permanent link to the past. That led to the birth of the *WMMS Classic Rock Saturday Night*, 7 p.m. to midnight, where we dug deep to find enough forgotten and unique tracks to make the show special—with BLF and his unique style right afterward, to keep the party going with a mix of old and new and, of course, the obligatory "Maggot Brain."

Jeff and Flash were already hitting their stride and ready for the big time when John Lanigan, a unique personality whose WGAR morning show dominated the market, left in 1984 for a station in Tampa owned by former WIXY owners Norman Wain and Bob Weiss. When he left, we started picking up his audience—and knew it because we were suddenly getting requests for "Kiss You All Over" by Exile and other CHR tunes. We played some of them, only in morning drive, to attract the disenfranchised Lanigan audience. It was a major opportunity. But even before then, and before it evolved to the *Buzzard Morning Zoo*, Jeff and Flash were winning younger Lanigan listeners as they migrated to FM.

We had borrowed the "Morning Zoo" name from Z-100, because it reflected the cast around Jeff and Flash. Casey Coleman was added to do sports, replacing WJW-TV colleague Dan Coughlin; Pat Brady covered traffic; Boom Goldberg added a voice of authority when topics threatened to become too silly, and quick-witted Ruby Cheeks added a woman's touch to what had been a male-driven show. I hired her before I even had an opening for her, and she'd won a following working weekends and fill-ins as our full-time part-timer.

And we had another unique character from the cleaning crew for our floor: Kenny Clean, who was literally the janitor who came in for the wastebasket every night. He was naturally funny, and I started working him into the show. His popularity soared along with his catchphrase, "Sho' you right," an affirmation that started much of what he had to say and became his trademark. People picked it up, and Jim Marchyshyn had buttons made with it, no name or call letters necessary. We'd play an R&B song every morning with Kenny running the "Soul Meter " to measure how much soul it had, every so often slipping in a deliberate dog.

Kinzbach was blessed with a perfect announcer voice, and as a former production director had an unparalleled sense of timing. It solidified a format that could reach well beyond the limits of the core WMMS audience. Tightly formatted in only commercial and segment placement, the show combined news and information with mass appeal humor and celebrity guests. It was also the most phone-intensive, audience-interactive show Cleveland had heard. Special features came from unusual sources. The first *Star Trek* movie provided one; its plot featured an alien craft destroying anything in its path. Driving back to the station from an afternoon screening of the film, I had the idea for a feature where listeners could call in to vent on the air and destroy something they don't like. Jeff brought up the Cleveland Mafia assassination of Danny Greene, killed when his car blew up, and that evolved to "Blow Something Up," which proved to be a celebrated, much-discussed and politically incorrect addition to the show. "Token Jokes" came from "Tokin' Jokes," an underground newspaper feature of pot-inspired humor from the seventies.

John Lanigan did not last long in Tampa. Though he showed a steady rise in ratings there, the rest of the station didn't. It changed to a format Lanigan wasn't compatible with, and he was out of work. We heard he'd been flown to Cleveland by WLTF. Their meeting went nowhere because they were far apart on money. But Larry Robinson heard Lanigan was in town, contacted him, and offered him morning drive on WMJI. Lanigan took the figure he had in mind and raised it, and Robinson didn't blink. WLTF heard of the deal and threatened legal action, but Robinson ended it by sending a check for the airfare and hotel room WLTF had provided. By September 1985, Lanigan was back, replacing the then husband-and-wife team of Dan Deely and Kim Scott on WMJI. It set the stage for a morning battle, but Lanigan's months away gave the Zoo a chance to gain the lead position.

One of our most ambitious projects was inspired by the all-star cast of Band Aid, which was organized by Bob Geldorf of the Boomtown Rats, performing the song "Do They Know it's Christmas" to raise money for charities to feed starving Ethiopians. The performers included Bono and Adam Clayton from U2, Phil Collins, Bananarama, and members of Duran Duran, Spandau Ballet, Ultravox, Frankie Goes to Hollywood, and Culture Club. A U.S. version, "We Are the World," followed; organized by Harry Belafonte and his manager, it was written by Michael Jackson and Lionel Richie, and featured Bruce Springsteen, Kenny Rogers, Lionel Richie, Michael Jackson, Tina Turner, Billy Joel, Steve Perry, and Bob Dylan. Then came a Canadian charity record organized by Bryan Adams and his manager, Bruce Allen: "Tears Are Not Enough," featuring Neil Young, Gordon Lightfoot, Burton Cummings, Anne Murray, Joni Mitchell, Dan Hill, Cory Hart, Bruce Cockburn, Geddy Lee of Rush, and Mike Reno of Loverboy.

Denny and I decided to do the near impossible: put together an all-star cast of Cleveland musicians—including native talent who had moved—and record our own charity song. We didn't consider it far-fetched. In fact, we thought we could score a national label to distribute it. We decided to help an Ethiopian relief charity, and also to send 10 percent of the profits to local food banks. Denny, Jim Marchyshyn, and I set up a lunch in late March at Jim's Steak House to run the concept by Marc Benesch, a local Columbia Records rep, to see if he'd be interested in pitching it to the label. He agreed to that much, and we were certain it would fly.

It wasn't that easy.

Denny spearheaded the project, contacting dozens of local acts and even former Clevelander Ben Orr of the Cars—who was living in Boston but had some Cleveland hits in the 1960s with the Grasshoppers, when Orr (nee Orzechowski) was known as Benny Eleven-Letters. Dennis Chandler—a musician who fronted the Stratophonics, an oldies cover band I hired as the house band for 14-K—pitched a song, "We Can Make It Happen." We invited WKYC-TV anchor and reporter Dale Solly, an occasional musician, to make a video of the performance. Denny booked the Beachwood Recording Studio to cut the track between April 15 and 26, and took a leave of absence from his weeknight show to supervise production.

As we started signing up performers, most of the performers felt the Chandler song wasn't resonant enough for a big chorus of singers. Michael Stanley was called in to write a new song, "Eyes of the Children," with the all-star group in mind. Only one ego outburst occurred, when it was Rocco Scotti's turn to sing and he was told what key to sing in. Scotti, an operatic performer famed for singing the National Anthem at Cleveland Stadium, lost his temper and said, "You don't tell me what key to sing in—I tell you what key to sing in," and stormed out of the studio.

We named the group C.A.R.E., for Cleveland Artists Recording for Ethiopia. CARE, the famed humanitarian organization fighting global poverty, initially objected but allowed us to use the name once we told them of our plans.

More than forty performers ended up participating, including Orr, Stanley, and Strongsville resident Ricky Medlocke of Blackfoot. It was a Who's Who of Cleveland music at that time. Musicians were the Michael Stanley Band: Tommy Dobeck on drums, Michael Gismondi on bass, Bob Pelander playing piano and synthesizers, Kevin Raleigh on synthesizers, and Danny Powers on guitarist. Vocalists were Medlocke; Pelander, Raleigh, and Powers; Skip Martin and Kenny Petus of the Dazz Band; Joe Vitale; Jennifer Lee; the Visions (Cianne Woods, Cherrelle Brown, Alecia Burton); Alex Bevan; Paul Fayreweather; Mimi Hart of the Bop Kats, and Donnie Iris. Chorus vocalists were Jim Bonfanti, Dave Smalley, and Wally Bryson, formerly of the Raspberries; Tom and Frank

Amato of Beau Coup; Billy Buckholtz and Steve Jochum of Wild Horses; Archie, Norris, Kenneth, Kevin and David Bell of You-Turn; Ellie Nore and Dave Smeltz of I-Tal; Audrey Goodwin; Shari Brown; Mark Addison Of Nation of One; Bill Pettijohn and Billy Sullivan of Moonlight Groove; Mary Martin; Mark Avsec of Donnie Iris & the Cruisers, and Dennis Chandler.

We premiered the "Eyes of the Children" single on June 26, and the C.A.R.E. video aired that evening on WKYC's news. WKYC also ran a "Making of the C.A.R.E. Sessions" special two nights later. It was Denny's baby right to the very end. He was even cutting and pasting labels on the tape boxes, which were being sent to other stations throughout Ohio. Though WGCL ignored it, WRQC added it.

After Columbia Records declined involvement, I approached Irv Azoff, president of MCA Records, whom I'd met when he managed the Eagles, Stevie Nicks, Joe Walsh, Dan Fogelberg, and many other quality acts. He agreed to distribute the song, even though it was fated to be only a regional hit. We revived our Buzzard Records and Filmworks label for the release. Thanks to Irv, we got it done. After four months of legal dealings and ego-smoothing, the song was released nationally on November 18 as both a single and a twelve-inch version. WKYC ran the video daily through the end of the year, and we managed to secure airplay on a couple of dozen stations outside of Cleveland. MCA got stock in the stores. It sold well, though primarily in Greater Cleveland, and I hope it did some good. Today, a mint copy of the twelve-inch goes for nearly $100 in collecting circles. The twelve-inch version also appears on a bootleg CD compilation of Cleveland artists that was sold in Europe.

CHAPTER 28

DEPARTURES AND DIVISIONS

Carl Hirsch, by design, had become less accessible and lost interest in the day-to-day operations at Malrite. By the summer of 1985, he was tired of making Maltz a wealthy man and being rewarded with constant goading and backstabbing, which started with the Jacksons concert and never let up. Carl resigned as president of Malrite Broadcasting to strike out on his own. He relocated to Los Angeles, where his new company, Regency Broadcasting, put up $11 million, a price then unheard of, to purchase KJOI-FM in Los Angeles. A few weeks later, Carl acquired a co-chairman and renamed the company Legacy. Within a few months, they were radio's fastest-growing and most successful chain.

The chair in Carl's office wasn't even cold when Milt Maltz began his campaign against Carl. He called me into his office less than a week after the KJOI deal and asked what I thought of Carl. I was honest. I said Carl was responsible for our success at WMMS and WHK and the overall success of Malrite. Milt sneered, and in what seemed to be a well-rehearsed routine, grumbled about how Carl "stole money from you and the company." From me? He started opening files from a thick pile on the table.

"Here's where CAR-R-L flew to LON-don on the CON-corde and stuck us with his expenses." Us? "Here's where Carl took a line of credit at a casino and gambled our money away." Our? No matter. It continued, Milt opening one file after another, showing me expenses while claiming that the spending was unauthorized. His tirade went on for twenty minutes. (I started worrying how Maltz would react if I ever decided to leave the company.) Milt finished with, "This is only a small example of how Carl robbed our company. Now, what do you think of Carl Hirsch?"

I said I doubted that Carl would engage in such activites.

Milt interrupted. He said he had Carl investigated, and suspected Carl had his own agenda ever since he lost the company over $300,000 on that Jacksons concert, which he never cleared through the board. "I am telling you," he sneered, "that Carl Hirsch put every radio and TV license we own in jeopardy. What do you think of Carl Hirsch now?"

I remained silent. I didn't want to be drawn into Milt's pissing contest. I finally said, "Well, Mr. Maltz, I didn't expect this." He stood. I stood. I shook his hand and walked out of his office. It was a harbinger of the year to come.

A few months later, *Crain's Cleveland Business* did an extensive front-page piece on Malrite, for which the writer interviewed station executives, past and present, with the exception of Carl Hirsch. I was asked about Carl and his aggressive attitude, and his quote that became the company's mission statement: We don't go to work, we go to war. I said, "Carl provided a certain spark and a certain enthusiasm. Carl definitely got you moving." The story continued with a quote from Joe Dorton, who was president of Gannett's radio division and who occasionally sparred with Carl over new acquisitions. He said, "Carl Hirsch had a great deal to do with (Malrite's) success."

Crain's was delivered to us every Monday morning. I had just arrived when Maltz's secretary paged me. Milt had to see me right away. When I walked in, he started bellowing about my comment: "There was NO REA-ZON for Hirsch's name to be mentioned! You could've talked about your stations and instead you talked about Hirsch?" I told him I was interviewed on a number of topics for at least twenty minutes. I was asked a question about Carl and answered it.

"Did you ever hear of NO COMMENT?" he yelled, claiming my

comment led the writer to contact Joe Dorton. "This turned into a Carl Hirsch story!"

I hadn't seen it yet, and asked to look at a copy. I read it quickly and said, "Two paragraphs after Joe Dorton's comments, it reads, 'Most analyst and industry sources said Hirsch's departure would have little effect on Malrite's future'—and the quote is from Jim Duncan of the *Duncan Report.*"

"I know who he is, and because of your comment about Carl, there were five"—holding up his opened hand—"paragraphs about Carl in this article, which is supposed to be about our future!"

I apologized, and promised not to bring up Carl's name up again—and, if asked, I would say "No comment." End of meeting. What a way to start a week.

Gil Rosenwald replaced Carl, but with a lesser title, "Office of the President." He did not get Carl's office, either. He also no longer had Carl as the buffer between him and Maltz. Carl usually knew how to contain Maltz's rancor and tantrums. Gil was different. He couldn't handle the overpowering and demanding Maltz and became Milt's punching bag. He grew tense. He never smiled. He started chain-smoking. He put on weight. He developed a very short fuse. Problems were exaggerated, good news was ignored.

In one meeting, Gil called Denny and me into his office, where he played us a generic TV spot for a rock station. It was produced by the Nashville-based Filmhouse Productions, which did national radio campaign spots where station call letters were inserted into an already-produced commercial.

We watched the spot, whose only socially redeeming value was a quick cameo by station friend Don Novello as Father Guido Sarducci. Otherwise, it featured quick cuts of sumo wrestlers and radios blowing up. It was strictly bottom-feeder material.

Gil asked what we thought of the spot. We told him we thought it was very adolescent and certainly not representative of WMMS. Gil said, "Too bad. I just bought that spot for Z-100 and I get a discount for putting it on WMMS, too."

Shortly after our format designation change, Gil set new guidelines that he claimed would be policy for all Malrite stations.

We added anywhere from three to seven—tops—new titles per week to our playlist. On average, of those titles, maybe half, at best, would end up becoming hits. I felt our position was to present new music—and information on the artist—and leave its providence to the court of public opinion, our listeners.

Gil now wanted to know the title and artist of every song we added on WMMS for airplay before notifying the labels and trade papers. He wanted the report immediately following my weekly Monday morning music meeting with Leo. This request reeked of influence peddling.

It got worse.

Gil did not listen to WMMS. He didn't know the music, nor did he ever pretend to. But a couple of weeks after we began reporting to the trades as a CHR, he instituted a Friday afternoon meeting to discuss new music we were considering for airplay. Soon he abbreviated the meeting, choosing instead to present me with a handwritten list of the songs he "suggested" I add. Never once did he order me to add a tune—and his suggestions never influenced me—but there were a few occasions when I told him we had added a local artist, something from an independent label, or a song he didn't list, and he unmistakably let it be known to me that he didn't agree with my choice.

Hirsch's departure was one of two losses I felt personally in 1985, though in the growing cauldron of discontent I knew both were going to happen. It was only a matter of when.

Jim Marchyshyn had more than earned his stripes, and his contributions in programming and marketing—where we were doing dozens of promotions, contests, appearances, and concerts a week—were unparalleled. He started getting offers from other stations but turned them down. Yet one from KSHE in St. Louis piqued his interest. They were offering more money, and their management was showing Jim more respect than he was receiving from

Gil. I wanted Jim to stay and arranged to meet for lunch with both him and Rosenwald. I did some number crunching ahead of time and showed Gil how our budget could be adjusted easily to accommodate a raise for Jim. But the meeting was a disaster. Gil refused to budge. He refused a raise or even the promise of one. Jim hated to leave but had to. After the lunch, Rosenwald portrayed him as a deserter and told people that Jim's promotional and marketing talents were spent.

Then in February 1986, Rosenwald started trying to get Kenny Clean fired. He claimed Kenny was dealing drugs, or that someone smelled alcohol on his breath. Another time he "heard," but wouldn't reveal his source, that Kenny showed up high at a personal appearance. After a few weeks of this, Gil called me to his office to ask why I hadn't fired Kenny. I told him I had no basis to.

A few days later, Rosenwald and WMMS station manager Bill Smith, without informing anyone, fired Kenny and told me he resigned. I learned months later that Kenny did not try to contact me when he was fired because of a threat from Gil that if he did, his family's cleaning company would lose the Statler Office Tower. When I pressed Rosenwald, he came up with a story that Kinzbach didn't like Kenny, had called his agent, Ed Keating, about it, and Keating called Rosenwald. Some staff members began referring to Rosenwald as Jerry Mahoney, Jim Wood as Knucklehead Smith, and Ed Keating as Paul Winchell, since it appeared that Keating was running the show. Rosenwald and Keating had become inseparable—a highly unusual relationship for a company president and a talent agent.

Creating rifts between managers became sport for Rosenwald. I wasn't sure if he feared Keating or just used him as an excuse to override my programming decisions. I was even told not to critique Keating clients Kinzbach and Kid Leo without Rosenwald present at the meeting. Keating, Rosenwald claimed, also insisted I not know what Leo's deal was; it made little sense, since the numbers not listed in the budget but shown in the totals equaled what Leo was making.

Leo had taken to wearing a golfer's wardrobe, which included a few loud-colored golf shirts and slacks. It wasn't my style but Leo carried it well. One morning I was standing in the hallway as Leo walked in. Gil walked up to me and whispered in my ear, "Here comes Bozo the Clown." The comment caught me by surprise. Why was he ranking Leo to me? Considering all of the developing conflict, I did not reply. "You have to keep an eye on him," Gil said after a few seconds of silence. "He's power hungry, you know and he's made some comments about the way you're handling things." I said, "Like what?" "Well, for one," Gil said, "you and Bill Smith are not going to be involved in any negotiating with Ed Keating on Leo's new contract. I'm going to do all future negotiations. That's the way he wants it and that's the way I want it."

We became a station of haves and have nots. The staff felt it was clear that Leo and Jeff Kinzbach were getting preferential treatment, and I was being called into Gil's office whenever Ed Keating felt his clients weren't being treated fairly. Some of the complaints were so preposterous I assumed Rosenwald and Wood were fabricating many to create conflict. Leo was often not available before his show due to golf commitments—even though, in his defense, he was golfing with the record weasels, which could be defined as work if the station got something out of it. Denny and Rhonda Kiefer had to take on more responsibilities to maintain our performance. In addition to her programming duties, Rhonda started meeting with the record guys Leo didn't like. On occasions when follow-through with a label was required, Leo would make calls during his show, which I felt compromised his on-air performance. There were also rumors, based on some odd budget figures, that Gil had to be getting a kickback from Keating's office.

I later learned the real reason why Rosenwald aced Kenny Clean: John Rio, better known as Mr. Leonard. Rosenwald had been strong-arming me to put Rio's Mr. Leonard character on WMMS. I was completely in favor of doing so but wanted the right setup to introduce him to the Morning Zoo crew. I had first heard him on John Lander's show on KKBQ in Houston, a rival station to one that Malrite had just acquired. I was impressed enough to steal Rio, who was not under contract at KKBQ, for our station. Under a separate deal, he already was doing bits for Scott Shannon at Z-100, and this put him fully in our camp.

After it happened, and Rio was on Malrite's payroll in Houston, Rosenwald admitted he "may have persuaded" Kenny Clean to resign because he needed Kenny's salary to add Rio to the Morning Zoo. He took it upon himself to make the programming decision that Kenny's character had run its course and was too close to Mr. Leonard's. (Rosenwald wanted listeners to believe that Mr. Leonard, who was white, was African-American, and he believed there wasn't room for two perceived African-American personalities on the program.) In fact, the morning show was coming in under budget and was sold out on commercial time. Clean's character was different from Rio's, and the two of them could and should have been together on the Buzzard Morning Zoo. Mr. Leonard, who was billed as the "assistant public service director" of WMMS, never showed up for work, and all of his bits were done on the phone. The Mr. Leonard character had a high-pitched voice, gave bad advice, and would do virtual interviews in the role of eccentric caller or, ultimately, sidekick. When he called in during a celebrity interview, he'd always ask, "How much money do you make?" He was irreverent, smart, and made a lot of well-deserved money.

By playing one side against another, Rosenwald had Maltz believing he was in control of the Malrite empire and putting out fires that Carl Hirsch never tended. Rosenwald's demands were starting to affect Malrite stations in other markets as well. Station programmers and managers were calling me to see if I could explain Rosenwald's insistence that WHK promotion director Cathy Bee, who was hired by Rosenwald while WHK had a country music format, oversee all Malrite stations' promotion departments, though she knew little about even the most basic rules of promotion and marketing. It was evident in WHK's invisibility in the press and at station-sponsored events, and in the way she set up promotions, often embarrassing ones, without notifying me or Bernie Kimble, who'd become WHK program director. Often, our production departments would flag questionable copy and call it to my attention. It was a poorly kept secret that Bee so murdered the English language, Rosenwald's secretary took over writing copy for her.

Hostility at the station took another upswing when the Sunday *Plain Dealer* ran a lengthy story on WMMS. Rosenwald called me to his office the next morning and accused me of "manipulating" the WMMS story to benefit me and asked why I didn't mention him, or Jim Wood and Bill Smith. He was insistent that I "controlled" his quote in the piece. I reminded him I didn't write the story and told him that most of what was in it was discussed over lunch at Jim's Steak House with *Plain Dealer* writer Joe Frolik a month earlier. He asked who paid for the lunch. I told him Frolik picked up the tab. Rosenwald called our business manager and asked her to bring in my expenses for the month, threatening to suspend me if I had paid for the lunch and expensed it. When Gil could find no such expense, he ordered the sales department not to use the *Plain Dealer* article for a "hype sheet," and referred to it as my "vanity project."

I was getting daily memos from Jim Wood, wanting detailed explanations of everything he heard on WMMS, from music to on-air delivery. His purported concern was "maintaining our success," now that we had achieved it. Denny said it best. "This is like Capitol Records telling the Beatles after the success of *Sgt. Pepper* that, 'You fellows have done a great job and achieved unparalleled success— and we want it to continue, so we're hiring these songwriters for you, and these producers, because we know what's best for your career.'"

When I suggested a new Helton-created TV spot, Wood claimed to have research that Claymation spots work better than animation. Rosenwald made it another one of his campaigns, this time against David Helton—who had done all our art from the beginning—asking why I hadn't found a better artist for a cheaper price.

Amid the needless chaos, we were rebuilding broadcast and production studios for WMMS and WHK under supervision of engineer Steve Church. Even then, we had to put up with Rosenwald sitting on purchase orders, just to let us know he was in charge. Church, a real innovator, was meantime inventing new devices to serve our needs that would be adopted by stations around the country. For our recorded *Rock & Roll Newsline*, he created an early version of a tapeless recording using audio circuits instead of tape; it also accurately counted the number of calls, which we could compile for potential sponsors. And we debuted his *Live Wire* talk show at 10 p.m. Sunday—a unique program whose likes had not been heard in the context of rock radio in Cleveland. One night he demonstrated "how songs are made" by recording a song, track by track, to the finished product at the show's end.

But our most time-consuming and politically charged project was keeping the fires burning for a Rock and Roll Hall of Fame in Cleveland—a campaign for which promotions assistant Gina Ior- illo and I were carefully guarding our plans. WMMS had pushed hard, locally and nationally, but getting the hall for Cleveland still was not a done deal.

CHAPTER 29

THE ROCK STOPS HERE

Defeat is an orphan, but victory has a thousand fathers. So it was with Cleveland getting the Rock and Roll Hall of Fame and Museum. Civic leaders, public and private institutions, entertainers, and everyday people all played large and small parts to bring the hall to the lakefront, and I was proud of the role played by WMMS.

But it was a victory that wouldn't have happened without one unsung hero. Long before there were campaigns, polls, and petition drives, he made the city's shot possible. His name appears in no histories, and most Clevelanders wouldn't recognize it: Edgar S. Spizel.

We knew him as Eddie Spizel, an advertising guy whose agency represented Cook United, the company that owned the Uncle Bill's discount chain and J.P. Snodgrass jeans and record stores. Jeff Kinzbach and Steve Lushbaugh did top-quality production, and Spizel ended up cutting most of his Snodgrass spots with us. When Cook United folded, he left town, moved to San Francisco, and built a successful agency there.

I hadn't seen him for years and was surprised when he called in 1984. Bill Graham, the famed rock promoter, was planning to build a rock and roll hall of fame in San Francisco, off Ghirardelli Square. "He's going to make it like rock and roll started with Haight-Ashbury," Spizel said, angry at the thought that earlier history might be ignored. His Cleveland pride was wounded. He said he was coming to town and wanted me to set up a meeting. The meeting included Kid Leo, Denny Sanders, and Bill Smith. Spizel made an impassioned pitch from the heart: Cleveland needed to beat Graham to the punch. "They can't be allowed to build it there," he said. "You're the biggest station, you can rally Cleveland."

It would be the ultimate Cleveland promotion, or a quixotic bust, and Spizel wanted us to roll the dice. We felt his passion and liked the idea but knew the station couldn't do it alone. First, I said, we needed to find out if we could get support from record labels for an alternative to what Graham was doing.

Enter the second unsung hero of the Rock Hall. One of the people I knew highest up the industry food chain was Tunc Erim. He was head of promotion and marketing at Atlantic Records and the right hand to Ahmet Ertegun, Atlantic's founder. Tunc, a good friend and a wonderful guy with a thick Turkish accent, came to Cleveland often. Cleveland was a rock and roll city, and it was his best market. He could bring a band like Roxy Music here, and they'd be treated like superstars. Audiences sat on their hands in New York and Los Angeles, but Clevelanders got excited about the music. Just as good, the musicians—and Tunc—knew they could stay at Swingos Keg & Quarter and get the privacy and "amenities" they didn't find elsewhere. For sex, drugs, and rock and roll, they said, Cleveland was the place to party. Tunc loved WMMS for being part of that and for breaking so much new music. He once told me, "You probably play more stiffs than hits, but you play them—and you figure out quick which are stiffs and which are hits." He considered it the record industry's version of Babe Ruth, striking out a lot but setting records for home runs.

I called him and explained the situation Spizel described. "You're close to Ahmet," I said. "How would we go about lobbying for a rock hall?"

"It's funny you bring this up," Erim replied, "because Ahmet is starting a rock and roll hall of fame." He said Ertegun had picked out a site in Manhattan, and the mayor, Ed Koch, was arranging a tax abatement. Ertegun planned to house exhibits, a library, and historical artifacts in the building, and to hold induction ceremonies. He had set up a foundation for it.

It was a complete surprise. A handful of people knew about it, outside Ertegun's circle of attorney Suzan Evans, the executive director of his Rock and Roll Hall of Fame Foundation, *Rolling Stone* publisher Jann Wenner, and some record company insiders. We learned later the foundation had been set up in 1983, spawned by the idea for an annual awards show like the Golden Globes. As Tunc explained it, it wasn't conceived as the grandiose thing it turned into.

And it would be in New York unless—what? "Tunc," I said, "if it's in New York, it's just another building. If you put it in Cleveland, it's going to be the centerpiece. It's going to be the focal point."

He said he'd talk to Ertegun. He called back the following day and said, "Ahmet has one question: What will Cleveland do for the Rock and Roll Hall of Fame?"

That was the question—and it was obviously one I couldn't answer myself.

The local music industry gave the idea a lukewarm response. Jules Belkin said, "Interesting, if it can be done." Hank LoConti at the Agora, who'd had plans drawn up for a museum in the Flats in 1981, was convinced we didn't have a chance. The record guys couldn't have cared less. Gil Rosenwald said I was wasting time on a dream. But Leo mentioned the calls with Tunc to Tim LaRose, whose family owned the House of LaRose, the local Budweiser distributor, which controlled a big ad budget. They advertised heavily on WMMS and co-sponsored station events. LaRose befriended Leo early in the relationship, and when LaRose talked, radio listened. He started calling other people. Word got around, and my phone call to Tunc Erim turned into "dialogue" with Ahmet Ertegun. LaRose was instrumental, through connections in both the public and private sectors, in calling attention to the proposal without it being looked upon as a Cleveland pipedream. We contacted the office of the mayor, George Voinovich, who saw the potential.

We told Jane Scott at the *Plain Dealer* about the meeting with Eddie Spizel and our plans to see if we could put any life into the project. Her story—under the headline "Cleveland to Get a Rock

Museum?"—ran on May 5, 1985, with a Hank LoConti quote: "I'm afraid New York will get it." The small story was noticed by Mike Benz at the Greater Cleveland Growth Association. He called to ask for details, which I glossed over lightly, and asked for connections to the music industry in New York. I told him I'd get back. I was soured on the Growth Association, which consistently favored WGCL and never treated us with respect. I shared information only after a friend at City Hall said she'd run interference so we wouldn't lose control of the project. I wanted to keep it from becoming another Growth Association campaign with WGCL on the inside track. But Tim LaRose had already obtained a list of industry contacts from Kid Leo and given it to Benz and others.

Once the idea went public, Clevelanders supported it. The effort brought in City Hall, Cuyahoga County, the state of Ohio, and the local congressional delegation, plus community groups and private interests. Everyone wanted a piece of it, and their names attached to it. Another unsung hero was Christopher Johnson, who became project coordinator of the campaign to get Cleveland the hall of fame. He put in endless hours, wrote scores of fundraising proposals, and chaired countless meetings with media and civil leaders.

Local media got behind the campaign and WMMS took the lead in promotion. Some of it might have been effective, some had questionable value. After the Growth Association insisted on a petition drive, in the summer of 1985, we joined other groups sending out interns to collect signatures. We gathered 650,000, but some of us wondered what it accomplished. More important, city and state officials were able to approach Ertegun's foundation by the fall of 1985 with the proposal for a major museum.

A number of high-ranking label executives and Wenner were flown into town a few weeks later on a tour of candidate cities. Tim Hagan, one of the Cuyahoga County commissioners, kept the meeting focused and united as a comprehensive proposal was outlined. But I remember cringing because the meeting, in the Clevelander

Club atop Erieview Tower, was in a room overlooking the bus station, not downtown and the lakefront.

One contact unique to us was Norman Durma, the Cleveland native and booster who'd become nationally known by his air name, Norm N. Nite, as a disc jockey and rock chronicler. After working at WGAR in the early 1970s, he left for WNBC and WCBS-FM in New York, and he turned the music history he gathered into the *Rock On* series of books. But he commuted back to Cleveland, and he offered his services as program director after we switched WHK to oldies. The job was already filled, and we couldn't meet his salary requirements for an airshift, but we bought a computer program developed from *Rock On*. Norm became unofficially involved with WHK, and he asked to be part of plans for the rock museum. He had impressive connections in the music industry. He helped pitch Ertegun and other connections for Cleveland. Norm stayed close to activities in New York, and he became a member of the Cleveland committee for the Rock and Roll Hall of Fame, along with me, Kid Leo, and Bill Smith of WMMS; Jules and Mike Belkin of Belkin Productions; Phil Locasio of WGCL, and record promoter Gary Bird.

As word spread, Cleveland's initiative made it look like the front-runner to get the hall, but we were far from a sure thing once other cities began to vie for it. Dick Clark said he couldn't understand why Cleveland would be chosen when Philadelphia was the birthplace of rock and roll because *American Bandstand* had started there. Detroit, Memphis, New Orleans, Chicago, and San Francisco also pitched the foundation, and most of them frankly had stronger claims than Cleveland's to being rock and roll's birthplace. Most of them also had a better image than Cleveland, which hadn't yet built the "comeback" identity of a decade later.

We based our claim partly on the fact that Cleveland was where Alan Freed popularized the term "rock and roll," and partly on something the recording industry could understand: the city's status from rock's earliest days as a "breakout" market for artists and records. Freed's Moondog Coronation Ball was considered the first rock concert. Cleveland was where Elvis Presley played his first concert outside the South, where Chuck Berry made his first public appearance, and the city where David Bowie broke out in America.

In dealing with the industry that invented hype, we weren't above using some hype ourselves. The assertion that Cleveland bought more records per capita than any other city, for example, was something that came up in one of our meetings focused on selling points for the city. To this day, I don't know if it was true. I'm not even sure how it could be proven. I said it, and I justified it, because when WMMS would play a record by an Alex Harvey or a Roxy Music, artists unknown to most of the country, it would sell well. The assertion was picked up and repeated, and it became another selling point.

Then there was the famous phone-in poll conducted by *USA Today*, which asked readers to pick the rock hall site from the eight major candidate cities. The poll had a certain legitimacy, because it was national and because each call to a city's 900 number cost 50 cents. It came down to civic pride: If you wanted the hall, you'd pay for the call.

Voting was on Monday, January 20, 1986. We pounded the phone number relentlessly on the air, as did other stations, and took the added step of setting up a phone bank downstairs, in the lobby of the Statler Building, where people could call at no charge—an idea neither authorized nor condemned by the Growth Association. People stood in line to make calls, and Cleveland jammed the lines, logging almost 38,000 votes by the end of the day. Memphis, in second place, drew about 1,500. *USA Today*, maybe knowing a good thing when they saw it, had a second day of voting. We pounded the number again, this time warning that other cities were getting a second chance to keep the rock hall out of Cleveland.

When voting closed, at 6 p.m. Tuesday, the tally was nothing short of astonishing. Cleveland had outpolled its closest rival by a margin of more than fifteen to one. The final results: Cleveland,

110,315 votes; Memphis, 7,268; San Francisco, 4,006; Nashville, 2,886; New Orleans, 2,500; New York, 2,159; Philadelphia, 1,044; and Chicago, 1,030. "The town loves rock and roll," Jann Wenner, who was president of the Rock and Roll Hall of Fame Foundation, told reporters. "I think Cleveland has the edge. I think this poll is really impressive. I think the city really wants this."

The hall of fame held its first induction ceremony two nights later at the Waldorf Astoria in New York City, honoring a group that included Alan Freed, Chuck Berry, and Elvis Presley. Norm Nite was the presenter for Freed.

By that time, my biggest fear was that Cleveland wanted it too much.

The odds against us were long.

I sent Denny, Bernie Kimble, and Jim Hale to cover the induction in New York, which Mayor Voinovich also attended. We were a little burned when we heard Mike Benz doing reports on WGCL, crediting that station with the Cleveland vote in *USA Today*, and learned he tried to lead TV reporters away from Denny. But the reporters knew who Denny was, and all three Cleveland newscasts carried his comments, including his perfect response to critics who said Cleveland was a poor choice for the Rock Hall because it hadn't produced any acts of note in nearly two decades: "Name a famous baseball player from Cooperstown, N.Y., or a famous football player from Canton, Ohio. It's not the players that played the game but the city the game was invented in."

The key was the term "rock and roll," as applied to a musical style by Leo Mintz of Record Rendezvous and popularized by Alan Freed, then dead twenty years. A memorial was going to be dedicated to him, and the Growth Association pushed for local media to organize citywide observances that would keep the Rock Hall campaign burning.

Promotions assistant Gina Iorillo and I came up with the idea of presenting a sequel to Freed's original Moondog Coronation Ball, held on March 21, 1952 at the Cleveland Arena. Finding that rights to the name "Moondog Coronation Ball" were not taken, we adopted it as our own and started planning a WMMS-WHK event on the anniversary, Friday, March 21, 1986. Station politics forced us to keep details under wraps; Gina's ostensible supervisor, Cathy Bee, would jealously attempt to thwart any event she tried to put together, and Gil Rosenwald and Jim Wood liked to create conflict. Once we revealed plans, the Moondog Ball did not sit well with the Growth Association, either; it was trying to present the Freed observance as its own creation.

I explained that we'd put on a free concert under the Moondog banner, featuring local bands and an oldies headliner. Chuck Berry was available. Eric Carmen, who had not played in public for a few years, agreed to appear, backed by Beau Coup, to perform "The Rock Stops Here," a benefit single for the Rock Hall he wrote with his brother Fred.

Even that wasn't without controversy. A week before the Moondog concert, WKYC-TV showed up unexpectedly at the station to interview me. We had world-premiered the "Rock Stops Here" single," and John Lanigan on WMJI accused us of paying off Eric Carmen to get the record first. Lanigan said it was "sickening when I hear other stations say we all have to work together and then they turn around and get all the credit that they can." Off the air, however, he told Fred Carmen he wasn't really that mad and just wanted to drum up publicity. It turned out that WKYC was upset because WJW-TV premiered the video version of the song.

The day of the show, we carried live remotes from a noon rally at Public Square, hosted by Denny, unveiling the plaque honoring Freed. Both Governor Dick Celeste and Congresswoman Mary Rose Oakar mentioned WMMS's contributions to Cleveland's rock and roll heritage. We also hired a plane to tow a banner reading "Happy Birthday, Rock & Roll from WMMS."

That evening, we carried "red carpet" coverage of notables arriving for what we called Moondog Coronation Ball II, on the first level inside Terminal Tower, and Oakar presented us with a copy of the Congressional Record honoring WMMS and Cleveland as the rock and roll capital.

Behind the scenes, it was a nightmare to the last minute; the stage for the concert couldn't be constructed until the last minute because building management neglected to get a required construction permit. But 3,000 people showed, including the governor. Local bands the Innocent, which featured a young Trent Reznor on keyboards, and Wild Horses played prior to Eric Carmen's performance with Beau Coup. Chuck Berry, scheduled to perform for his customary thirty minutes, stayed on for almost an hour and a half. Acoustics were marginal, but no one seemed to mind.

About thirty other related events took place throughout the city, including a showing of *Go, Johnny, Go*, an early rock film with Alan Freed, and Chubby Checker and Norm N. Nite spinning oldies at the Palace Theater. For WHK, we held a "sock hop" at Brooklyn High School, whose original auditorium was where Elvis had performed. We co-sponsored fireworks in the Flats with WKYC-TV, sponsored Moondog nights at Peabody's Down Under, the Akron Agora, and the Mining Company clubs, and set up a rock and roll midnight movie at the Hanna Theater.

We didn't have the Rock Hall yet, but we were getting there. No other city came close to matching what was done in Cleveland.

The call came to the station on Thursday, May 1, that the foundation's board had met and decided. The wait was over. We won the beauty contest. Cleveland had the Rock and Roll Hall of Fame. The official announcement would come on Monday, allowing time for a delegation to get to New York, but we spent the weekend announcing we had the inside track—and get ready to celebrate.

We were the Rock and Roll Capital of the World. And now the world would know it.

CHAPTER 30

KNOW YOUR CLOSE

Arbitron's fall ratings results came three days into 1986. Despite predictions that no station would ever again achieve double-digit numbers, WMMS had an unbelievable 14.5 percent share of the audience—up two points from summer and almost double the nearest competitor, easy-listening WQAL. Another survey company, Birch, released its results a few weeks later, showing us with an even larger 19.7 percent of the market—three-tenths of a share from owning 20 percent of the total market.

It was the dream come true. WMMS had become one of the highest rated and most respected stations in America. It was vindication for Denny, who had kept the station together during the Malrite mass exodus, while everyone was stuck with bottom-tier wages. It was vindication for me, going back to the years when Denny and I had pitched every FM station in Boston to try our format—and made broad predictions it could become the biggest station in the city. Well, we'd done it. Not in Boston, but in Cleveland. But we'd proved it could be done.

Distribution of our weekly WMMS Top Tracks survey reached nearly all record outlets in the five-county Metro Cleveland area, plus Summit and Stark counties. The survey was a personal favorite, because it hearkened back to those Top 40 radio surveys distributed to record stores in the fifties and sixties. We were getting constant local and national media exposure. Ruby Cheeks was picked as one of *Cleveland* magazine's "86 Most Interesting People," and the Sunday *Plain Dealer* did a feature on her. Leo represented the station on WEWS's *Morning Exchange* the next day. *Radio & Records* did a feature story on WMMS in its next issue, on our latest Arbitron ratings victory and our campaign for the Rock and Roll Hall of Fame. *Billboard* magazine followed with its own piece. Mary Strassmeyer, who once considered WMMS the microcosm of everything wrong in Cleveland, called Rhonda weekly to get the latest station gossip for her *Plain Dealer* column. Even BLF consented to a rare interview for the *Plain Dealer*, and the writer called him "one of the most unique people I ever interviewed."

We kicked off our tenth annual *Plain Dealer*/Camelot Records readers' poll. Voters had the chance to win hot electronic items of that era, but the biggest prize, one that would only increase in value, was the WMMS autograph book. It was a Rhonda Kiefer idea. Acts visiting the station would sometimes sign an office wall. Instead of that, she thought, why not have a book that could be seen by more people—and given away at the end of the year? Considering the number of celebrities visiting—musicians to politicians to comedians to actors—it became a major collection with well over 200 autographs. The only thing we forgot was to make two sets and keep one for posterity.

Don Novello called, asking us to send WMMS paraphernalia to *Saturday Night Live* for a *Miami Vice* parody skit, "Cleveland Vice." We locked up visibility in the movie *Light of Day*, which would be set in Cleveland and star Michael J. Fox and Joan Jett; Fox's character would wear a custom WMMS satin jacket in a few scenes.

We were spontaneous, living the reality of what was once a fantasy: that if you were not listening to WMMS you were missing something.

Pat Benatar's husband, Neil Giraldo, called Leo to announce her WMMS-sponsored concert in February; to punch up the announcement, we immediately gave away the entire front row of seats on the air—plus dinner before the show. The day of the concert, we presented the couple a cake for their fourth anniversary. Leo emceed the show and thanked Pat and Neil for their $16,000 donation in WMMS's name to local children's charities connected to her "Hell Is for Children" hit. Tom Cousineau and Bob Golic of the Browns presented them with a gold record and football jerseys from the team and WMMS.

Word came from *Rolling Stone* magazine that we had won "station of the year" in their readers' poll for the seventh straight year, this time with 40 percent of the vote. We held back from announcing it on the air until we locked up an appreciation day to thank Cleveland. In less than a week, we secured a free concert at Public Hall, featuring the band Night Ranger with local favorites Beau Coup opening. It was a full team effort. Nina Blackwood gave it the national spotlight on MTV and flew in as guest emcee. Vince Lombardi of the mayor's office gave WMMS a key to the city. Wanting to promote on all available levels, we also held a WMMS/*Rolling Stone* magazine party at the Mining Company and carried *Rolling Stone*'s awards show on a satellite feed from MTV.

Though we were unable contractually to land WMMS co-sponsorship, we got behind Jay Leno's appearance at the Front Row Theatre, notified his management what we were doing, and got Ruby to emcee the show—and Leno to thank WMMS from the stage for our support.

For our commitment to local talent, we sponsored the first Cleveland Rockers Hall of Fame Jam at Blossom Music Center, featuring the Michael Stanley Band; Donnie Iris & the Cruisers; the Innocent, featuring a young Trent Reznor; Nation of One; Wild Horses; and the band Cleveland.

Arista Records, which had done "best of the morning show" albums for Z-100 in New York and KKBQ in Houston, approached us to do a similar project for the *Buzzard Morning Zoo*. It was relatively easy since we had archived the morning shows. Arista would distribute it in Greater Cleveland market as a specialty item and earmark profits for charity. We planned its release to coincide with the fall ratings period and Christmas shopping season.

"The Best of Token Jokes of the Morning" were collected in a book. Promoted by Jeff and Flash in a series of store appearances, it went through three more pressings to keep up with demand. Jeff and Flash also hosted a day-long marathon of *Twilight Zone* episodes after I lobbied JC for more WMMS visibility on Malrite's WOIO, Channel 19.

Flash had our news department on top of every important story, and we built a "news as it happens" image with greater coverage than the AM news-talk station—leading Flash to be named news operations director for both WMMS and WHK. We never hesitated to interrupt a program at any time, day or night, if something happened worthy of a "Stand by for a WMMS Buzzard Bulletin." Pat Brady, flying a plane adorned with our call letters and the Buzzard, gave us the best traffic reports in the city—and made us the station that others now listened to for updated reports. We added a daily business report from Shearson Lehman Brothers, which provided its report in exchange for a mention. We had to be one of very few rock and roll stations, if not the only one, to do so.

We were covering all the bases. Creative dayparting let us serve multiple demographics. We knew our older demos were getting married, having kids, and settling down. We didn't want to lose them through lifestyle changes. When the Sesame Street tour had come to Public Hall the previous year, we had had had Kenny Clean host the show and give milk and cookies to 2,000 in attendance age twelve and younger.

Even our throwaway promotions got support. We did one with the Cavs, who at the time were a poor draw, giving participants a $2 discount on $8 and $10 seats. We expected 100 at the most, and 600 showed. Boom emceed at halftime and gave away a trip to Disneyland. It wasn't even our promotion, but he made it sound like it was. We remained frugal, compared to other stations, in spending promotional and marketing dollars, but we spent money when we had to—such as buying local commercial time in the Super Bowl, one spot in each half.

The annual Cleveland ski fair at Public Hall was produced by the same agency that handled WRQC, and our booth was set up off the main route in a lightly trafficked area. Gina Iorillo convinced a few of her friends to wear skimpy bikinis and roller-skate around the fair passing out WMMS items. Nothing in our agreement with the organizer preventing us from doing so. I nicknamed them the Buzzard Bikini Beauties, and they definitely brought WMMS the most attention at the show.

These promotions were gravy on our seasonal run of new WMMS Buzzard shirts, augmented by Buzzard sunglasses and key chains, and Buzzard Morning Zoo T-shirts. We earmarked profits from our spring-themed Buzzard T-shirts for the Rock and Roll Hall of Fame and Museum Foundation, ran 7,500 to cover advance orders, and had to order 5,000 more to meet demand. We looked into releasing Baby Buzzard Wear to add to our merchandising. After discussion with both major department stores, May Company and Higbee's, we went with the latter as exclusive retailer. We carried beverage coolers and beach towels sold exclusively at Blossom Music Center, and marine flags sold at boating stores. We had a half-million bumper stickers readied for spring; they cost $34,000, but the cost was underwritten by clients who were given coupon placement on the back of the stickers and mentions on-air.

We co-sponsored the Revco Marathon, providing each runner with a WMMS plastic bag holding a sticker and button enclosed, and sponsored the "Midwest Race of Champions" at Norwalk Raceway. In a promotion with Cedar Point, we printed up 5,000 visors for our annual Buzzard Day, logged as one of their busiest days of the year. At rival Geauga Lake, we did a "show us your Buzzard" promotion offering discounted admission to anyone wearing something with the Buzzard on it; attendance doubled to 8,000 from 1985.

We launched our first food item, a cheese curl snack called Buzzard Bites. It sounded better than it tasted. Driving past a Dairy Queen one day, I noticed a sign for the Blizzard, their signature shake, and thought it read Buzzard. That led me to suggest they promote the "Buzzard Blizzard." They went for it.

We were involved in a dozen different charities through various marketing campaigns and co-sponsorships.

The Greater Cleveland Growth Association tried to discourage national acts at its Parties in the Park because of pressure from WGCL, which was still smarting over the previous year's lip-synch humiliation and was no longer able to get national acts to perform for the event. We got around that by going directly to the mayor's office to propose a free concert of our own on May 23rd with Blue Oyster Cult and Platinum Blonde—billing the event as Cleveland Indians Day. The Tribe, playing Toronto that evening, was suffering the worst attendance in its history; rumors that they might move increased when we broke the story that the American League did not want the team to sign a long-term lease with the stadium. Mayor Voinovich and County Commissioner Virgil Brown supported our event. Mike Benz at the Growth Association and Kim Colebrook at WGCL were furious and tried to halt the concert. But we had all the necessary permissions and permits, and because it wasn't a Party in the Park promotion there was little they could do. As a last resort, Benz called City Hall, claiming Blue Oyster Cult was a "heavy metal band using satanic lyrics" and warning of likely disturbances. We held our ground, and 35,000 showed up for the free concert on Mall C, while the Indians drew more than 9,000 walk-up ticket sales. With no disturbances and not a single arrest.

In a crowning achievement the same week, Governor Dick Celeste appeared as a guest DJ on the *Buzzard Morning Zoo*. He arrived at 5:30 a.m. and stayed for the entire show, acting as part of the team. He was either a regular listener or had an astounding advance crew. He knew all the morning show bits, all the characters and their personas, and even kept political comments to a minimum. He was one of the best guests the Zoo ever had.

Working at the station, however, had become unbearable. The environment was toxic, each day was worse than the day before. Blame games were so common, I came up with the "Malrite salute"—fold your arms and point your fingers in opposite directions Memo wars and turf battles raged out of control. Morale, which should have been at an all-time high, was plummeting.

Cathy Bee was making promotional commitments without appropriate paperwork, which created confusion at both WMMS and WHK. Gina Iorillo and Maureen Duffy, who were supposed to handle WMMS promotion, found themselves being forced to fulfill commitments Bee had set up that we'd known nothing about. We had to outsource work to our first promotion director, Dan Garfinkel, to help straighten out the mess. Working until midnight and on weekends was commonplace, and Rosenwald refused to allow the hiring of any assistants, even though there were line items in the budget for those positions. It was as though he took pleasure in the problems.

In mid-May, *Los Angeles Times* writer Patrick Goldstein arrived in Cleveland to do a story on the city's successful quest for the Rock Hall and WMMS's unique radio format. I offered him complete access to the station. He talked to almost everyone on the WMMS staff and sat in on Denny's show. The result of his visit was a feature story in the *Times* Friday *Calendar* entertainment supplement.

The headline read, "Cleveland Is on a (Rock 'n') Roll."

Goldstein praised the wide variety of music he heard on WMMS, including everything from the Fabulous Thunderbirds and Van Halen to Prince.

Goldstein captured Cleveland and WMMS. Corporate felt otherwise. Gil was furious that Jim Wood had not been interviewed since he was also from California. He also asked why there were no quotes from Kid Leo or Jeff Kinzbach and how that would be explained to Ed Keating.

I told him Goldstein had been provided full access to the station and talked to a number of people. "If what you say was true," Gil said. "why are the only two people quoted you and Denny?" He also asked why Malrite wasn't mentioned in the article as the owner of the station—"and that we have two stations in Los Angeles, too."

Rosenwald and Jim Wood started grilling me about our music rotation format. I explained my system more than once—how every hour had different categories, how weekdays and weekends were different, how holidays, seasons and even weather might alter the categories, and how rotations were changed daily so no one could duplicate us. Rosenwald and Wood refused to believe that our "secret" was having great talent to execute the format. Rosenwald's eyes glazed over during the explanation. Wood said, "This doesn't make any sense." I replied, "A 14 share does."

A few weeks after that, I was called to another meeting with them and a former WMMS engineer who had built a computer program that he claimed could duplicate our format. It was a crude program that couldn't come close to handling our rotations, which were done with a card file augmented daily by hand, and it would be an unnecessary expense at best. Rhonda and Leo agreed we didn't need the system, but Rosenwald's pitch turned into a hard sell.

He stopped just short of ordering us to buy it, though he managed to get other Malrite stations to commit to it. Later I confirmed through a third party that Rosenwald had part ownership of the company selling the program.

A station that had never had secrets now had many.

In early July, I got an unexpected phone call from Tom Shovan, who edited and published *Pulse,* a weekly radio management trade magazine based in New York.

"Have you heard anything about Maltz putting Cleveland up for sale?" he asked. He told me a rumor was circulating that Milt had a deal that would allow him to sell WMMS and WHK in order to get full ownership of the WOIO-TV license, which Malrite then shared with other partners.

I brought the rumors to Gil Rosenwald, who wouldn't confirm, deny, or discuss them.

A week later I got a memo from Gil demanding a complete inventory of WHK and WMMS—covering everything from how many albums and CDs we had to the number of desks and chairs. And it was due in one week.

I started taking those "for sale" rumors seriously.

My relationship with Gil had become adversarial. We barely spoke. It was the complete opposite of working with Carl Hirsch, where there were no secrets and, above all, no bullshit politics.

My relationship with Leo had also changed. I don't know what he had been told, if anything, but he began distancing himself from me. We still had our Monday music meetings, but they had become routine and strictly business.

.   .   .

I was tipped off to a rumor about a new Detroit company negotiating to buy an AM-FM combo in Cleveland, most likely the troubled WGCL and WERE properties.

Denny, Rhonda, and I did some research and built a file about the Detroit company, to be ready to counterattack a new competitor if that rumor turned out to be true. We began in May to plot our programming, promotion, and marketing plans for the fall Arbitron, which wouldn't start until September. We considered it a given that we would face new competition.

We didn't get very far in our investigastion of the company rumored to be buying into the market. The new company contacted us, confirmed its purchase of WGCL and WERE, and, as the saying goes, made us an offer we couldn't refuse. It was far more money than Denny, Rhonda and I were making at Malrite—and it came with the promise of being able to run the stations the way we did when Carl Hirsch was in control. No interference, no politics, a decent budget, and the understanding that the new station would not go up directly against WMMS. They had, instead, identified a "hole" for a contemporary format which would share only a minimal number of song titles with WMMS.

I also received an offer from Carl Hirsch, but by then I had committed to the new company, Metropolis Broadcasting. It already owned WDTX, a Detroit station whose innovative programming was creating a buzz.

During this turmoil, we were putting the finishing touches on what would be one of our biggest WMMS Appreciation Days of the year, with INXS and the Del Fuegos. It was a bittersweet event. The band had crossed into star status—and we had them at the height of their career.

This was my final promotion with WMMS—and a farewell I could share with no one. I stood at the side of the stage, looking at the close to 20,000 people in the seats and on the grass. In my mind was a newsreel counting down the past thirteen years. Before INXS went on, the entire staff was invited onstage. It was the final time

I'd represent WMMS in public. To our listeners, we were still writing rock and roll history. Behind the scenes, politics and ego were eroding the foundation.

It was the most difficult moment of our careers. Denny and I were leaving the station we helped create, which had become one of the most respected in the country. On the other hand, we'd be leaving at the top of our game—the way Jim Brown did with the Cleveland Browns, when Art Modell ordered him to report to training camp instead of finishing work on the movie *The Dirty Dozen*. Brown went out a winner. Gil Rosenwald was our Art Modell, and we'd leave as winners, too.

I knew that the moment I left the building, Milt, Gil, Chaffee, and Jim Wood would launch character assassinations against me similar those leveled at Carl Hirsch. I expected them to be vicious and inexorable.

Just before I resigned, Lonnie Gronek, a former sales manager, replaced Bill Smith as general manager. Although I didn't know him well, I liked Lonnie and knew him to be a no-nonsense nose-to-the-grindstone manager. He avoided petty politics and was results oriented.

The first order of business with the new general manager was to finalize the fall ratings plans. It put me in an unusual position since I was only days away from being an enemy of the station.

I confidentially told a few people at the station of Denny's and my plans to resign on August 15. Someone was loose-lipped, which I learned when a memo was issued to the entire WMMS and WHK staff—as well as corporate—for a mandatory meeting in the corporate conference room for the same day. It was an unusual request since Maltz rarely spoke to or even acknowledged the peons.

Surrounded by Gil Rosenwald, John Chaffee, and Jim Wood, Milt, with a forced villainous smile, stood on his tip toes and began by growling about his love for everyone, thanking each and every employee for building Malrite into a "broadcasting empire"—and vowing that the empire would continue to grow and prosper.

Then his voice turned to a snarl. "But there are EN-im-ees among us trying to dee-STROY your company."

He mentioned the article written by Tom Shovan in *The Pulse*. "Do you know who owns *The Pulssse*?" Milt roared. "I'll tell you. Bob SILL-erman. And do you know who Bob SILL-erman is?" Sounding rehearsed, Jeff Kinzbach said, "He's Carl Hirsch's partner at Legacy." Milt thanked Jeff and spent a couple of minutes attacking Hirsch.

Then he launched into a tirade against Sillerman, who most of the staff didn't know. "He-e-e STEALS from his PART-ners and puts them out of business," Milt bellowed, apparently suffering from selective memory loss about how he seduced and abandoned his partner, Bob Wright, less than twenty years earlier, leaving him with a small Tiffin, Ohio station while he took the rest.

"I spoke to the gentleman there who wrote the story," Milt said in his guttural voice, "and he told me the story originated here. Now, who-o-o-o would try to hurt our company by spr-r-r-reading such a rumor—and what should we do to those res-PON-sible?"

Leo's turn. "They shouldn't be working for us."

Denny whispered in my ear, "We were set up."

In a private meeting with Milt and Gil following Milt's grandstanding meeting, I turned in my resignation "to concentrate on my radio consultancy" with the understanding that Denny would be joining me in that endeavor.

Milt said nothing. Gil said nothing.

Finally, Gil stood up, shook my hand, and said, "Good luck" in a manner that translated to, "the elevator is at the end of the hall," and I walked out of Milt's office, down the corporate side of the corridor, opened the door, walked into the hallway, pressed the down button, and got on the elevator, knowing I would never return.

I resigned from WMMS and WHK effective August 15. Rhonda and Denny resigned the same day. Nine other staffers, also tired of the Malrite politics, followed us in the days and weeks to come.

END OF AN ERA

When was the golden age of WMMS? You could ask ten people and get ten answers. Creative radio is about change. An age rarely lasts long, and it doesn't become golden until it's over. But if I had to pick a date when WMMS was "over," it would be February 25, 1988. A front page story in the *Plain Dealer*, complete with Buzzard logo, reported that the station had stuffed the ballot box to win the *Rolling Stone* Readers' Poll as "station of the year" for the ninth time by buying hundreds of magazines and having station employees cast votes.

Busted. Stuffed. Stoned.

The station was defensive and defiant. Listeners felt betrayed and angry. The respect they had for the station vanished. The exposé became a national scandal. I received a number of calls that day from people I knew at WMMS, WHK, and even Malrite corporate, telling me that Gil Rosenwald was openly—but wrongly—blaming me for leaking to the *Plain Dealer* the memo that led to the story. They also asked for advice on how to put out the fire. I said, "There's an old saying about when you're in a hole—the one thing you should *not* do is keep digging."

Here's what happened.

Gil Rosenwald was concerned that WMMS's dropping ratings and declining loyalty could cost votes from listeners in the *Rolling Stone* poll. Losing, he believed, would give ammunition to competing stations, which were already citing the ratings dip that caused some clients to demand lower ad rates.

I'd seen it coming. I don't care how successful something is, everything has a shelf life. WMMS peaked in 1985 and 1986. Eventually it would start to slide. Months before I left the station, I met with Gil to warn that we could not continue trying to be all things to all people. A new generation was coming up, rock and roll was still rebellious, and WMMS had become the establishment. We needed to continue reinventing ourselves. I even suggested buying a station—WDBN, the Medina station that became WQMX, was available—to create our own competition. Gil was livid that I brought it up, but more furious that I thought WMMS was peaking.

They'd come to believe their own hype. They thought they were invincible. They had to win at all costs. In November 1987, when the *Rolling Stone* Readers' Poll edition reached newsstands, Gil ordered WMMS general manager Lonnie Gronek to purchase 800 to 1,000 copies of the magazine through Rosie's, a downtown store. The number was set at 800 after a budget meeting.

This was new. For years, we had promoted the *Rolling Stone* poll on the air and encouraged listeners to vote. Our biggest effort was the year a roadie for the band American Noise brought several dozen magazines to a WMMS show they were playing at the Agora. The roadie worked for George R. Klein News Company, the newspaper and magazine distributor, and the magazines were unsold copies that would be discarded after the covers were removed and sent back to the publisher for credit. (It's cheaper than sending the whole magazine.) We invited listeners to fill out the ballots. I readily admitted to the *Plain Dealer* that I probably filled out four myself. But there was never any grand plan to purchase *Rolling Stones* in bulk.

This time, though, there was a plan. Gronek directed WMMS promotion director Maureen Duffy to purchase those 800 magazines, and to get the check from the station's business manager. Duffy made the request in a memo. A second memo strongly suggested that all station employees fill out ballots in the Malrite conference room, promising free pizza to those participating.

The first memo, from Duffy, was leaked to reporters Michael Heaton and David Sowd at the *Plain Dealer* by Walt Tiburski, WMMS's former sales chief, who was now co-owner of WIN Communications, which owned WQAL in Cleveland.

A copy of the same memo was also leaked by a part-time employee at WMMS, which confirmed its authenticity.

Gronek initially denied buying the *Rolling Stones.* Shown the memo, he told the *Plain Dealer*, "We buy the magazine and we distribute them to the staff and our family and friends and relatives. The company gets behind it. We take copies of the magazine to outside events and distribute them. I've filled a number of them myself." The quote became fodder for competitors, who joked about WMMS and Malrite having trouble coming up with 800 family, friends, and relatives.

Gronek also defended his decision by claiming that "if we didn't buy the copies, some other city would. We just do it bigger and better." That brought comment from stations like WNEW-FM in New York, which ran second in the poll. Program director Mark Chernoff told the *Plain Dealer*, "We absolutely do not, never have, and never will hand out or fill out ballots. That would be tainting the poll results . . . We don't even campaign." Mike Craven, the general manager of third-place WMMR in Philadelphia, called the WMMS move "less than above board." In fact, when the 800 bogus votes were removed from 1987 poll, WMMS had received only 200 votes deemed legitimate by *Rolling Stone.* WNEW-FM had 800.

Making a dreadful situation worse, Rosenwald and Gronek told Jeff and Flash to suspend regular programming to discuss the *Plain Dealer* exposé. The official statement, repeated throughout the morning, was that if WMMS was guilty of anything, it was "overzealousness on Cleveland's behalf." Kid Leo said, "We did it for Cleveland," a quote that backfired badly on WMMS. Worse, when TV stations confronted him for a sound bite, Leo wrote off the incident by saying he had filled out so many ballots that he had writer's cramp.

The next day's *Plain Dealer* had a second front-page story, with the headline, "*Rolling Stone* drops award after 'cheating' by

WMMS." It also had a full-page ad that WMMS took out for about $9,000. Under its six-inch heading—"SECRET?"—a six-paragraph statement said the station campaigned hard for nine years to win the Best Radio Station poll, openly talked about it, and "always urged its own employees to participate in the balloting—all at the station's expense, keeping in mind that the rules allow multiple entries."

It said they "realized long ago that the positive recognition of the station translated as a source of pride for Cleveland," and that they wouldn't be "intimidated" by "jealous competitors." It claimed that "overwhelmingly positive response . . . leads us to believe that you want us to continue in this effort for the city and the station. As usual, WMMS will act in partnership with you to maintain Cleveland's image as the rock and roll capital of the world."

If Leo's "We did it for Cleveland" comment was the coffin, this full-page ad provided the nails. The *Wall Street Journal* picked up the story, under the headline, "Repeat After Me: I Like WMMS, I Like WMMS." Brent Larkin's editorial column in the *Plain Dealer* said WMMS made a bad situation worse by defending the ballot-stuffing, giving Cleveland negative exposure nationally. Stations in other markets complained that Cleveland didn't deserve the Rock and Roll Hall of Fame. Even the City Club of Cleveland satirized the incident in its annual Anvil Revue broadcast on WCLV. (That upset Milton Maltz, because WCLV was one of the few stations he listened to for pleasure.)

Someone had to take the fall. Gil Rosenwald chose to sacrifice promotion director Maureen Duffy and contest coordinator Steve Legerski. Duffy was guilty only of reluctantly following orders. Legerski was whacked because Bee didn't like him either. Lonnie Gronek and Kid Leo objected that the firings would make them fall guys, when Malrite was posturing it did nothing wrong. Rosenwald initially refused, and then he agreed to rehire Legurski but not Duffy.

If there was a funny part of the story, it was that Malrite could have saved the $2,400 it spent buying *Rolling Stone* magazines, and avoided detection of vote-stuffing, if its legal department had reviewed the plan in advance. To boost interest in the poll, *Rolling Stone* tied it to a sweepstakes. Because of that, according to Federal Trade Commission regulations, voters did not have to buy the magazine for an official ballot. WMMS could have stuffed the ballot box with postcards and photocopies.

A revolving door, in management and on the air, had replaced the consistency that once was the most enviable thing about WMMS. Politics flooded the station, and staff aligned with whomever they thought held the highest ground. Too many people were making programming decisions. The station reminded me of a rock band that continues using its famous name long after most of the original musicians have left. A valued brand name has lost its class.

WMMS was no longer the soundtrack to Cleveland. It was just another FM rock station.

ACKNOWLEDGEMENTS

My deepest gratitude to the greatest fans in the world, our listeners. And to the staff of WMMS—renegades unequalled. Ours was the greatest team in radio and truly a family affair. We worked hard, played hard, and took our creative freedom to heights that will never be duplicated.

Thanks also to:

Carl Hirsch for encouraging creativity, artistic freedom, and for running interference from those who fell "short" or were too "plain" to comprehend.

Rhonda Kiefer, the protective curator of WMMS saga. This book wouldn't have happened without your immeasurable organization, assistance, support, knowledge, and unwavering programming assistance. Thank you for the preservation of the memos and documents of that era.

Denny Sanders, my confidant from the day we met in Boston in early 1970 to the greatest of years. You were the conscience of the Buzzard. WMMS would not have been the extraordinary achievement it was without your incessant perseverance to the cause.

Ed "Flash" Ferenc, whose work in our news department and public affairs programming provided evidence that our listeners wanted to be informed as well as entertained.

Len "Boom" Goldberg, whose voice perfectly articulated the Buzzard's personality. Thank you for our many chats and e-mails, which helped fill in a few blanks. You will forever be remembered, respected, and honored.

Murray Saul, who may be turning 80 but retains the mind and manner of a twenty-year-old. You're a close friend and confidant. Thank you for asking, almost daily, "Is that book finished yet?"

Betty "Krash" Korvan, who went from Catholic school girl to a Machiavelli quoting, rock-and-rolling, sizzlin' sovereign of night time radio.

Dia Stein, for helping connect the dots to some of the most astounding memories of those astonishing times. You made the weekends never end!

Tom O'Brien—Aw Me! Caw, Caw! My, my, my! What is I gonna do now? Penitentiary! I quake! Chihuahua, Chihuahua, Chihuahua!

Gaye Ramstrom-Coakley, our sweet Swedish sales sensation for remembering many of the events the rest of us forgot and for your banned Memorial Day weekend O.

Joel Frensdorf, for stirring those mind-boggling memories and airchecks especially from those early days at 50th and Euclid.

Dan Garfinkel and Jim Marchyshyn, the greatest ministers of propaganda in the history of radio. You wrote the playbook for media marketing and promotion.

David Helton, whose Buzzard was once Cleveland's most recognized and revered (and rightly so!) icon, representing WMMS and Cleveland as the rock and roll capital to the rest of the world. You gave him life.

B.L.F. Conversation with you is always a unique pleasure and experience.

Frank Foti and Steve Church for providing the auditory attacks that matched our energy and determination to dominate the airwaves.

Jim Davidson, radio historian and collector extraordinaire.

Phil Christie, my mentor at WHDH-FM and WNTN in Boston.

All the influential radio stations in Boston and New York to which my transistor radio was tuned day and night in the fifties and sixties. And the great Cleveland stations of the fifties, sixties, and early seventies—they set the bar high.

Billy Bass, Denny Sanders, David Spero, Martin Perlich, Shauna, Tree, and Joyce Halasa, the WMMS airstaff of the early 1970s. They rallied community support from listeners to block WMMS from changing its format to country. Without them, we would not have had the foundation to build upon.

Anastasia Pantsios, Janet Macoska, Dan Keefe, Fred Toedtman, and Bob Farrell for the incriminating photographic evidence.

The South Boston Barracudas: Tom Gosse, Tony and Cookie Liebl, John Grant, Larry Lerch, Doris and Ronnie Segal—lifelong friends.

John and Sandy Lanigan for the use of your Clearwater hacienda where I delineated this book (and Sandy for consistently "reminding" me to get it finished).

And special thanks to Tom Feran for making sense of what was initially a fifteen-hundred page manuscript. You made me look better than I have any right to expect.

—John Gorman

Primi et ultimi in bello
First and last in war
(MacGorman motto, 804 A.D.)

CAST OF CHARACTERS AT WMMS

BLF Bash (Bill Freeman)—Overnight air personality.

Bracanovich, Tom—National chief engineer, Malrite Communications.

Chaffee, John, Jr (JC)—National program director, radio and, later, National Program Director, television, Malrite Communications.

Clean, Kenny—Former janitor who became a sidekick on the *Buzzard Morning Zoo.*

Cheeks, Ruby—Weekend air personality, later member of the morning show team.

Church, Steve—Chief engineer; replaced Frank Foti.

DeCapua, Dave—National sales manager, WHK-WMMS.

Duffy, Maureen—Promotion director.

Ferenc, Ed "Flash"—News director and morning drive co-host.

Fisher, Hal—Vice president/general manager, WHK-WMMS .

Foti, Frank—Chief engineer.

Freeman, Bill—*See* B. L. F. Bash

Goldberg, Len "Boom"—Air personality and "official voice."

Gorman, John—Music director; program director; operations manager, WHK-WMMS; Consultant, Malrite Communications.

Halper, Donna—Music director, weekend air personality, host of the *Prisoner Request Show.*

Hirsch, Carl—Vice president and general manager, WHK-WMMS/ Cleveland; later, president, Malrite Communications.

Iorillo, Gina—Promotions assistant.

JC—*See* Chaffee, John.

Kendall, Charlie—Music director, morning show host.

Kid Leo—(Lawrence J. Travagliante) Overnight and, later, afternoon drive air personality and music director.

Kiefer, Rhonda—Assitant programmer.

Kinzbach, Jeff—Production director; later, morning drive air personality.

Korvan, Betty—(Betty Bezkorovan) Late-night air personality.

Koski, Al—(Jeff) Weekend air personality.

Lapczynski, Matthew—*See* Matt the Cat.

Gronek, Lonnie—Sales manager; later, general manager.

Lushbaugh, Steve—Air personality and production assistant; later, production director.

Maltz, Milton—Co-founder and chairman, Malrite Communications.

Marchyshyn, Jim—Promotion and marketing director.

Matt the Cat (Matthew Lapczynski)—Afternoon drive and, later, midday air personality.

Mr. Leonard (John Rio)—Former KKBQ/Houston morning show sidekick who was signed by Malrite to do his character voice for WMMS/Cleveland and WHTZ (Z-100)/New York.

O'Brien, Tom—Production director

Perdue, Jimmy—Overnight air and Saturday morning air personality

Rio, John—*See* Mr. Leonard.

Rosenwald, Gil—(John) Account executive, WHK; sales manager, WHK-WMMS; vice president and general manager, WHK-WMMS; office of the president, Malrite Communications.

Rothman, Archie—Hosted Sunday night *Time Machine* program, which featured a wide variety of eclectic entertainment.

Sanders, Denny—Air personality; later, program director, programming assistant, and creative services director.

Saul, Murray—Account executive; later, "Get Down man" and host of public affairs shows *Jabberwocky* and *We, the People.*

Sharpe, Gary—Two-time chief enginner, WHK and WMMS.

Smith, Bill—Account executive; later, local sales manager, national sales manger, vice president and general manager, WMMS-WHK.

Spero, David—Afternoon drive air personality, WMMS; later, morning drive air personality, M105.

Stein, Dia—Production assistant, music assistant, weekend and vacation air personality.

Stile, Shelly—Music Director and weekend air personality.

Thacker, Dean—National sales manager, WMMS; later, vice president and general manager, WHTZ (Z-100)/New York.

Tiburski, Walt—Local sales manager; later, national sales manager.

Travagliante, Lawrence—*See* Kid Leo.

Ullman, Debbie—Morning drive personality.

Warren, Verdelle—Receptionist extraordinaire.

Wood, Jim—National program director, radio (replacing John Chaffee), Malrite Communications.

INDEX

ABC News, 174

ABC Rock Radio Network, 198

AC-DC, 183

Adams, Bryan, 143-145, 147, 243

Adamson, Stuart, 145-146

Aerosmith, 78, 167

AFTRA (American Federation of Television and Radio Artists), 127-128

Agency Recording, 30, 136

Agora, x, 30, 47, 68, 72-73, 97, 122, 129, 132, 135-138, 142-143, 146, 159-160, 162, 172, 180, 185, 195, 200, 257, 263, 276; *P25*

Akron, 37, 91, 106, 115, 122, 133-134, 156, 158, 172, 176, 183, 187, 191, 219, 239, 241, 263

Allen, Bruce, 144-145, 243

Allen Theatre, 30, 35, 47, 72-74, 134-135, 160

Allman Brothers, 30, 203, 239

American Noise, 143, 177-179, 276

Arbitron, 38, 122, 155, 163, 178, 186, 203, 216, 264-265, 272

Arista Records, 226, 266

Atlantic Records, 200, 208, 256

Audience Research Bureau, 38-39, 43, 46, 64

Auger, Brian, 29-30, 37, 47

Azoff, Irv, 144, 200, 245

Bass, Billy, 49, 53, 61, 139

Bassette, John, 47, 71, 139-140

BBC (British Broadcasting Company), 29, 35, 97, 195, 201

Beach Boys, 75-77, 86, 100-102, 109, 167

Beatles, vii, 11, 34, 95, 109, 148-149, 151-153, 175, 184, 194-195, 231, 253

Beau Coup, 245, 262-263, 266

Beck, Jeff, 203

Bee, Cathy, 252, 262, 269

Bee Gees, 34

Belkin, 9, 29, 47, 72, 74-75, 77-79, 104, 108, 141, 159-160, 178-181, 212, 232, 257, 259

Belkin, Jules, 72, 74-75, 77-79, 159, 232, 257

Belkin, Mike, 141, 178-181, 259

Belkin Productions, 9, 47, 74, 159, 212, 259

Benatar, Pat, 167, 170, 182, 204, 265

Benz, Michael, 223, 258, 261, 269

Bergman, Pete, x

Berry, Chuck, 260-263

Bevan, Alex, 71, 107, 139-140, 142, 178-179, 244

Billboard, 68, 92-93, 119, 136, 154, 159, 236-237, 265

Bird, Gary, 166, 190, 218, 259

Black Sabbath, 169

Blackfoot, 146, 244

Blackwood, Nina, 182, 185, 266

B.L.F. Bash (see Freeman, Bill)

Blossom Music Center, 73-96, 180-18l, 266, 268

Blue Oyster Cult, 30, 78, 167, 169, 269

Bohn, Rodger, 29, 105

Bole, Larry, 98, 112

Bono, 94, 121, 205, 243

Boomtown Rats, 154, 243

Boston, (musical group), 159,

Bowie, David, 44, 68, 95, 131-132, 208, 222, 260

Boxcar Willie, 95, 143-144

Bracanovich, Tom, 1, 40

Brady, Pat, 227, 241, 267

Buzzard Beatles Blitz, vii 148, 152-153

Buzzard Day, 70-71, 268

Buzzard Morning Zoo, 214, 223, 233, 241, 252, 266, 268-269

Buzzard Theater of the Air, 107, 153, 222

C.A.R.E. (Cleveland Artists Recording for Ethiopia), 244-245
Capitol Records, 150-151, 177, 204, 217, 232, 253
Carmen, Eric, 179, 262-263
Celeste, Dick, 262, 269; *P28*
Chaffee, John, 6, 13, 119, 122, 168, 186, 188-189, 234, 273
Cheap Trick, 160-161, 178
Cheech and Chong, 11
Cheeks, Ruby, x, 241, 264; *P28*
Chi Pig, 176
Chicago (musical group), 75-76, 100, 102
Christie, Phil, ix, 21-22
Christmas Carol, A, 106-107
Church, Steve, xi, 253
Clean, Kenny, 222, 242, 250-252, 267; *P27*
Clear Channel, 224
Cleveland Boys, 136-137, 179
Cleveland Browns, 4, 15, 75, 77, 169, 187, 191, 200, 211-212, 266, 273
Cleveland City Council, 138, 229
Cleveland Indians, 4, 15, 63, 89, 158, 177, 212, 269
Cleveland Metroparks, 71, 114, 197
Cleveland Plaza, 124, 129, 141
Cleveland Press, 9, 14, 29, 41-42, 75, 77, 149, 161, 168, 195, 210
"Cleveland Rocks," 87-88, 179
Cleveland Stadium, 30, 73, 74 76, 177, 190, 212, 232-233, 244
Cleveland State University, 3, 30, 26, 52, 68, 178
Coffee Break Concert, vii, x, 45, 97, 139-146, 150, 178-180, 186, 200, 205, 227
Colebrook, Kim, 219, 223-224, 269
Coliseum, 73, 89, 114, 120, 134, 138, 169, 180, 187, 201, 206, 232
Columbia Records, 8-9, 87, 121, 132-133, 135-137, 160-161, 217, 222, 243, 245
Cousin Brucie, 11
Cousineau, Tom, 200, 265

Damnation of Adam Blessing, 92
Darden, Thom, 169, 200, 211
Dazz Band, 244
DeCapua, Dave, 42, 54, 58, 80
Dee, Gary, 55, 128, 156

Deep Purple, 227
Def Leppard, 78, 204
Devo, 106, 176
Dr. Hook & the Medicine Show, 75, 102-103
Duffy, Maureen, 269, 276, 278
Duran Duran, 182-183, 204, 236, 243
Dylan, Bob, 48, 63, 72, 74, 131-132, 140, 243

Eagles, 44-45, 47, 74, 94, 156, 166, 171, 204, 245
Electric Light Orchestra, 37, 78
Elvis Presley, 177, 260-261
Epic Records, 180, 220
Erim, Tunc, 256-257
Ertegun, Ahmet, 256-257
Euclid Beach Band, 179

Father Guido Sarducci (see Novello, Don)
FCC (Federal Communications Commission), 3, 12, 33, 86, 117-118, 190
Ferenc, Ed "Flash," 33-34, 48, 52, 76, 107, 116, 121-123, 125, 139, 162-163, 168, 173, 189-190, 197, 200, 209-210, 214, 220-221, 230, 241, 266-267, 277; *P26, P28, P33*
Ferry, Bryan, 36, 47, 51, 74; *P9*
Firesign Theatre, 11, 27-28
Fisher, Hal, 4, 7, 40, 53-54, 56, 151
Flash (see Ferenc, Ed)
Fleetwood, Mick, 114; *P19*
Fleetwood Mac, 96, 110-114, 156, 171, 178, 200, 231
Fogelberg, Dan, 245
Foghat, 47, 143, 147
Foreigner, 78, 207
Forward, Dewey, 146
Foti, Frank, 109, 169, 181
Fox, Michael J., 265
Frampton, Peter, 186
Freed, Alan, 10, 259, 261, 263
Freeman, Bill (B.L.F. Bash), 116-119; *P33*
Funkadelic, xi, 59, 118

Garfinkel, Dan, 71, 100, 104, 107, 158, 211, 270
Get Down, vii, xi, 80, 82-83, 85-88, 102-104, 107, 119-120, 133, 139, 153, 239

Glass Harp, 47, 139
Goldberg, Len, xi, 5-6, 10, 14, 28,
    43, 46-47, 58-60, 62, 87-88, 93-94,
    107-108, 140, 167-168, 196, 206-207,
    209, 214, 226, 241, 267; *P4, P26, P33*
Golic, Bob, 265
Grateful Dead, 144
Greater Cleveland Growth Associa-
    tion, 219, 223, 258, 268
Gronek, Lonnie, 273, 276, 278

Halper, Donna, 25, 32, 59, 99
Harvey, Alex, 37, 68, 230, 260
Helton, David, xi, 66, 69, 115, 120, 172,
    188-189, 207, 214, 221, 226, 253; *P26*
Hirsch, Carl, 54, 69, 91-92, 102, 112,
    120, 126, 128, 158, 163, 187, 193,
    196, 203, 213, 226, 228, 231-232,
    234, 246-248, 252, 271-274; *P24*
Hunter, Ian, 74, 87
Hynde, Chrissie, 172, 176

Iorillo, Gina, 212, 254, 261, 267, 269
Isley Brothers, *P10*

Jackson, Michael, 185, 202-203, 214,
    230-232, 243
Jacksons, The 202, 231-234, 246-247
Jagger, Mick, 10, 121, 149, 191, 215,
    231
James Gang, 77
Jett, Joan, 127, 265
Journey, 24, 78, 167, 183, 187, 206-207

Keating, Ed, 125, 129, 250-251, 270
Kendall, Charlie, 35, 93, 99, 103, 107,
    110, 115, 134; *P14*
Kent State University, 48, 54, 103, 115,
    132
Kid Leo, x, 7, 12-13, 25, 27, 45-48, 50,
    53, 58, 74, 82, 100, 102, 107, 127,
    131-132, 159, 169-170, 172, 188,
    190, 200, 220, 234, 250, 255, 258-
    259, 270, 277-278; *P2, P8, P9, P10,
    P14, P20, P23, P24*
Kiefer, Rhonda, 122, 152, 167, 174,
    183, 191, 207, 228, 230, 251, 265;
    P18, P26, P33
Kinzbach, Jeff, 6, 26-27, 54, 65, 107,
    110, 116, 134, 153, 170, 185, 203,
    240, 251, 255, 270, 274; *P2, P6, 10,
    P14, P22, P28, P33*

Kiss, 24, 73, 114, 148, 155, 165, 171,
    183, 198, 241
Kissell, Zeke, 16
Knack, The, 38, 149, 177
Korvan, Betty, x, 52, 60, 98, 100, 107,
    116, 120, 123, 163, 175, 210; *P6, P33*
Koslen, Jonah, 47, 143, 178-179
Kucinich, Dennis, 3, 138

Lanigan, John, 99, 156, 241-242, 262
Lapczynski, Matthew, x, 12, 13, 46, 53,
    58-59, 91, 99-100, 107, 132, 140-141,
    145, 163, 179, 211, 221, 230; *P7, P14,
    P16, P26, P27, P33*
Laughner, Peter, 31, 38, 49, 139
Lauper, Cyndi, 143, 161, 185, 236
Led Zeppelin, 34-35, 52, 106, 120, 166,
    174, 200-202, 204, 208
Lee, Geddy, 172, 243
Lennon, John, 136, 149, 151-152,
    174-175
LoConti, Hank, 30, 73, 142, 212, 257-
    258
Love, Mike, 75, 87, 101
Love Affair, 143, 177-179
Lushbaugh, Steve, 13, 26-27, 59, 107,
    116, 153, 255; *P2, P14*
Lynyrd Skynyrd, 29-30, 36, 75, 105,
    123, 167

M105, 61, 89, 91-96, 99, 109, 123, 141,
    155, 157-163, 165-168, 170, 177,
    190, 192-198, 207, 216, 218-219
Macoska, Janet, 31, 87, 195
Madonna, 131, 185, 202, 219
Malrite, 3-4, 6-7, 10, 35, 43, 54-55, 61,
    66, 91-92, 103, 105, 109-110, 120,
    126, 147, 153, 187, 213, 228, 231,
    233-234, 239, 246-249, 251-252, 264,
    267, 269-278
Maltz, Milton, 7, 24, 38-44, 54-55, 69,
    83, 89-91, 94, 103, 124, 127, 186,
    203, 231, 233-235, 246-248, 252,
    271, 273, 278; *P24*
Marchyshyn, Jim, 211-212, 221, 242-
    243, 249; *P26, P33*
Matt the Cat, (See Lapczynski, Mat-
    thew)
Michael Stanley Band, 47, 141, 143,
    178-180, 244, 266
Mintz, Leo, 149, 261
Modell, Art, 15, 75, 77, 273

Moondog Coronation Ball, 259, 261-262
Morning Exchange, 128, 265
Morning Zoo, 213-214, 223, 233, 241, 251-252, 266, 268-269
Mott the Hoople, 29, 47, 53, 74, 95, 132
Mountain, 13, 35, 47
Mr. Leonard, 214, 251-252
Mr. T, *P22*
MTV, 142, 182-185, 199, 203, 241, 266
Municipal Stadium, 73-75, 101, 148
Music Grotto, 68-69, 92, 98
Music Hall, 30, 73, 205

National Lampoon Radio Hour, 61-62, 64-66
Nationwide Broadcasting, 30, 41-42, 156
NBC, 133, 175, 181
New York Dolls, 37, 59-60, 73, 131-132
Nicks, Stevie, 113-114, 245
Novello, Don, 172-173, 248, 265; *P23*

O'Brien, Tom, 153, 220, 240; *P18, P26, P33*
One Trick Pony, 173

Peaches, 122, 145, 189
Perdue, Jimmy, 52, 58
Pink Floyd, 78, 167, 204, 208
Plain Dealer, 5, 9, 14, 29, 42-43, 49, 127, 130, 136, 149, 161-162, 178, 199, 207, 210, 253, 257, 264-265, 275-278
Plant, Robert, xi, 208
Playhouse Square, 4, 30, 104, 142
Popovich, Steve, 87, 135
Pretenders, The, 167, 172, 182, 209
Prince, 185, 202-203, 229, 232, 270
Public Hall, 73, 148, 173, 180, 266-267

Radio & Records, 103, 136, 177, 218, 223, 237, 265
Raspberries, 94, 244
Record Rendezvous, 149, 261
Record Revolution, 36, 49-51, 91, 100, 161
Recordland, 145
Reed, Lou, x, 49, 50, 51
Rezny, Tom, 195, 196; *P26, P33*
Richfield Coliseum, 89, 232

Robinson, Larry, 192, 195, 242
Rock and Roll Hall of Fame, 254-257, 259, 260-263, 261, 263, 265, 268, 270, 278
Rolling Stone, 21, 152, 190, 210, 257, 266, 275-279
Rolling Stones, x, 61, 73, 109, 111, 116, 166, 182, 185, 190-191, 225, 276-277
Rosenwald, Gil, 58, 119, 126, 152, 169, 187, 203, 228, 231, 248, 257, 262, 271, 273, 275, 278 *P34*
Roxy Music, 37, 47, 51, 74, 204, 256, 260
Rush, 34-35, 78, 95, 99, 161, 172, 226, 243

Sanders, Denny, xi, 3, 21, 28, 82, 100, 107, 111, 132, 134, 140, 149, 154, 255; *P3, P6, P10, P14, P18, P27, P33*
Saturday Night Live, 149, 172-173, 186, 211, 265
Saul, Murray, xi, 58, 60, 80, 93, 100, 119, 133, 169, 239 *P5, P11, P15*
Schliewen, Peter, 36, 49, 100
Scott, Jane, 9, 29, 49, 127, 149, 257
Smiling Dog Saloon, 29-30, 68, 97, 102, 105
Smith, Bill, 211, 250-251, 253, 255, 259, 273; *P26*
Southside Johnny, 95, 115, 121, 125, 134, 138, 171
Southside Johnny and the Asbury Jukes, 138
Spaceman Scott, 222
Spector, Phil, 101, 132, 149, 226
Spero, David, 13, 35, 44, 46, 107, 132, 162
Spizel, Eddie, 255, 257
Springsteen, Bruce, 72, 83, 94-95, 131-138, 137, 161, 166-167,171, 205, 243; *P14*
Stanley, Michael, 31, 37, 45, 47, 74, 107, 133, 139, 141, 143, 178-180, 244, 266;
Stein, Dia, xi, 168, 169, 281, 284; *P21, P26, P27, P33*
Stile, Shelley, 103, 107,113, 115, 119, 142; *P11*
Strongsville, 116-117, 146, 244
Styx, 186
Swingos, 102, 111, 120, 137, 256

Talking Heads, 178, 182, 185
Tiburski, Walt, 6, 13, 29-30, 37, 43, 53, 62, 68, 74-75, 78, 82, 87, 92, 100-101, 155, 161, 211, 277; *P26*
Tin Huey, 176
Tokyo Shapiro, 62, 64, 75, 91
Tom O'Brien, 108, 112, 127, 153, 220, 240
Travis, Bob, 166, 190, 218, 224
Tubes, The, 115, 151

U2, 73, 94, 121, 143, 205, 243
Ullman, Debbie, 25, 32-33, 49, 59, 86, 98
Upbeat, 42, 45, 126, 227

Van Halen, 165, 186, 203, 270
Velvet Underground, 49
Voinovich, George, 229, 257

Wain, Norman, 92, 149, 193, 241
Waitresses, The, 129, 176
Walsh, Joe, 29, 35-36, 44-45, 75, 94, 245
Warren, Verdelle, 65, 107, 140, 151
WBBG, 155, 192
WBCN, 21-22, 25, 120, 136, 193
WBZ, 20, 22, 63
WCAS, 25, 34
WCBS-FM, 259
WCLV, 91, 278
WCOZ, 193-194
WCSB, 26, 52
WCUE, 54, 92, 115
WCVB-TV, 33
WDBN, 91, 276
WDMT, 157, 229
WDOK, 91, 228
WDTX, 272
WDVE, 136
WEBN, 136, 188
WEWS-TV, 45, 128, 265
WGAR, 42-43, 99, 125, 128, 156, 158, 168, 241, 259

WGAR-FM, 155
WGCL, 9, 36, 43, 64, 95, 156-157, 160, 165-168, 190, 199, 201, 203, 207, 210, 212-213, 216-224, 227, 238, 245, 258-259, 261, 268-269, 272
WHK, 1, 4, 10, 39-40, 42-43, 45, 54-55, 68-69, 99, 105, 119, 123-124, 126-129, 150-151, 154, 156, 168-170, 197, 225-226, 235, 246, 252-253, 259, 263, 267, 269, 271, 273-275
WHK-FM, 135
WHK-WMMS, 4
Who, The, 10, 24, 122, 167, 201
WHTZ, 213-215, 221, 241, 248, 252, 266
Williams, Wendy O., *P21*
Wild Horses, 143, 177-178, 187, 245, 263, 266
Wilson, Dennis, 86-87; *P15*
WIXY, 7, 9-10, 28, 36, 43, 64, 69, 78, 92, 109, 149, 155, 157, 168, 193, 241
WJW-TV, 142, 210-211, 241, 262
WKYC, 63, 245, 262
WKYC-TV, 172, 244, 262-263
WLTF, 157, 225, 242-243
WLYT, 64, 165-167, 198
WMJI, 196, 225, 242-243, 262
WONE-FM, 239-241
Wood, Jim, 228, 231, 234, 250, 253, 262, 270, 273; *P34*
World Series of Rock, vii, 72-73, 76-78, 88, 100, 102, 105, 114, 116, 166, 190
WQAL, 91, 211, 264, 277
WQAL-FM, 165
WRQC, 198-199, 210, 229, 245, 267
WZAK, 229
WZZP, 156-157

Young, Jesse Colin, 47, 77, 139
Young, Neil, 30, 46, 77, 96, 140, 156, 162, 167, 243